TAKE A STAND

JORGE RAMOS

TAKE A STAND

LESSONS FROM REBELS

BERKLEY

New York

For the rebel in you

To my mom, the first rebel I knew

BERKLEY
An imprint of Penguin Random House LLC
375 Hudson Street, New York, New York 10014

Copyright © 2016 by Jorge Ramos
Translation by Ezra E. Fitz

ISBN 9780440001294

The Library of Congress has cataloged the Celebra hardcover edition of this title as follows:

Names: Ramos, Jorge, 1958–
Title: Take a stand: lessons from rebels/Jorge Ramos.
Description: New York: Celebra, 2016.
Identifiers: LCCN 2015038892 | ISBN 9781101989630 (hardback) |
Subjects: LCSH: Ramos, Jorge, 1958– | Television journalists—Mexico—Biography. |
BISAC: BIOGRAPHY & AUTOBIOGRAPHY/Political. |
BIOGRAPHY & AUTOBIOGRAPHY/Editors, Journalists, Publishers. |
BIOGRAPHY & AUTOBIOGRAPHY/ Rich & Famous.
Classification: LCC PN4973.R36 A3 2016 | DDC 070.92—dc23
LC record available at https://protect-us.mimecast.com/s/oX1gB6CLOgW4so

Celebra hardcover edition / March 2016
Berkley trade paperback edition / February 2018

Printed in the United States of America
1   3   5   7   9   10   8   6   4   2

Cover photo by Deborah Feingold
Cover design by Anthony Ramondo
Book design by Tiffany Estreicher

CONTENTS

INTRODUCTION   On Rebels, the Powerful and Otherwise   1

ONE   Taking a Stand in 2016   15

TWO   Barack Obama's (Unkept) Promise   27

THREE   Two Bushes, Two Wars: Don't Trust Them
If They Send You to War   47

FOUR   Fidel Castro: Treat a Dictator like a Dictator   63

FIVE   The Power of "No": Lessons from Cuban Dissidents   75

SIX   Hugo Chávez: I Am Not the Devil   91

SEVEN   The One Who Loses Is the One Who Tires First:
Leopoldo López and Lilian Tintori   119

EIGHT   Carlos Salinas de Gortari: Mexico's Favorite Villain   129

NINE   Dilemmas of a Masked Guerrilla:
Subcomandante Marcos   143

TEN   Enrique Peña Nieto: Saving Mexico?   153

ELEVEN   Alvaro Uribe: The Irascible Survivor   169

TWELVE   The Cost of Rebellion: The Case of Ingrid Betancourt   179

THIRTEEN   Daniel Ortega, or the Revolution That Left
Everything the Same   187

CONTENTS

FOURTEEN   Money Isn't Everything: What the Super-rich Can
Teach Us: Bill Gates, Richard Branson, and Jorge Pérez   195

FIFTEEN   Don't Let Them Discriminate Against You:
Sonia Sotomayor   213

SIXTEEN   Spike Lee and Doing the Right Thing   221

SEVENTEEN   Do Your Homework—Lessons from Three
Great Journalists: Barbara Walters, Oriana Fallaci,
and Elena Poniatowska   231

EIGHTEEN   Devoting Your Life to a Dream:
Benjamin Netanyahu and Hanan Ashrawi   247

NINETEEN   Know That You Will Win: Desmond Tutu   259

TWENTY   America's DREAMers: The First Step
Is Losing Your Fear   265

TWENTY-ONE   Final Lessons: What I Learned from
Thirty Years of Interviews   277

APPENDIX   Author's Speech to the Committee to
Protect Journalists, New York, November 24, 2014   289

Acknowledgments   293

On Rebels, the Powerful
and Otherwise

We must take sides. Neutrality helps the oppressor, never the victim. Silence encourages the tormentor, never the tormented.
—ELIE WIESEL

ALL REBELS HAVE something in common: they challenge and they confront. They put aside silence and fear.

Their principles are very clear:

I won't shut up.

I won't sit down.

I won't go away.

All rebels take a stand. They decide and they act. Neutrality is not an option.

I don't want to be neutral. That's not where change takes place. Happiness and love and success aren't found in neutrality. On the contrary, they are their own forms of rebellion.

Being neutral isn't enough, whether in journalism or in life.

We all need a little bit of rebelliousness.

I first learned about rebels and rebellion through journalism. In fact, the best journalism rebels against power and the abuse of it. Being objective and neutral—simply "professional"—isn't enough. Good journalism always antagonizes power.

I love being a journalist. It's the only profession in the world whose description includes being both rebellious and irreverent. In other words, being a journalist keeps you forever young. As the Colombian writer and Nobel laureate Gabriel García Márquez once said, it's the best job in the world. But we can and should use the media as a weapon for a higher purpose: social justice.

Life never finds a perfect balance between two points of view. It's not black and white. It's not a bunch of verifiable data. Life doesn't progress in a linear fashion, and it isn't headed to a particular destination. It's not divided between good and evil, rich and poor, the rulers and the ruled. Life isn't fair. It will never meet you halfway. We are never in perfect balance with it.

An argument doesn't always have a moral counterpart. The truth can't necessarily be found between two opposing views. It doesn't lie in the method itself. That would be too easy. The truth exists elsewhere. And in order to find it, we have to bravely take sides. We have to take a stand.

We achieve the most in journalism—and in life—when we are engaged, when we question those in power, when we confront the politicians who abuse their authority, when we speak up and denounce injustice. The best of what we are is revealed when we side with the victims—the most vulnerable ones, those whose rights have been neglected or abused. And the best journalism comes, of course, when we stop pretending that we are neutral and recognize our moral obligation to sing the truth to those in power.

"Journalism," as Truman Capote wrote in the preface to *The Dogs Bark*, "can never be altogether pure . . . [P]ersonal perceptions, prejudices, one's sense of selectivity pollute the purity of germless truth."

Life is not pure. Yes, I'm advocating for the practicing of journalism with perspective. This means being transparent and acknowledging to the audience—to our readers—that we have opinions, as well as a code of ethics. We don't live in a vacuum. We make moral decisions all the time, whether it's before an interview, before an investigation, or before covering a story. It's perfectly acceptable to take a stand, to refuse to be neutral. In fact it's an imperative. One of the best interviewers in history thought so.

"I do not feel myself to be, nor will I ever succeed in feeling like, a cold recorder of what I see and hear," wrote Oriana Fallaci in her book *Interview with History.* "On every professional experience I leave shreds of my heart and soul; and I participate in what I see or hear as though the matter concerned me personally and were one on which I ought to take a stand (in fact I always take one, based on a specific moral choice). So I did not [write] with the detachment of the anatomist or the imperturbable reporter."

I am arguing here for point-of-view journalism.

We must take a stand when dealing with those in power. Yes, we have to make an ethical decision to side with those who do not hold the reins of authority. If we have to decide between being the friend or the foe of a president, a governor, or a dictator, the decision should be easy: I am a reporter, and I'm not here to be your friend.

There are six arenas in which we must always take sides: racism, discrimination, corruption, public lies, human rights, and dictatorships or other authoritarian regimes. You cannot remain neutral when someone attacks a minority, when someone is discriminated against because of gender or sexual orientation, when politicians or business owners use their position to enrich themselves, when a public figure lies, when basic human rights are being violated, when a ruler commits fraud or imposes his will upon the majority.

Not taking sides under these circumstances would, in effect, be condoning unethical behavior and the abuse of power. Silence always helps those on top, never those who are being crushed underneath. As Archbishop Desmond Tutu has pointedly said, "If an elephant has its foot on the tail of a mouse and you say that you are neutral, the mouse will not appreciate your neutrality."

But taking sides does not mean being partisan. That would be promoting propaganda, or something even worse: using the profession to enable others to come to power, and to remain there.

More than anything, taking sides means refusing to remain silent in the face of injustice. The worst thing we can do in this profession is to choose silence.

"Non-co-operation with evil is as much a duty as is co-operation with good," Mahatma Gandhi said during the Great Trial of 1922 when he was charged with "bringing or attempting to excite disaffection towards his Majesty's Government established by law in British India." Gandhi believed in nonviolent protest, and in never remaining silent, even when the law was against him.

When journalists remain silent, lives are lost. Many journalists were silent before the Iraq War in 2003, and thousands of U.S. soldiers, along with tens of thousands of Iraqi civilians, died unnecessarily. We have to learn from that. Standing silently before injustice is the worst sin a journalist can commit.

(I talked about exactly this in a speech I gave to the Committee to Protect Journalists in New York, which can be found at the end of this volume.)

Professor Jeff Jarvis of the City University of New York's Graduate School of Journalism is one of the most reasoned and influential proponents of the need and obligation for journalists to take sides. "If it isn't advocacy, it isn't journalism," he wrote in his book *Geeks Bearing Gifts: Imagining New Futures for News*. There, Jarvis argues that whether we are covering fraud on Wall Street, the poor and disadvantaged, or even ways to prevent cancer or lose weight, we are taking sides. Simply collecting data, publishing beautiful pictures of cats, or reporting gossip is not real journalism, Jarvis argues. And he's right.

Taking sides is an ethical decision which requires a specific behavior from journalists. The way you start is by calling things by their true names.

A dictator is a dictator is a dictator. That's what you have to call one when you see one, and you have to treat him as such. You cannot treat a tyrant the same way you treat the victims of his tyranny. When reporting a story, I cannot give the same weight to a priest who rapes a child that I give to the child who was sexually abused.

Events like the Holocaust, massacres of civilians, and violations of human rights have no ethical justification. Therefore, we can describe and explain the murky motives of the perpetrators, but what we cannot do is present them as part of a reality that has two morally comparable versions.

As many others have said before, the problem isn't the bad; it's the indifference of the good.

The inspiration for this book came from a quote from the writer and Holocaust survivor Elie Wiesel. During his 1986 Nobel Peace Prize acceptance speech in Oslo, Wiesel told us that we must take sides. "Neutrality helps the oppressor, never the victim. Silence encourages the tormentor, never the tormented. Sometimes we must interfere," he said. "When human lives are endangered, when human dignity is in jeopardy, national borders and sensitivities become irrelevant. Wherever men and women are persecuted because of their race, religion, or political views, that place must—at that moment—become the center of the universe."

Wiesel laments that the world knew of the horrors of the Holocaust as they were being perpetrated, and yet, despite that knowledge, remained silent. "And that is why," he said, "I swore never to be silent whenever and wherever human beings endure suffering and humiliation."

That resolution to never remain silent and to always speak out against injustice is what encouraged me to write this book. Throughout my career, I have met many people—some of them true rebels— who have refused to keep quiet, who have risked everything up to and including their own lives to defend what they consider to be morally correct and true.

A rebellion is not something that needs to be prevented or suppressed. In fact, rebellions are essential to the advancement of humanism in this world.

Rebels are good. Rebels make us better.

GOD AND REBELLION

I grew up with a strong and imposing father—what child doesn't see his father as an all-powerful being? My father offered me two choices in life: accept and follow the rules to a T, or rebel.

I chose to rebel.

My first conscious act of rebellion was refusing to go to church on Sundays with the rest of the family. I know it sounds insignificant. But for me, a young boy growing up in predominantly Catholic Mexico, it was a real challenge. (Much later in his life, my father and I made our peace, and I remember him as being loving and changed.)

Other, similar acts followed. In elementary school and high school, I rebelled against Catholic priests who hit us on the hands and buttocks as punishment. The particular priest who was in charge of discipline was the same one to whom we had to confess every Friday. The individual who beat us for minor infractions and intimidated us by raising a shoe to our faces was the man who was to hear my sins.

So I resisted. Oftentimes I'd make up sins—sort of a celestial savings account—and sometimes I would simply lie to the confessor. Those were, for me, two ways of rebelling.

But beyond the abusive priests I had to face at school, there was the issue of God. How could it be that such a perfect being would have representatives here on earth who were so despicable and violent? And how do you explain wars, children dying from terrible diseases, and the brutality of dictators? A generous, compassionate, almighty God would never allow something like that.

As a child, I had to make countless prayers to a God who was distant, unattainable, and—quite frankly—impossible to verify. Masses and collective prayers were, to me, a boring, hypocritical exercise in uselessness. Nobody could prove to me the existence of heaven, hell, or a higher power who dictated or evoked everything. But they asked—they demanded, often under threat of beatings—that we dedicate our lives to this belief.

I couldn't do it.

I grew up without faith. Faith is something you either have or you don't. It is not something that can be imposed. I would have liked to believe. I suppose it might have made my life easier, but that's not the way it was.

Finding myself unable to confirm the existence of God, His powers, and His absolute goodness threw me into the realm of the skeptics. Even as a child, I realized that—for me—religion was just a well-told story. It was up to me to believe it or not. And I chose not to.

Things don't happen for a reason, nor are they part of a Creator's great design. We have to give meaning to our lives ourselves.

I absolutely respect those who believe, follow, and promote religion. It's entirely possible that they have it right. I expect one day I will find out. But I myself became an agnostic even before I knew the word.

So, as a challenge to my father, to the priests in my schools, and to the certainty of the God they tried to impose upon me, I could only choose a profession based upon questioning everything: journalism.

Journalism is, fundamentally, conducted in the face of life and everything it forces you to confront. It forces you to question everything and in doing so it philosophically pits you against the mighty, it morally forces you to report abuse, and—in practice—it turns you into a rebel.

Journalists live every single day with the word "why?" on the tips of their tongues.

To put it in religious terms, journalism was my salvation. My career didn't promise me eternal life, but at least it provided me with a more honest and intense mortal existence. Whatever might exist beyond that is impossible to know.

Very early on I learned that rebellion brought me closer to truth and justice than obedience did. And that, I think, is why I chose a profession that requires one to doubt and question the world.

I hope I have explained where my admiration for those anti-establishment types who question everything comes from. But it's also important to make a point of clarification.

This is not a book about me. It's a book about the lessons I learned covering rebels and acts of rebellion as a journalist. There are few things that make me happier than listening to—and reporting on—the stories of people who rebelled and won.

THE NEW REBELS

I use the term "rebel" in its broadest sense: someone who breaks with the established rules and carves out a new path. We must disarm the word "rebel" so that we can use it without fear in our daily lives. The classic definition suggests an armed individual standing in opposition to either a dictatorship or a democratically elected government. And his intention was often to seize power by the use of force.

We have to recognize that we have been disappointed with the results of many revolutions initiated by former rebels who conform to the stereotype. The Cuban Revolution culminated in a horribly bloody dictatorship, and (with the exception of Tunisia) the Arab Spring put regimes in place that were even more repressive and intolerant than the ones they toppled.

Today, we can remove the connotations of violence and destruction from the term "rebel." It is possible to disrupt and transform the world without destroying and killing it. Every successful act of rebellion pre-supposes that something dies. But the goal of many new rebels is to abandon authoritarianism, stereotypes, and political and religious impo-sitions in order to create a space for democracy, freedom, and equality.

The rebels included in this book are not necessarily revolutionaries, and they aren't always politically motivated. But in all of these cases, their words and actions have had a disruptive and transformative effect upon the societies in which they live.

These days, it is the "millennials"—that is, young people between the ages of eighteen and thirty-four—who are rewriting the rules of jobs, industries, and interpersonal relationships. And we have witnessed the emergence of a new ideology of disruption. The old rules no longer apply.

Having been born in the latter half of the previous century, I worked my way very slowly through the labor market: I went from as-sistant editor to editor, and from there I became a reporter, before fi-nally, much later, hosting a news program. My increases in salary were as gradual as they were painful. But that was the way forward. Thou-sands of people had taken these same steps before me. First you take a low-paying job in the town where you grew up, and then eventually you move on to a better job in a bigger market. It took me at least a decade to play that game with much success. For some people, it took even longer.

But today that's no longer the case. A meritocracy has been im-posed. The young journalists with whom I work every day are no lon-ger willing to wait their turn or follow the traditional ways forward. Their premise is that the best ideas should be the ones that are coming to the forefront, and that audacity can take the place of experience. The one who wins is the one who has the best idea and knows how to de-velop it. Age and experience no longer determine anything. They are merely secondary considerations.

Making mistakes doesn't matter because you can keep trying until you succeed. Decades ago, former U.S. president Franklin Delano Roosevelt put it better than anyone else when he said, "It is common sense to take a method and try it. If it fails admit it frankly and try another. But above all, try something."

We live in a new, developing culture that rewards rebels: the ones who take risks, who aren't afraid, who decide to break the rules. Being obedient—waiting patiently for progress to be made—is now viewed with skepticism. Large companies and entrepreneurs aren't looking to hire menial employees. They're looking for leaders, people who take responsibility for things both good and bad, and who are searching for new solutions.

Ideologies don't carry the weight they once did. Left and right, communism and capitalism—these mean less and less in a world where the consensus seems to be finding concrete solutions to concrete problems. And the rebels are the ones who manage to cast aside the hackneyed ideas in favor of finding new ways of seeing the world. It's not about having large or small countries or companies; it's about having effective and influential ones.

Technological advances have democratized rebellion. Instead of armed revolutions like the ones in Cuba and Colombia, just to name a couple of examples, the revolutions we are seeing today are digital.

The recent student rebellions in Venezuela and Hong Kong were made possible by social networks. Authoritarian governments in Caracas and Beijing were forced to use repression and negotiation with non-state operatives and demonstrators who were using cell phones as weapons.

Rebels are no longer forced to have clandestine meetings high in the mountains or deep in the jungles or in dark city basements. In the early twenty-first century, rebellions are being formed in cafés, classrooms, dorm rooms, garages—anywhere else you have an Internet connection or a phone signal. iRevolutions are forged in cyberspace.

The democratization of rebellion, however, is not limited to just the political arena. Rebellion has become a more essential element to our society at large. Governments, businesses, nongovernmental organizations, philanthropic institutions, museums, and small businesses—everyone is looking for rebels, for people to incite rebellion within their own confines. Sometimes, this rebellion turns the public servant or business into a leader. Other times, this same rebellion explodes inward, requiring radical transformations.

But in either case, nonviolent rebellion has become an indispensable part of our lives. Again, we're not talking about revolutions aimed at overthrowing governments and institutions, but about individuals who are willing to break the rules in order to move us forward as a people and help us all to live better lives.

ALL OF THE interviews collected here—around thirty of them—were conducted during the past thirty years of my career in the United States as the host of the programs *Noticiero Univisión* and *Al Punto*, and of the program *America* on the Fusion network. Most of them were first developed for television.

It was on Monday, November 3, 1986, at six-thirty in the evening, that I gave my first news broadcast for the Spanish International Network, which would later become Univision. I could barely read the teleprompter and had never interviewed a president. I was twenty-eight years old.

For a long time, I thought this would only be a temporary job before I returned to being a reporter and foreign correspondent, which is what I really loved doing. I always assumed that my bosses had the same doubts about me that I had about myself. So every time I went on vacation, I left my desk completely clean and clear. After thirty years in television, the one thing I know is that nothing is certain. The only thing that keeps you on the air is the people who watch you and believe in you. Nothing else.

These past three decades have given me the opportunity to interview the most interesting people in the world. Some of them were powerful rebels who changed our lives. I have spent many years collecting the material for this book and squeezing out the lessons I've learned from my interviewees. This, after all is said and done, represents what I've learned in three decades of my work as a journalist.

Some of the interviews here and the lessons learned from them are truly dramatic, life-and-death situations. Other times it's as simple as a leader setting his or her neutrality aside, encouraging the rest of us—by example—to take risks and defend our own points of view.

From the DREAMers, we learn to let go of our fears. From Justice Sonia Sotomayor, we learn to never give up. Spike Lee teaches us to raise our voices against injustice. Barbara Walters demonstrates the importance of being prepared for big opportunities. Cuban dissidents have the strength to say no to power. Venezuelans refuse to tire in the face of adversity. Subcomandante Marcos exemplifies patience as a virtue of the warrior. Ingrid Betancourt shows us the high costs rebels occasionally have to pay. Billionaires are proof that money isn't always the most important thing in life. And Archbishop Desmond Tutu encourages us to know that, in the end, we will win.

Not every rebel reaches a position of power, and not everyone in a position of power was once a rebel. But I also include the mighty: presidents and political leaders who at some point showed signs of rebelliousness, or who had to confront the status quo and were forced to confront serious moral dilemmas.

So I delve into the election of America's first African American president, Barack Obama, and the promise he made in order to win the Latino vote; into the circumstances that led the two Presidents Bush into starting wars; into the feared, hard-line security team of Cuban dictator Fidel Castro; into the lack of preparedness of and serious errors committed by Mexican president Enrique Peña Nieto; into the unusual and highly criticized ways in which Mexico's favorite villain, Carlos Salinas de Gortari, operates; into the peculiar style of exercising power employed by former Colombian president Alvaro Uribe; into the terrible irony of Sandinista leader Daniel Ortega, who fought against the Somoza regime only to end up looking very much like them; into the differences and similarities—yes, there are some—between Israeli prime minister Benjamin Netanyahu and Palestinian leader Hanan Ashrawi.

What all of these people have in common is that, at some point in their lives, they chose not to remain neutral, they took a stand, and they continued to fight for what they believed in. There's certainly a lot we can learn from them. These are the lessons of the rebels.

Your mission is clear: Life is too short to bask in the warmth of ambiguity. Dare to explore. Refuse to be neutral.

ONE

Taking a Stand in 2016

"**A**RE YOU AN activist or a journalist?"

I have been asked that question many times recently, and I understand why. When a journalist takes a stand—as I have done when it comes to immigration and human rights—and confronts public figures—as I have done with presidents, presidential candidates, and all kinds of politicians—then the line between advocacy and journalism is a little more difficult to define. But there are clear differences.

To take a stand does not mean to be partisan. Don't be a Republican or a Democrat, just be a journalist. To take a stand simply reaffirms the conviction that our most important social role as journalists is to denounce the abuse of power when we see it so that it can be prevented. To always offer two opposing points of view—as is the case in many newscasts on TV—does not guarantee that the truth will prevail.

The 2016 presidential campaign has given us plenty of opportunities to test the ethical limits of what journalists can and should do. So let me start by answering the query at the beginning of this chapter. I am the latter—just a reporter asking questions.

However, I have not stayed neutral about the immigration debate and the importance of Latinos in the United States. I took a stand. And that is perfectly acceptable in journalism. The best examples of great journalism that we have in this country—Edward R. Murrow, Walter Cronkite, and the *Washington Post* reporters Bob Woodward and Carl Bernstein—always involve a journalist making an ethical decision and taking a stand.

To take a stand does not mean that I cannot write, analyze, conduct interviews, and report with full independence like any other journalist. I can and I do do that every night on Univision's newscast and weekly on Fusion's *America*. But the fact that I am an immigrant and a Latino has an influence on what I do as a journalist (and I am completely transparent about it). No journalist works in a vacuum. "I am I and my circumstance," wrote Spanish philosopher José Ortega y Gasset in 1914.

So let me give you an example of how I have taken a stand during the presidential campaign of 2015–16. During the incredibly intense summer of 2015 when there were seventeen Republicans and four Democrats running for the White House before the election—our country experienced one of the most xenophobic and anti-immigrant moments that I remember since I arrived here as a student more than three decades ago.

Immigrants are an easy target for vote-seeking presidential hopefuls, TV talking heads, and social media pundits. After all, the undocumented amongst them usually cannot defend themselves. When was the last time you saw an undocumented immigrant on TV responding to criticism leveled at him by a candidate vying for the White House? That scenario is extremely rare. A vast majority would rather stay silent in order to avoid deportation.

Many Republican candidates attacked undocumented immigrants, calling them "illegals" and trying to make gains in the polls by abusing a segment of the population that, by definition, has no political representation. At times they seemed to be trying to outdo one another with the fierceness of their rhetoric. Nothing is easier—and more unfair—than to blame immigrants for the worst problems in a country. Crime, unemployment, and budget overruns in schools and hospitals, among many other absurd charges, were being directly linked to the most vulnerable and defenseless group of the population.

In contrast to the Republican candidates, all the presidential hopefuls on the Democratic side supported a path to citizenship for the majority of the 11 million undocumented immigrants and offered some temporary protection to those already here (in case Congress didn't act soon on comprehensive immigration reform). But they did so quietly. Other than giving a few strong responses when asked about the question in the media, the Democratic candidates let Republicans destroy themselves in front of the growing Hispanic electorate. Democrats knew that without a substantial part of the Latino vote, no Republican candidate could reach the White House.

The misinformation about Latin American immigrants was not consistently challenged in the media, in the presidential debates, or at political rallies. Many outrageous statements were being presented as truths. The verbal attacks on Mexican immigrants were particularly violent, accusing some of them of being criminals, drug traffickers, and rapists.

Other than the falsehoods and lack of evidence presented by the candidates, what surprised me most was the silence of the Mexican government and the passivity of many elected officials. They were not complicit with the xenophobes, but their inaction allowed for the anti-immigrant campaign to continue unchallenged

Where was the indignation? In the streets, in almost every conversation between immigrants, in the social media, among artists, writers, and journalists, Latinos were very upset. But many professional politicians, the White House, Congress, and the Mexican government maintained a detached attitude.

Following an old script, they thought that if they ignored the attacks and did not respond directly, the prejudiced charges would disappear in the next news cycle. But that did not happen. The false accusations kept on coming, and the mood of the country seemed to shift to the right before our very eyes. Clearly, the tactics of appeasement were not working. Without any significant resistance, the anti-immigrant forces were having a field day.

The pendulum had swung the other way. Long gone were the days when the Senate approved a plan—by a 68–32 vote—for comprehensive immigration reform. That was June 2013—a lifetime ago in politics. The bipartisan plan—14 Republican senators crossed the aisle to support it—would offer a path to citizenship for millions of undocumented immigrants, a new and improved technological system that would verify legal employment, streamline the process to accept legal immigrants, and as a nod to conservatives, reinforce the security at the border with Mexico.

That plan, unfortunately, never came to a vote in the House of Representatives. Despite the fact that many Republicans were willing to join the Democratic majority, the Speaker, John Boehner, refused to bring the Senate proposal for a vote. That was the closest we had been to fully restructuring our broken immigration system since Republican president and icon Ronald Reagan granted amnesty to more than 3 million people in 1986.

There were so many falsehoods and insults being thrown about. So we had to take a stand. And we did.

Accusations of crime, threats of mass deportations, plans for building a wall at our southern border, and efforts to deny citizenship—those were the main items on the laundry list for the anti-immigrant movement. The only way to deal with that was by confronting the candidates, calling them out, and reporting the facts.

After doing my research, I took a stand on TV, in press conferences, and in my weekly column distributed by *The New York Times* Syndicate on these issues.

Fact number one: Immigrants do not import crime. It's a myth that the influx of undocumented immigrants leads to more crime in the United States. The vast majority are not criminals or rapists. In fact, research shows that while the undocumented population has increased over the years, the crime rate in the United States has decreased.

Between 1990 and 2013, the number of undocumented immigrants in the United States rose from 3.5 million to 11.2 million, according to data from the Pew Research Center and the Census Bureau. During that same period, according to the FBI, the violent crime rate decreased 48 percent.*

It's also false to say that immigrants are more violent and prone to crime than native-born Americans. In fact, males between the ages of 18–39 born in the United States have an incarceration rate of 3.5 percent versus a rate of 0.86 percent for those born outside the United States, according to the Migration Policy Institute.†

Also, there is no evidence—none, not a shred!—that the Mexican government is somehow conspiring to send criminals to the United States.

It's obviously unfair to blame all undocumented immigrants for crimes that just a few of them commit, just as it would be unfair to make all Americans shoulder the blame for the massacre of nine people in a church in Charleston, South Carolina, in 2015, for the killing

---

* Walter Ewing, "Immigrants Are Less Likely to Be Criminals Than the Native Born," American Immigration Council Immigration Impact, July 8, 2015, bit. ly/1RlaTte.

† Rubén G. Rumbaut, Roberto G. Gonzales, Golnaz Komaie, and Charlie V. Morgan, "Debunking the Myth of Immigrant Criminality: Imprisonment Among First- and Second-Generation Young Men," Migration Policy Institute, June 1, 2006, bit.ly/1zIXind.

of twelve people in a theater in Aurora, Colorado, in 2012, or for the shooting of twenty children and six adults at the Sandy Hook Elementary School in Connecticut in 2012.

The bottom line is simply this: immigrants, in this country through legal means or otherwise, do not commit crimes at a higher rate than the rest of the population.

Fact number two: Immigrants contribute far more to the economy than they take out in services and benefits. Let's use, as an example, the Mexican immigrants living in the United States.

According to the Pew Research Center, about 33.7 million people of Mexican origin lived in the United States in 2012 (or about 65 percent of the Hispanic population). Of course the vast majority who reside here today are not drug dealers or rapists. On the contrary, the reason most immigrants are here is to work. In fact, about 570,000 businesses owned by Mexican immigrants in the United States generate more than $17 billion every year, according to data from the Mexican government.

With regard to the economy, undocumented immigrants contribute a lot more than they get back in health care, social services, and educational benefits for their children. They pay taxes. They create jobs. They harvest our food, build the houses we live in, and take care of our children. They do the jobs that nobody else wants to do.

In fact, offering a path to legalization for most undocumented residents, as the Senate proposed in 2013, would generate about $700 billion in gross domestic product in the first ten years, according to the Congressional Budget Office.*

Of course, anti-immigrant activists will brush those facts aside and insist that since the undocumented people broke the law simply by coming here, they need to be punished. Undocumented immigrants

---

* "The Economic Effects of Administrative Action on Immigration," Executive Office of the President, November 2014, 1.usa.gov/1LS5t4l.

broke the law, that's true. But they did so because thousands of American companies want to hire them. Remember that those American companies also broke the law, and continue to do so every single day. And, as hurtful as it may sound, we are all accomplices. Millions of people—including you and me—benefit from the labor of the undocumented.

Fact number three: It is an absurd idea to build a wall along the 1,954-mile border with Mexico. Building walls is bad business—they are expensive and they don't work as a deterrent. According to estimates reported in the *New York Times*, each mile of the border wall would cost about $16 million. (There are already fences and walls along 670 miles of the border. So to build a wall along the remaining 1,284 miles would cost, at least, $20 billion.)

It's also worth pointing out that the nation's borders are already pretty secure. The number of undocumented immigrants in the United States dropped from 12.2 million in 2007 to 11.3 million in 2014, and more than 18,000 agents are patrolling the southern border.

And let's not forget that the number of undocumented Mexicans arrested at the southern border has dropped from 1.6 million in 2000 to 229,999 in 2014—the lowest number in four decades, according to the Pew Research Center.

In fact, in 2013 more undocumented immigrants from China entered the United States (147,000) than from Mexico (125,000), according to a recent report in the *Wall Street Journal*. A wall is useless without a solid immigration policy.

Here's the most compelling argument against a 1,900-mile wall at the southern border: almost 40 percent of the undocumented immigrants in the United States are people who simply overstay their legally obtained visas, and many of them, quite possibly, arrived by plane. How would a wall stop them?

Fact number four: It is impossible to deport 11 million people in twenty-four months, a time period that was mentioned in the Republican race. This vision is nonsense, better suited as the plot of a creepy sci-fi movie than as a political platform.

Just consider the logistics. For the United States to deport 458,333 immigrants every month or 15,277 per day would be the equivalent of filling up at least thirty 747 airliners every single day for two years.

To even contemplate such a move would involve the government subjecting the country to a reign of terror. Imagine authorities across the country raiding homes, workplaces, and schools, violating the human rights of millions of men, women, and children. The government would have to send soldiers, police officers, and every agent from Immigration and Customs Enforcement to round up immigrants. After these brutal raids, the undocumented would need to be held in stadiums or other large facilities while they waited to be put on buses or planes back to their countries of origin.

And how much would this all cost? About $137 billion, or $12,500 per immigrant, according to one estimate from ICE.

And what about due process? What would happen with families in which some members are legal and some are not? The courts would be overwhelmed.

This twisted dystopia of walls and hate and mass deportations looks nothing like the America I know. This grand scheme would not lead to a greater nation; it would only give birth to a realm of bigotry, xenophobia, and divisiveness. Is this the kind of America that the vast majority of the population really wants to live in? It conjures up images of the kinds of regimes that most Americans have abhorred.

Fact number five: You cannot deny citizenship to the children of undocumented immigrants born in the United States. Simply put, their rights are protected under the Fourteenth Amendment of the Constitution. They are as American as each one of the presidential candidates. We are talking about 4.5 million children who would have to leave the country if the proposal to take away citizenship is enacted retroactively. This would apply to everyone from newborn babies to students getting ready to attend college.

Aside from the legal and ethical issues, this is a practical minefield. What if a child's father was from Mexico and his mother was from Honduras? Where do you send a kid without a country or a passport?

It is true that the majority of countries do not have birthright citizenship. But the United States of America is a unique country founded, created, and built by immigrants. In that sense, it is an exceptional country with a tradition of protecting immigrants and their children. The Fourteenth Amendment, which helped make America what it is, should not be changed for political purposes.

Fact number six: Words matter. When presidential candidates use the public platform that they are afforded to spout hatred and bigotry against an ethnic group, it is very dangerous. As they drum up support and ratchet up the invective, other people may be moved to violence.

Many of the candidates kept using the word "illegal" instead of the term "undocumented immigrant." First of all, no human being is "illegal." It is simply a double standard to call these people "illegals" and not to use the same language with the thousands of American companies who hire them and with the millions of U.S. citizens who benefit from their work.

A similar situation occurred with the derogatory term "anchor babies" used during the presidential campaign in reference to the children born in the United States to undocumented parents. Yes, there is a better term: U.S. citizens.

Help on this issue came from the Vatican.

When Pope Francis—born in Argentina to immigrant parents from Italy—gave a speech in the U.S. Congress in September 2015, he tackled the issue with assertiveness, offering us the full context in which we should view this issue: "We, the people of this continent, are not fearful of foreigners, because most of us were once foreigners. I say this to you as the son of immigrants, knowing that so many of you are also descended from immigrants."

There is nothing more cruel than for an immigrant who has benefited from the opportunities this country offers to close a door in the face of someone seeking the same opportunities for himself.

TAKING A STAND on immigration during the 2016 presidential campaign meant speaking up for those who didn't have a voice and challenging those who were seeking power. Candidates are not the only participants in presidential campaigns. Journalists have the grave responsibility of separating myths from facts and denouncing the candidates who aim to win votes or points in the polls by attacking minority groups with falsehoods.

In the end, immigration is an economic, social, and multinational problem that urgently requires a political solution. We need to realize that it's absurd, inhumane, and impossible to deport 11 million people and break apart thousands of families. We also need to realize that hateful words and speeches laden with lies and prejudice do nothing to help this situation.

Sadly, every time a major election rolls around in the United States, it seems as though undocumented immigrants are painted as Public Enemy No. 1. But that is wrong. I hope that this time the debate sparks some sense of urgency so we can solve this serious problem once and for all.

Presidential candidates should keep in mind that Latino voters are well aware of the value of immigrants, legal or otherwise, in this country, and they won't vote for anyone who attacks them.

It's a very simple concept: Latinos won't vote for a candidate who says that he or she is going to deport their parents, their friends and neighbors, their coworkers, children and students. More than 26 million Latinos will be eligible to vote on November 8, 2016. That number is more than enough to decide an election. President Obama won the 2012 election by fewer than 5 million votes. It is now an established fact in politics is that no one can make it to the White House without the Hispanic vote.

Great nations are defined not by how they treat the rich and powerful, but by how they care for the most vulnerable. In today's political climate, undocumented immigrants and their children are the most vulnerable.

I cannot ignore injustice when I see it—I'm just a reporter asking questions. But if we don't question authority, how are we ever going to change anything?

TWO

Barack Obama's (Unkept) Promise

I'm president. I'm not king. —BARACK OBAMA

IT ALL STARTED with a promise. And, as often happens, the person making the promise didn't keep it.

This promise wasn't made in a vacuum. Here's the context: in May 2008, Barack Obama, then a United States senator from Illinois, was on his way to becoming the Democratic Party candidate for president. But his closest opponent, Hillary Clinton, hadn't conceded yet. It was still mathematically possible for her to win the nomination, and therefore she still had hope. But miracles don't often happen in the world of politics, and the numbers clearly favored Obama. His campaign had been much more disciplined than Hillary Clinton's, and his lead in terms of numbers of delegates had him just a step away from the nomination.

In late May, Barack Obama was already thinking about the presidential election on November 4. But he had two serious problems. Surveys were indicating, first, that many of Hillary's supporters wouldn't necessarily vote for him, and second, that the majority of Latino voters favored her over Obama. And without a strong majority of the Latino vote, he would never make it to the White House.

This last fact is why, I believe, he decided to speak with me at a school in Denver, Colorado, on May 28, 2008. Obama needed the Latinos who supported Hillary Clinton to vote for him come November. But his strategy to achieve that goal was a complicated one.

Historically, there have always been tensions between the black and Latino communities. The rapid growth of the Hispanic population in just the past few decades has seen them passing African Americans as the largest minority group in the country. In practice, this meant that some jobs that were previously performed by African Americans were now held by Latinos. In the streets of major cities—as I personally experienced when I lived in Los Angeles—gangs comprising their respective ethnic groups waged a constant, violent war over territory. Could the first African American presidential nominee win the support of millions of Latino voters?

There were a few precedents, on a local level. For example, the former mayor of Los Angeles, Tom Bradley, an African American, always enjoyed strong support from the Latino community and its leaders. But Bradley's tenure marked the beginning of the Latino Wave—the demographic revolution marked by millions of new immigrants from Latin America and a high birthrate among them—and there was no precedent for an African American candidate running for president from either major party.

What Barack Obama was trying to do was something completely new and different, and he couldn't win the White House without strong Latino support. According to the Pew Hispanic Center, Latinos numbered at least 45 million people, making up 15 percent of the U.S. population. In a very tight election, 10 million Latino voters showing up at the polls could decide the winner.

In 2008, it was a new rule in American politics was that you couldn't win the presidency without winning the Latino vote. For a Republican, that meant earning at least a third, while a Democrat would need twice that.

The big question was whether Republicans were going to maintain the inroads they had made in the previous two presidential elections. Their mantra was that, yes, the Latino vote was practically divided, and because of that, they would win the day. These hopes were based on the relatively high percentages that George W. Bush had received in 2000 (35 percent) and 2004 (44 percent).

Bush had achieved what no previous Republican candidate had done. In 2000, he hired a Hispanic advisor, Sonia Colin, who helped him work on his spoken Spanish. The RNC also spent record amounts of money on ads in Latino media outlets. During interviews, Bush would always try to toss out a few sentences in Spanish, and while the result wasn't always entirely successful, the efforts he put into this communication strategy shone through.

And not only that. As the former governor of Texas, Bush had a good understanding of the Latino community, and from the beginning he expressed support for the idea of helping undocumented immigrants. And he went further than any other Republican politician by initiating a dialogue with the government of Mexico on a possible immigration accord.

All of that, of course, fell apart after the September 11 terrorist attacks. But during the 2000 campaign, Bush still knew how to reach out to Latinos. And that, ultimately, handed him the election. A few more Cuban American votes in Florida—and a little help from the Supreme Court—were enough to put him in the White House. Four years later, Bush increased his support among Latino voters by nine points, to 44 percent, an unprecedented number in the political history of the Republican Party.

That's what Barack Obama was facing in the 2008 campaign. Nobody knew whether the Republican candidate—Senator John McCain of Arizona—had at his disposal the same base of support among

Hispanics that Bush had enjoyed. McCain fully understood the importance of the Latino vote, and early on he supported comprehensive reforms that would legalize millions of undocumented immigrants. He hoped that this stance would earn him at least a third of the Latino vote. McCain couldn't speak Spanish, nor did he even put in the effort that Bush had, but his experience when it came to border issues was indisputable. It was believed that a substantial percentage of Latinos were ready to vote for the senator from Arizona over the one from Illinois.

As a candidate, Barack Obama had a serious problem with Latinos. When he was a senator, he had voted in favor of a bill that would extend the construction of the fence separating Mexico from the United States. (Actually, it was several separate fences built at various points along the 1,954-mile border.) That set him at odds with many Latinos who didn't believe that more walls were the solution to the nation's border problems. And when we sat down for our interview, I told him so.

"Some Latinos are concerned about your position about the fence," I said. "You voted for the fence at the border with Mexico. Although many experts think that a fence won't stop immigration. Not only that. Many people are dying at the border because of the fence. Would you, if you become president, order to stop the construction of the fence?"

"Here's what I would do," Obama replied. "I want to figure out what works. I've been a leader on immigration reform . . ."

"But a fence works?" I interjected.

"I don't know yet. And that is why I think . . ."

"But you voted for the fence," I cut in again.

It's true, I'm not afraid to interrupt someone I'm interviewing. But I only do it when it's necessary to emphasize a point, to highlight a contradiction, or when an answer doesn't quite make sense. How could Senator Obama have voted in favor of erecting a fence along the border and then tell me, in an interview, that he didn't know whether or not it would actually work? He should have investigated that before making the decision to vote. The other interpretation, of course, is that he did in fact believe that it would work, but he simply didn't want to say as much on a Spanish-language news network.

"Well, I understand. I voted for authorization to start building fencing in certain areas on the border. I think there might be areas where it makes sense and it can actually save lives if we prevent people from crossing desert areas that are very dangerous."

"But four hundred people die every year [trying to cross the border]," I countered.

"That is one of the reasons why we have to resolve the immigration issue," he replied.

"Senator Clinton promised to send a comprehensive immigration reform bill to Congress within her first one hundred days [as president]. Can you match this promise?" I asked.

"Initially it was in her first term," he recalled. "Then, I think, I said I would do it in the first year. She upped the ante and she said one hundred days."

"Can you do it in one hundred days?" I asked.

"I cannot guarantee that it's going to be done in the first hundred days," he said. "But what I can guarantee is that we will have, in the first year, an immigration bill that I strongly support, and that I am promoting, and that I want to move forward as quickly as possible."

And so Senator Obama made his promise. That's what he said to me on May 28, 2008, at a school in Denver, Colorado.

We both knew this would be a very tough commitment to keep. And immediately I said as much. This was his chance to amend, adjust, or even qualify his response. But he insisted that, yes, he could get it done.

"Many people think that is going to be very difficult," I cautioned. "Not only because of the economy, but also because you have the war in Iraq. Those are other priorities."

"That's why I don't want to make a hundred-day promise," he said.

So there was no doubt about the promise Obama had just made to me. A comprehensive immigration bill would be before Congress during his first year as president. It wouldn't be during his first one hundred days—as Hillary Clinton had proposed—but it would be within that first year. That promise would come to define his relationship with the Latino community, and it would raise enormous conflicts and tensions during President Obama's eight years in the Oval Office.

Another issue would be deportations. Before bringing the interview to a close, I asked Senator Obama if he was willing to suspend deportations and raids by U.S. Immigration and Customs Enforcement (ICE) until an immigration reform bill was passed by Congress. In this case, he wasn't willing to compromise. However, he did say, "I don't believe it is the American way to grab a mother away from her child and deport her without us taking the consequences of that." Years after uttering that sentence, Obama would become the president on whose watch more immigrants were deported—more mothers and fathers torn from their children—than ever before in the nation's history.

Before the election, on September 27, 2008, I had the opportunity to interview Obama along with his vice presidential nominee, Joe Biden, in Greensboro, North Carolina. It was the typical sort of interview one might expect just days after the first presidential debate. Obama seemed tired but satisfied. We talked for several minutes and at no point did Obama look to renege on the promise he had made to me four months earlier. His plan remained unchanged.

OBAMA'S PROMISE ON immigration reform worked. He won 67 percent of the Latino vote in the November 2008 elections. Three-quarters of the registered Hispanic voters who had supported Hillary Clinton in the primaries ended up voting for Obama. John McCain and his running mate, Sarah Palin, on the other hand, managed only 31 percent. McCain had come up short.

President Obama's inauguration ceremony on January 20, 2009, was a historic event. His victory was interpreted by many as a sign that great social change was coming to the United States. A country that had maintained slavery for the first ninety years of its existence, followed by decades of racism and official discrimination, had chosen a black man as its president. The United States—and this was the dream—could now enter a post-racial era in which skin color did not matter.

The election of Barack Obama seemed like a collective act of rebellion by the voters of America. The election of an African American man to the highest office in world politics would have been unthinkable a hundred, fifty, maybe twenty years before. The American electorate had set aside the question of the candidate's color and elected the man they believed to be best qualified for the job.

The sense of optimism in the United States and in the world was so overwhelming that nothing seemed impossible. Barack Obama had become Super Obama. He was the most famous man on the planet. Despite the major challenges he faced, expectations were very high: he could end the worst global financial crisis since the Depression, put an end to the wars in Iraq and Afghanistan, find a way to achieve peace between Israel and Palestine, ease the tensions with the Arab world, stem the spread of nuclear arms, eliminate terrorist attacks, reduce global warming, connect the people of the world through technology, eliminate extreme poverty and inequality, promote democracy, and end dictatorships. . . .

He was not promising to fix everything, but the agenda the world had set for Obama seemed endless. He was a salesman with a briefcase filled with hope. And if he could achieve the impossible in the United

States—overcoming racism and racial prejudice—then perhaps he could do the same for the rest of the world. This spirit was such that he was awarded the Nobel Peace Prize after just eight months in office.

In this climate of optimism and dreams, realizing President Obama's promise on immigration reform actually seemed feasible in 2009. Even more so, given the fact that the Democrats controlled both chambers of Congress. No, not all congressional Democrats would vote in favor of comprehensive immigration reform, but there was a small but significant number of Republicans willing to help the cause. It was just a question of getting it done.

At least, that's what we thought.

In 2009, I had two opportunities to interview President Obama in the White House. In the first, on April 15, he still sounded optimistic.

"Are you going to keep your promise, despite the economic times that we are facing right now?" I asked.

"I am absolutely going to keep my promise that I am going to push for a comprehensive immigration reform," the president replied. "I already met with the Congressional Hispanic Caucus and reaffirmed my commitment. My administration and key congressional leaders are already beginning the work of how do we shape a package that could have the opportunity of getting through both the House and the Senate. Now, you're absolutely right: the economic crisis has meant that I have been putting a lot on Congress' plate . . ."

"But you will try?" I pressed.

"What I can guarantee is that we will have a package and we will be moving forward, because I continue to believe that is in the interests of everybody," he replied.

That was on April 15, 2009. But when I spoke with him again, in an interview that aired on September 20 of that same year, the president's tone had changed. This was exactly four months before January 20, the one-year anniversary of the inauguration and the sell-by date on his election promise. This time the president was no longer absolutely certain, and he even opened the door to the possibility that he might not be able to deliver.

"This is your promise," I reminded him. "Are you going to keep your promise? Can you do it before January 20?"

"Whether the bill gets introduced on November 15, December 15, or January 15, that's not really the issue. I mean, it would be easy for us to get a bill introduced. The challenge is getting the bill passed. And there I've been realistic . . . I'm not backing off one minute from getting this done. But let's face it. I've had a few things to do: we had an economic crisis that almost saw a financial meltdown; health care has taken longer than I would have liked."

Finally, the truth. The president was not going to keep his promise on immigration reform.

The debate over the Affordable Care Act—Obamacare—had demonstrated just how difficult it can be to get the minimum required number of sixty votes in the Senate for a filibuster-proof majority. Despite the fact that the Democrats held a majority in both chambers, the death of Senator Edward Kennedy on August 25, 2009, made things much more complicated for his party in terms of simple math. The election to choose his replacement was won by Scott Brown, a Republican, and that victory made it impossible for the Democrats to get the sixty votes on their own.

After a series of legislative maneuvers, Obamacare was passed by both the House and the Senate and signed into law by the president on March 23, 2010. But, with that same signature, hopes of comprehensive immigration reform went up in smoke.

The debate over Obamacare left Congress hopelessly divided. The Republicans were highly resentful of the way passage of the new health care system was managed, and they were not prepared to cooperate on any new legislation with the president. Immigration reform was dead.

Hillary Clinton had been right. Immigration reform should have been proposed during the first one hundred days in office. If Obama had done that, it's possible that he could have earned the support of a number of House and Senate Republicans. And that support would have been crucial.

The fact is that Obama had from January until August of 2009 to put together an immigration proposal, and it would almost certainly have been approved in both the House and the Senate, yet he did not. He waited too long, and his political capital ran out. The passage of Obamacare—coupled with the election of Scott Brown—ended any chances of fulfilling his immigration promise.

OBAMA NEVER PUBLICLY acknowledged his mistake. His strategy failed. Delaying the introduction of an immigration reform bill was a terrible political miscalculation.

Shortly after Obamacare was signed into law, the tone of the language coming from the White House began to change. Instead of acknowledging their strategic error, the administration started blaming the Republicans for refusing to bring immigration up for debate. Indeed, the Republicans in Congress were blocking any possibility of legalizing undocumented immigrants. This time it was on their watch, and Hispanic voters were not going to let them forget it. But the fact of the matter is that President Obama and the Democrats made a huge tactical blunder in failing to fulfill their immigration promise of 2009. And Obama would spend the rest of his presidency trying to rectify that mistake.

The president naively believed that there would be some space for maneuvering and that he could pressure the Republicans. But once again, he was mistaken. This time, his strategy to gain GOP support was to dramatically increase the number of deportations. The argument was that if he could show himself as being strong when it came to enforcing the law by deporting hundreds of thousands of immigrants every year, the Republicans would be more inclined to come to the table and make a deal.

But they didn't budge. Meanwhile, thousands of Hispanic families were being torn apart and destroyed on President Obama's watch. According to the Department of Homeland Security, in 2009, Obama's first year in office, more than 392,000 deportations were carried out. This was a nearly 10 percent increase from 2008, which was George W. Bush's final year in office.

The number of deportations continued to grow, and along with it, the Latino community's anger. In 2010, President Obama deported 382,000 undocumented immigrants, and in 2011 that number rose to 387,000. No American president in history had ever deported that many people.

Obama visited Brazil, Chile, and El Salvador in March of 2011. His promise of comprehensive immigration reform was all but forgotten. The issue now was deportation, and I brought that up in an interview I held with him on March 22 of that year in San Salvador.

"You have been deporting more undocumented immigrants than ever before to Latin America," I said. "Would you consider putting a stop to those deportations, especially students?"

"Well, first of all, Jorge, I don't always get to see you on TV, but I know that you've been giving me a hard time on television, which is fine," the president began. "With respect to deportations, Jorge, I've been very clear. We have refocused our efforts on those who have engaged in criminal activity. We aren't going around rounding up students. That is completely false."

Well, not completely. Take that year, 2011. According to official data from the Department of Homeland Security, of the 387,000 people who were deported, 189,000 had criminal records. That means that 198,000 did not. In other words, in 2011, more innocent immigrants than criminals were deported.

One week after that interview, on March 28, I brought up the topic again with the president during a meeting with high school students in the Columbia Heights neighborhood of Washington, D.C. The "town hall"–style meeting was centered on themes such as education, and several students were invited to ask Obama questions. And as the moderator, I also had that opportunity. Immigration reform wasn't going to pass, and the two parties were fighting, which put pressure on the president to act unilaterally by utilizing an executive order, as was his right.

"With an executive order, would you be able to stop deportations of students?" I asked him.

"With respect to the notion that I can just suspend deportation through executive order, that's just not the case, because there are laws on the books that Congress has passed," he replied. "For me to simply, through executive order, ignore those congressional mandates would not conform with my appropriate role as president."

After Obama's broken campaign promise, and Congress's failure to pass any sort of immigration reform, thousands of undocumented students known as DREAMers began taking a series of radical steps to demand protection from their president and their representatives. The movement began on January 1, 2010, when four students—Gaby Pacheco, Felipe Matos, Carlos Roa, and Juan Rodríguez—decided to march from Miami to Washington. Other marches, protests, and sit-ins in congressional offices took place across the country. The argument was simple: there was no prospect of comprehensive immigration reform, but legislators could legalize the status of undocumented students—those who had been illegally brought to the United States as children by their parents—through the so-called DREAM Act.

Despite a number of legislative attempts in 2010, the DREAM Act never gained the necessary votes to be approved in either chamber of Congress. The blow was twofold: comprehensive immigration was dead, and so was the DREAM Act.

But the DREAMers refused to give up. They changed their tactics and focused their pressure on the White House. Their objective was to convince the president that he did, in fact, have the power to protect them from deportation and allow them to work and study in the United States legally.

The president was not convinced. He had, on several occasions, publicly stated that he had no legal authority to halt deportations. He insisted that he was bound to enforce the laws passed by Congress and could not stop the deportations of any one group in particular.

The DREAMers believed otherwise. They intensified their campaign and their protests. They showed up everywhere the president and members of Congress appeared. And they turned the slogan Obama had made famous during his election campaign—Yes We Can—back on the president.

Obama was facing a dilemma. Many Hispanics were upset with him because of his broken campaign promise, and his administration was deporting more people than any previous president. Although it was the Republicans who were blocking any hope of meaningful immigration reform, including the DREAM Act, Obama still needed support from Latino voters if he wanted to be reelected on November 6, 2012.

His Republican opponent, Mitt Romney, had clumsily and confusingly said that he was in favor of "self-deportation" for millions of undocumented immigrants. That all but guaranteed he would lose the Latino vote. But Obama didn't just need to win that demographic; he would need a commanding victory in order to earn reelection.

And that's how what was a resounding "no" from President Obama ended up being the most significant immigration move of his first term in office. After several months of consulting with his legal team, and still feeling the heat from the DREAMers, on June 15, 2012, Obama announced a program of deferred action for childhood arrivals—DACA—which could benefit up to 1.7 million undocumented students, according to data from the Pew Hispanic Center.

The decision was almost unilaterally rejected by congressional Republicans, while being met with nearly universal support among the Hispanic community, as several polls showed. And so it came as no surprise that Obama won 71 percent of the Latino vote in the 2012 presidential elections, versus 27 percent for Romney. Once again, Hispanics had showed their loyalty to Obama, but they wanted something in return.

Helping the DREAMers was welcome, but it wasn't enough. If Obama had a legal basis for helping hundreds of thousands of students, he should also be able to apply those same principles to protecting millions of others. The president was afraid that DACA would generate false hopes and enormous expectations among the Latino community. And in this case, he was right.

Once again, the first to pressure the White House were the DREAMers. They wanted the president to help their parents with another executive action. Others were looking for legal protection for undocumented parents of children born in the United States, and for all of those who had been living and working here illegally for years. The hopes and dreams of 11 million undocumented immigrants were in the president's hands.

He quickly took up a defensive posture. "I'm president. I'm not king," he said in one interview. "I'm not the emperor of the United States," he said in another. And he reaffirmed his belief that he didn't have the authority to go any further than he already had by offering deportation relief to the DREAMers. That was his limit.

Meanwhile, Obama still held out hope that an immigration reform bill—which had been passed by the Senate in June 2013—would make its way through the House of Representatives. This bill would legalize the majority of undocumented immigrants in the country. But the Republican Speaker of the House, John Boehner, refused to put the bill to a vote for more than five hundred days.

In late 2014—after the Republicans had taken control of the Senate at the midterm elections—it was clear that a vote would never come. It was then, and only then, that Obama decided to act.

On November 20, 2014, President Obama made the most important immigration policy move of the last fifty years. He announced protection for nearly 5 million undocumented immigrants through a new deferred-action program called Deferred Action for Parental Accountability, also known as DAPA. The majority of the beneficiaries—who would have their orders of deportation suspended and be granted work permits—were the undocumented parents of children legally born here in the United States. This measure was broader and more encompassing than the amnesty promoted by Ronald Reagan in 1986, and would positively affect 3 million people.

After all this time, President Obama had finally done exactly what he had said he could not do. He had changed his mind. But why? Clearly, he had an outstanding debt to pay to the Latino community. That's my interpretation. After failing to keep his campaign promise, and after seeing that comprehensive immigration reform was dead on arrival in Congress, the president was feeling the pressure to do something for the millions of undocumented immigrants in this country. DACA, and later DAPA, were his responses. Obama did, in fact, have the authority to take executive action to stop millions of deportations. Meanwhile, in the time it took his legal team to make this decision more than 2 million undocumented immigrants were deported, and thousands of families were destroyed. Someday he would have to answer for that.

CLEARLY, PRESIDENT OBAMA did something the Latino community wanted him to do. According to a survey conducted by Latino Decisions, 89 percent of Hispanics supported his executive action to halt the deportations of nearly 5 million undocumented immigrants. In this way, Obama turned out to be true to his word.

A few days after the announcement, on December 9, 2014, President Obama traveled to Nashville, Tennessee, to celebrate with the growing and thriving Latino community in that city. After the event, I had the opportunity to speak with him. The president, I suppose, was hoping for something of a party.

There was, of course, much to be grateful for. He had finally dared to do what he himself had said he could not do. The lives of millions of people were transformed in the blink of an eye. Gone were their years of fear and living in the shadows. They wouldn't have to hide anymore. Finally, parents could say good-bye to their children in the morning and tell them, with certainty, that they would be there when they got home that evening. All of this was made possible through Obama's executive action. No, it wasn't permanent, but revoking an order of temporary action is a rarity in the United States.

The interview took a strange turn, and ended up being far from a celebration. The president did not seem to be in a very good mood; indeed, he was surely preoccupied by the repercussions of the Senate's report on the CIA's use of torture, which had been released the same day as his announcement. According to the report, the United States had indeed tortured dozens of post-9/11 detainees.

But I wanted to talk about other things.

"Seventeen governors have filed a lawsuit against you, trying to block your executive decision," I began. "They say you are 'abdicating your responsibility to faithfully enforce the laws' and that you are 'violating your constitutional duty.' Are you concerned about being impeached?"

"No," Obama replied, "because what we've done is not only lawful—based on the evaluations of the Office of Legal Counsel—but is the same type of action taken by every Democratic and Republican president over the last twenty, thirty years."

"I understand that," I said. "But many times you said that you didn't have the legal authority to go ahead. You said, 'I'm not a king,' 'I'm not the emperor of the United States.'"

"Yeah."

"Even in March 2011, on a Univision town hall meeting, you told us, and I quote, 'With respect to the notion that I can just suspend deportations through executive order, that's just not the case.' Well, that's exactly what you did," I pointed out.

"No, Jorge," he countered. "What I've said clearly, consistently, is that we have to enforce our immigration laws. But that we have prosecutorial discretion given limited resources. And we can't deport eleven million people."

"So it's not that you changed your mind?" I asked. "Or that you were convinced otherwise?"

"What was clear," he said, "was that we could prioritize how we deploy the limited resources we have to focus on the borders, to focus on criminals . . ."

"But if you, as you were saying, always had the legal authority to stop deportations," I pressed, "then why did you deport two million people?"

"Jorge, we're not going to—," he began.

"For six years you did," I interjected.

"No, listen, Jorge—"

"You destroyed many families," I pressed. "They called you 'Deporter-in-Chief.'"

"You called me 'Deporter-in-Chief,'" he said.

"It was Janet Murguía from La Raza," I corrected.

"Yeah, but let me say this, Jorge—"

"Well, you haven't stopped deportations," I said.

"No, no, no."

"That's the whole idea."

"That's not true," the president said. "Listen, here's the facts of the matter."

"You could have stopped them."

"Jorge," he said, "here's the facts of the matter. As president of the

United States, I'm always responsible for problems that aren't solved right away . . . The question is, are we doing the right thing, and have we consistently tried to move this country in a better direction? And those, like you sometimes, Jorge, who suggest that there are simple, quick answers to these problems, I think—"

"I didn't say that."

"Yes, you do," Obama maintained, "because that's how you present it."

"But you had the authority."

"When you present it that way, it does a disservice. Because it makes the assumption that the political process is one that can easily be moved around, depending on the will of one person. And that's not how things work—"

"What I'm saying is—"

"We spent that entire time trying to get a comprehensive immigration reform bill done that would solve the problem for all the people," the president said in conclusion. "So right now, by the actions that I've taken, I still have five million people who do not have the ability to register and be confident that they are not deported."

PRESIDENT OBAMA: THE LESSONS

Things did not end well. After the interview, while a whole team of photographers from the Univision and Fusion channels took pictures, President Obama said that he was very upset with the way I had brought up my questions. He felt that he had done something very positive for the Latino community—protecting millions of people from deportation—while I was focusing on the more negative issues, such as his changing position and the 2 million people who had been deported.

No interview should be a celebration of the person being interviewed. You always have to ask the tough, uncomfortable questions. But clearly the president had wanted this to be a moment of celebration, a time to highlight the advances he had made on immigration issues.

This had been a long road for President Obama. He wasn't able to keep his 2009 campaign promise. But five years later, he was able to give the Hispanic community an executive order protecting millions of undocumented immigrants from the threat of deportation. And he wanted—and hoped, with good reason—that he would be publicly acknowledged for that during this interview. But I could never quite get to that point. We moved on to discuss other issues, and in the end, the atmosphere in the room was tense, to put it mildly.

On a personal level, I was in full agreement with the president with regard to his executive action. But that didn't matter. As a journalist, I had to point out the conflict and contrast between his previous statements—denying he had the authority to stop deportations of a particular group of people—and the executive action he had just ordered, namely, suspending those same deportations. The contradiction between his statements and his actions is clear.

Further, there was the painful issue of the deportations that actually did take place. If he had the authority to stop them all along, then why wait and allow so many mothers and fathers to be torn from their children? No president in history has deported more people than Obama. Why wait until 2014 to do what he could have done in 2009? The pain, the destruction of thousands of families, caused by these deportations seems as pointless as it was preventable. And this kind of damage can't be repaired.

It's awful to think that all of this suffering was the result of pure politics, of a blind desire to follow an ambiguous political process. The president could have stopped deportations in 2009 while Congress drew up an immigration reform bill. Doing so would have put extra pressure on the members of Congress. But he didn't.

Ultimately, President Obama changed course, he did the right thing, and he made peace with the Latino community. But for the thousands of broken families, it was too late. After more than 2 million deportations, many Latino immigrants will remember him for failing to deliver on what he guaranteed during his campaign.

I shared the optimism that millions felt at President Obama's election. But on this issue that means a great deal to me, I had to take a stand and try to hold the president accountable. Lesson learned: no matter who you are, don't make promises you can't keep. "A promise is a promise," I told President Obama during a forum in Miami in September 2012, "and with all due respect, you didn't keep that promise."

THREE

Two Bushes, Two Wars: Don't Trust Them If They Send You to War

I don't want to see a single shot fired.

—GEORGE H. W. BUSH

I have my father's eyes but my mother's mouth.

—GEORGE W. BUSH

W E HAVE HAD two presidents named Bush and both sent me to war. With the first, George H. W. Bush, it was the Gulf War. With the second, George W. Bush, it was Afghanistan and Iraq.

I have interviewed every American president since 1990, and what impresses me the most is the enormous power presidents hold in their hands when it comes to making life-and-death decisions for thousands—perhaps millions—of people. I understand that a soldier is bound to follow the orders of his commander in chief. But it's a different matter when a reporter like me, born in Mexico, ends up in a foreign war because of choices made in the Oval Office in Washington.

This is the story of my interviews with Bush 41 and Bush 43, and how—without actually intending to—they shipped me off to war.

GEORGE H. W. BUSH

My first interview with any U.S. president was on November 20, 1990, in the White House. George Herbert Walker Bush was preparing to strike Iraq. Saddam Hussein had invaded Kuwait on August 2 of the same year, and the United States (along with a sizable international coalition of forces) was not going to allow Saddam to go unpunished.

Guillermo Martinez, Univision's vice president and director of news, knew that I had a thick accent when speaking in English. But even so, he offered the interview to me. "If you feel you're ready for it, it's yours," he said generously. I took it as a personal challenge; I memorized the pronunciation of all the questions I wanted to ask, and I booked my flight to Washington.

The White House had approved the interview as a means of promoting a trip that President Bush was making through South America. In December, he would be visiting Venezuela, Brazil, Uruguay, Argentina, and Chile. The idea was to promote free trade and democracy in the region. But the trip—which had been planned months in advance—was coming at a bad time. President Bush didn't have his mind set on South America; all of his attention was focused on Iraq.

While planning the interview, my news director gave me some advice that I still value to this day: "First we get the news, and then comes everything else." In other words, focus on the conflict in Iraq, not the trip to South America, though many of my viewers would be very interested in that. And that's what I did.

The United Nations had approved thirteen resolutions against Saddam Hussein's regime. War was rapidly approaching, and no diplomatic solution seemed to be in sight. Iraq considered Kuwait a historic part of its territory, while the world considered Saddam Hussein a dictator who was brutally taking advantage of a smaller, weaker nation.

Still, there were many in the United States who thought we had to give sanctions more time to work and to force Saddam out of Kuwait that way. Washington had little appetite for war. But Bush was ready for a fight.

We began and ended the interview by talking about Iraq.

"Why do you insist on putting a deadline to Saddam Hussein or face war?" I asked.

"[The] United Nations has defined what Saddam Hussein must do," the president replied. "We have given sanctions four months. We're willing to give him more time. But he must leave Kuwait. We have failed to make him realize what he has done. The world will prevail. He won't."

"Why not sit down with Saddam Hussein and negotiate a solution to this crisis?"

"You might make that case," he said. "But you have to see all the people that have tried it. What he wants to do is to present this as Iraq against the United States. It is not. It's Iraq against the world."

"Are we going to war?" I asked succinctly.

"I'm still very hopeful of a peaceful solution," Bush said. "This is an international problem. So it is my hope that Saddam Hussein recognizes that he can't stay in Kuwait. That's what I hope for. I don't want to see a single shot fired. We [are] still trying through diplomatic means, we are still trying very hard. But the American embassy is under siege. American citizens are being held. This brutal hostage situation has to stop and it has to stop now."

On the news later that night, November 20, 1990, I stood in front of the White House and said it was my impression that war was on the horizon. "The clock is counting down, and Saddam Hussein is the only one who can stop it," I said.

Saddam didn't. The United States and the Coalition forces launched their first air attacks against Saddam's troops on January 17, 1991. Next, a fast-moving ground offensive—lasting only one hundred hours and beginning on February 24—ended any territorial ambitions Iraq might have had for Kuwait.

I arrived in the war zone one day later, in a C-130 military transport plane that nearly crashed; one of the engines failed, and we had to make an emergency landing in Jeddah, Saudi Arabia. From the Saudi border, I traveled in a caravan along with other journalists until we reached Kuwait City. It was destroyed, blackened, and it smelled of smoke and death. In an act of vengeance, Saddam's few remaining soldiers had set fire to a number of buildings before fleeing the city.

But even amid the rubble, you could see the first few signs of liberation. A few Kuwaitis took to the streets of the main avenue in their port city and fired their rifles into the sky to celebrate the end of six months of occupation. "Thank you! Thank you!" they cried out to every foreigner they saw.

This was my first experience of war in the Middle East. I was terrified and excited at the same time. Nothing was normal. Unidentified bodies piled up in makeshift morgues while a number of different armed groups tried to impose some semblance of order in the streets. One tense night, I managed to get a Kuwaiti fighter to stop pointing his gun at my chest by offering him a piece of chocolate. He wanted to see my press credentials, and I couldn't find them. Life wasn't worth much in Kuwait. Well, it was worth the price of a candy bar and I'm glad for that.

In a harrowing and delayed retreat, thousands of Saddam's soldiers tried to flee along the road that connected Kuwait City to southern Iraq. But they were bombarded by the U.S. Air Force and its Coalition allies. There, along the "Highway of Death," I picked up a few spent shell casings, a car's license plate, and a necklace made of black stones. I still have those mementos of the war that George H. W. Bush unwittingly shipped me off to.

GEORGE W. BUSH

Two decades later, the first President Bush's son, George W. Bush, would send me to Afghanistan, and then, shortly thereafter, back to Iraq.

I met W, as he was universally known, in Austin when he was governor of Texas. He hobbled into the room where we would be having the interview in November of 1999. Everything was hurting, and it was with good reason. Three days before, an overloaded truck had run off the road and nearly hit him while he was out for a jog.

At fifty-three, W wanted to be the Republican candidate for the presidency, but there were a number of factors stacked against him. In one interview he couldn't name either the prime minister of India or the dictator who ruled Pakistan. This lack of knowledge served only to heighten the concerns of those who thought he wasn't ready to be president.

And with me, he didn't want to talk about his past. He'd made it known to the press that he hadn't had a drop of alcohol in thirteen years, but he refused to say whether he had ever tried marijuana or cocaine. "I've already answered that question," he told me. "I've already said everything I have to say about that." He added that his past had been thoroughly investigated, that there was no evidence to that effect, and that "respectable journalists" don't ask those sorts of questions.

Bush's strategy was to not talk about things that made him uncomfortable, and to question the motives of journalists who disagreed with him. And that was the same strategy that he employed later as president in the buildup to the war in Iraq: don't question the commander in chief.

Inevitably, when we sat down in Austin, I asked W about his father. What was the biggest political error his father had made, and what had the younger Bush learned from him? Politically, he replied, his father's biggest mistake was his statement that became the famous quote "Read my lips. No new taxes."

So you won't be making promises like that, I asked? No, he said, but history will judge my father for having been a great president and a great man.

Bush maintained a good-natured tone throughout the interview. That was his strength. The cliché at the time was that Bush was the kind of person you'd like to have a beer with (although, of course, it would have to be a nonalcoholic beer).

I also noted something different from other interviews I had conducted in English. Bush often injected Spanish words. Some of them came off well, while others didn't. He began the interview by saying, "*Puedo hablar un poquito pero no quiero destruir un idioma muy bonito. Por eso, voy a hablar un poquito en español, pero mucho en inglés.*" ("I can speak a bit but I don't want to destroy a very beautiful language. So I'll speak a bit of Spanish but mostly in English.")

It wasn't a spontaneous thing. He worked hard at it, but still, he tried. And he ended the interview by saying, in Spanish, "I have my father's eyes but my mother's mouth." With that, he let out a burst of laughter.

Bush's Hispanic media advisor, Sonia Colin, was also there for the interview, and she smiled from ear to ear upon hearing those words come out of her boss's mouth. Sonia was constantly teaching him new Spanish phrases, and Bush would shamelessly repeat . . . and destroy them.

This wasn't a case of a curious Spanish student. Bush had taken classes in high school, but had forgotten almost everything since then. He was working his plan to earn the Latino vote by speaking the language that's spoken at home by most Latino voters.

Bush served two terms as governor of Texas. Both he and his advisor Karl Rove understood the importance of the Hispanic community in the state elections. The same would be true, they surmised, at the national level. At the time, throwing out a few poorly pronounced Spanish words was enough to demonstrate an interest in the Hispanic community's issues. It was a show of recognition after decades of rejection and discrimination. A candidate who could speak Spanish (or even Spanglish) was something very new and welcome.

The governor did not agree with offering amnesty to the 6 million undocumented immigrants living in the United States back in 2000. "Not now," he said. "I wouldn't do it. I would want to know more about the subject."

Bush did, in fact, know all he needed to know about amnesty. He knew that President Reagan had granted amnesty back in 1986—with mixed results—and he knew that if he proposed to grant amnesty now, he would lose his party's nomination for the presidency. Thus, his strategy for winning Hispanic voters was set: we'll speak a little bit of Spanish, but we're not going to offer amnesty.

The strategy worked. What caught the attention of the Univision audience was not his rejection of amnesty for undocumented immigrants, but the fact that he spoke Spanish, such as it was. The sentence he threw out—"I have my father's eyes but my mother's mouth"—was repeated so many times in our news recaps that it ended up defining Bush for our viewers. Yes, here was a candidate who could speak Spanish . . . or, at least, one who tried.

Of course, those of us who worked in Spanish-language media were guilty of allowing Bush to define himself in such a way. Instead of demanding concrete commitments to the Latino community—like amnesty, better educational and health care programs, programs to combat extreme poverty, and improved relations with the countries of Latin America—we settled for a few poorly spoken catchphrases in Spanish. Bush's message wasn't in what he said, but in how he said it.

Bush's friendliness prevailed over an extremely conservative agenda. He told me he completely understood why a father earning fifty cents a day in Mexico would want to come to the United States and earn fifty dollars a day instead. Still, he was not about to offer any sort of protections to this poor, anonymous Mexican immigrant.

Bush perfected the art of saying "no" with a smile. Considering he was not an expert in global affairs like his father, much of his campaign was based on his exceptional ability to connect with ordinary voters, and on the fact that he did not put on airs of intellectual pretension.

What nobody knew at the time was that we were electing a president who would have to confront the worst terrorist attacks in our nation's history, and who would eventually lead us into two wars.

Bush won the Republican nomination without any serious problems. I interviewed him again, on a train in California, during his national campaign. The candidate who just a few short months before had nervously spoken a few words in Spanish now did so with absolute confidence. It wasn't a personal matter. It was a clear strategy to win the Latino vote.

Most Latino voters are of Mexican descent. But Bush and his advisor Karl Rove knew that the election against Democratic candidate and former vice president Al Gore would be extremely close and could be decided by the state of Florida and its Cuban American voters. And Bush understood them better than Gore did.

After a visit to Cuba, the governor of Illinois, George Ryan, proposed ending the U.S. embargo. It had been a failure, he said. Bush disagreed.

The Republican candidate opposed lifting the sanctions. He said that investing in Cuba would only reinforce Castro's dictatorship, and he didn't support the idea of allowing American citizens to travel to the island nation. First, he would have to see democratic changes, the release of political prisoners, and freedom of worship and expression.

Bush was closing ranks with the more traditional Cuban exiles and their conservative views. He wasn't willing to compromise on anything when it came to dealing with the Castro brothers. He wasn't interested in doing what President Nixon had done when he went to China in 1972. What he cared about was winning the Cuban American vote in Florida, by as large a majority as possible.

Indeed, the November 7, 2000, presidential election did end up being decided in Florida, where the Republican campaign had spent far more than the Democrats in Spanish radio and television advertising. After more than two weeks of recounts and lawsuits, the state of Florida declared Bush the winner by a mere 537 votes. Shortly thereafter, the Supreme Court—by a ruling of five to four—confirmed this result.

Those 537 votes that gave Florida—and the presidency—to Bush may well have been cast by Cuban Americans. Bush and Rove's Hispanic strategy—speaking Spanish, investing in Spanish-language advertising, and unconditionally supporting the standing U.S. embargo on Cuba—put them in the White House.

BUSH, GRATEFUL FOR the support he got from the Hispanic community—he won 35 percent of the Latino vote—asked me to be the first journalist to interview him as president. Mexican president Vicente Fox had invited him to San Cristóbal in Guanajuato, and I spoke with Bush on February 16, 2001. He showed up without a tie, wearing black boots and his trademark smile.

"Do you think you won the election thanks to the Cuban American vote in Florida?" I asked.

"Yes," he replied. "I think they had a lot to do with that. I'm very proud and thankful for their support and *por eso nunca voy a olvidarlos.*" ("That's why I will never forget them.")

"During your campaign, you said you wanted to be a compassionate leader," I said.

"*Sí.*"

"Don't you think it would be a compassionate decision to give amnesty to six million undocumented immigrants in the United States, who are the poorest of the poor and the most vulnerable?" I countered.

"Jorge," he replied, "I think the best policy for our country is to recognize that there are people who want to work, and work with employers to make sure they are able to find jobs. Have that be called a 'guest worker program.'"

Bush had been president for less than a month, and his positions on Cuba and immigration hadn't changed. But his true obsession—Iraq—was about to rise up and stand out for the first time.

According to evidence gathered by U.S. government agencies, Saddam Hussein had tried to kill former president George H. W. Bush with a car bomb when he visited Kuwait in 1993. The attempt failed, but President Bill Clinton ordered a series of bombing raids against Iraq in retaliation.

Saddam had tried to kill W's father—who was commander in chief of the Coalition forces fighting against Iraq's invasion of Kuwait—and now that he was president, W had the Iraqi leader in his sights.

In a bizarre decision, made well before he arrived in Mexico, W had authorized a series of air strikes against Iraq. Why would the U.S. president choose to bomb Iraq on the same day that he was making an official visit to Mexico? The strikes were a response to attacks made against international coalition planes protecting the no-fly zone.

Shortly before noon on February 16, George W. Bush kissed President Fox's mother, Mercedes, on the cheek, and twenty-four American and British planes bombed military targets in Iraq. There were dozens of victims.

Kisses and killings on the same day. Kisses for Mexico, and killings in Iraq. Only too happy to get the "theme of the day" on the agenda, President Bush's administration sent a double-edged message: affection for our friends and beatings for our enemies.

"Is it your intention to do away with Saddam Hussein?" I asked Bush. He didn't want to respond directly, but later he did say that if he caught Saddam with weapons of mass destruction, he would react with force.

That direct threat to Saddam, and that reference to "weapons of mass destruction," made after just twenty-seven days in office, would become key to understanding the rest of George W. Bush's presidency.

THE 9/11 TERRORIST attacks changed everything. President Bush was stunned and overwhelmed. He received the shocking news at an elementary school in Florida, and the memorable images of that precise moment are a president facing a threatening and uncertain future.

Nearly three thousand people died when members of Al Qaeda hijacked four commercial airliners and crashed them into the Twin Towers in New York, the Pentagon in Washington, and a field in Pennsylvania.

President Bush ordered a withering attack against the Taliban regime in Afghanistan for supporting and protecting the Al Qaeda terrorists. And that took me to Afghanistan in December 2001, one of the most foolish things I've done in my life. When my bosses at Univision decided not to send me to cover the war in an official capacity, I requested some vacation time and went on my own. I flew to Pakistan, crossed the border into Afghanistan, and—along with my translator, Naim—headed for the Tora Bora region of the mountains.

For $100, I hired three guerrilla fighters under the command of the tribal leader Haji Zaman, and in an old Toyota van we drove to Jalalabad, some fifty miles from the border. Halfway there, one of the fighters, a young man barely twenty years old named Kafir, told me in very rudimentary English something that chilled me to the bone. "I am a follower of Osama," he said, referring of course to Osama bin Laden, the leader of the group that had perpetrated the terrorist attacks against the United States.

Kafir looked me straight in the eye and continued toying with his weapon, a Kalashnikov. As the bumpy drive went on, in a cruel sort of game, Kafir would occasionally point his rifle at my chin. This seemed to amuse him. Of course, it wasn't surprising to find Afghanistan full of Bin Laden supporters. For years, the Taliban regime had trained and protected them.

Four international correspondents had been killed on an Afghan highway just a month before, and I didn't want to be the next one. Guerrilla fighters knew that journalists would be traveling with cash. Afghanistan was not a land where Visa or American Express would get you very far. With my stomach in knots and cold sweat on my brow, I looked at Kafir and said, "If you take care of me, I'll take care of you."

I don't know if he understood. But he stopped pointing his rifle at my face. When we got to the hotel in Jalalabad where a number of foreign journalists were staying, Kafir waved his weapon in a sign to follow him. But I didn't want to stray very far away from the van. I reached into the plastic bag where I kept my cash, counted out fifteen bills, and gave them to him. (One of the best pieces of advice a fellow correspondent had given me before I left for Afghanistan was to carry small bills.) Kafir looked at the money. This might have been the first time in his life he had ever seen a dollar bill—and with a glance and the slightest of gestures with his rifle, he indicated the entrance to the hotel. I quickly walked toward the hotel and never looked back. Fifteen dollars. That was it. Life is cheap in this part of the world and that was what my life was worth in Afghanistan.

The journey from Jalalabad to the Tora Bora mountains was at least another hour along all but impassable rural roads. "Where is Osama bin Laden?" I asked a group of guerrillas. They pointed their rifles toward the horizon. I saw a massive mountain range perforated by hundreds of caves. It was clearly a perfect hideaway.

* * *

THE CAMPAIGN IN Afghanistan was a necessary war, a retaliation for the terrorist attacks against the United States. But the Iraq War was not. That was a war invented by George W. Bush.

The nation's sense of vulnerability in the wake of September 11, coupled with a surge of patriotism and militarism, paved the way for President Bush to attack Iraq.

The 9/11 attacks led to the formulation of a new doctrine: the Bush Doctrine of preemptive strikes. The idea was to attack before you are attacked. And Saddam Hussein had become the perfect target.

The Bush administration accused Saddam of being in possession of weapons of mass destruction—the same thing the president had said to me during his first month in office—and having ties to the Al Qaeda terrorists. Both accusations were later proven false.

Not many journalists dared to question the official version of the facts. Numerous speeches were made—the most famous being Secretary of State Colin Powell's address to the United Nations in February 2003—but no evidence was presented. Despite the objections and concerns of many other nations, and the requests for more time for UN inspectors to demonstrate whether or not there were weapons of mass destruction in Iraq, Bush decided to attack in March 2003. "We will, in fact, be greeted as liberators," Vice President Dick Cheney said on television. But that didn't turn out to be the case. I was in Iraq during the first days of the war, and the United States was seen by many as an invader.

I saw no flowers being waved and I heard no music heralding the American soldiers. Following a convoy carrying food to Iraqi refugees, I crossed the border from Kuwait into Safwan, Iraq. We continued deeper into Iraqi territory and there, with the people, I saw the first U.S. military vehicles. There was silence. Almost complete silence. That's how the Iraqis greeted the American "liberators."

There is no doubt that Saddam Hussein was a brutal dictator and murderer. But he had nothing to do with the 9/11 terrorist attacks, nor was he in possession of weapons of mass destruction in 2003. It was all an invention of George W. Bush and his administration.

It turned out to be a very expensive invention. More than 4,000 American soldiers died needlessly in the Iraq War. And according to IraqBodyCount.org, an estimated 133,000 Iraqi civilians lost their lives between 2003 and 2014.

PRESIDENT BUSH: THE LESSONS

George W. Bush was one of the worst presidents we have ever seen. His mistakes were incredibly costly, both in terms of dollars and in terms of human lives. He left behind the most dire economic crisis since the Great Depression in 1929. He sent the country into wars in Afghanistan and Iraq, the latter of which was completely unnecessary. The humanitarian crisis in New Orleans in the wake of Hurricane Katrina reflected that ineptitude of his administration during important historical moments.

While he cannot be held personally responsible for the deadliest attack of our lives, which took place on his watch, his response, in the form of the invasion of Iraq, was ill-conceived and disastrous. In many ways the geopolitical catastrophe that is the present-day Middle East was created by that response.

The blame for all of this lies, in part, with us. The first lesson is that journalists should have asked more questions of him. Many more. We should have questioned everything. We shouldn't have allowed him to do anything and everything under the guise of national security. Even today, we are suffering the consequences of such a policy. Our private lives became just another area of investigation for the national security complex. We, as journalists, didn't serve as a counterpoint. Instead many journalists lined up obediently and abandoned our mission to seek the truth no matter the cost. That was our mistake. And it was a serious one

However, it is important to recognize that some journalists did express their opposition to the war and did it in very clear and unambiguous terms. They were, no doubt, a small but courageous minority.

After I returned from the war in Iraq, I reported what I had seen. There was no way to justify the military invasion. And I gather that my criticisms—both on television and in my columns—were not much appreciated by the administration. Despite submitting multiple requests, I was never able to interview President Bush again. I even stopped receiving invitations to social events at the White House, like the Cinco de Mayo party and the Christmas festivities. Access denied.

I do, however, have to thank him for accelerating my decision to become an American citizen. That's my other lesson. I planned on voting in the 2008 elections. I wanted to fully participate in this nation's democracy. I wanted to contribute—even with a single vote—to the hope that the United States would never again find itself in a useless war like the war in Iraq.

The third and final lesson—and I learned it from Bush 41 and Bush 43—is very simple: don't trust them if they send you to war.

FOUR

Fidel Castro: Treat a Dictator like a Dictator

Nobody knows where the world is heading right now.
—FIDEL CASTRO

WE KILL FIDEL Castro several times a year in Miami. Rumors of his death are so common that the local TV stations have a plan of action in place and ready to employ for whenever it actually happens. But up to this point, Fidel has survived a dozen U.S. presidents, and will doubtlessly go down in history for resisting every attempt to remove him from power.

And the United States tried it the hard way: with the Bay of Pigs invasion in 1961, with the economic embargo the United States put in place the following year, and apparently with multiple assassination attempts. Every one of them failed.

In December 2014, President Barack Obama did the unthinkable: he reestablished diplomatic relations with Castro's regime in Havana. Doing so broke with the half-century-long belief that the only way to deal with his dictatorship was through sanctions. And the justification Obama gave when he made the announcement was solid: we can't keep doing the same thing and expect different results from Cuba.

Shortly thereafter, I read a poll in the *Miami Herald* showing that the Cuban American community in South Florida was divided on the issue: half of the respondents supported Obama's move, believing that more contact with the island would, over time, promote democratic reforms, while the other half was staunchly opposed.

Having lived for more than two decades in Miami, I have come to understand the Cuban exile community. While Obama's new methods could, in a best-case scenario, put an end to the Castro regime, those who have been the victims of that regime are not willing to concede any ground to the dictatorship. It's a simple matter of principle: they believe that you have to stand up to dictators and fight them, not negotiate with them.

For President Obama, however, it wasn't about principle; it was a question of getting results. The embargo failed to remove Castro from power, as have the sanctions. Those efforts had succeeded only in causing economic hardship among the people of Cuba and making it impossible to explore other, diplomatic alternatives.

In early 2015, the price of oil had dropped so low that economic aid from Venezuela to Cuba became a purely symbolic gesture. This put the Castro brothers—Fidel and Raúl—in a very vulnerable state. Without the protection of the former Soviet Union, and without the financial support of Venezuela the regime was running a serious risk of collapsing or seeing Cuba become an even more impoverished state, like North Korea. Considering these circumstances, Obama decided it was time to act.

At first, he asked for little in return: the release of two American prisoners in Cuba—government contractor Alan Gross and intelligence agent Rolando Sarraff Trujillo—in exchange for three Cuban spies being detained in the United States. But the long-term bet was that more contact—between citizens and between governments— would lead to the end of the Castro brothers' dictatorship. Clearly, Obama was trying something new and distinct from the strategies of all the presidents who had preceded him since the Cuban Revolution in 1959.

One thing that caught my attention is that when news of the reestablishment of diplomatic relations broke in both countries, Fidel Castro remained silent. Officially, he had ceded power to his brother Raúl in 2006. But Fidel was still the historic leader of the Cuban Revolution.

Official announcements were made by Barack Obama and Raúl Castro. With Fidel, it came down to speculation, as it always did: did his silence signify a rejection of the agreement with the United States? Was he too sick to speak? Or could he even be on the verge of death? I will never believe this last rumor until I can see it with my own eyes. Fidel has buried many people who had bet on his death.

In fact, my credibility as a journalist depends on not being mistaken when it comes to Fidel's actual death. I've often told the story of a Cuban couple shopping for groceries at a Miami Publix supermarket. Not realizing that I was standing behind them in line, they were arguing about Fidel's apparent death, which had been reported once again. The woman was convinced that he was gone, while the man denied it. "I won't believe it until I hear Jorge Ramos say it on *Noticiero Univisión*," he said. So I'd better not be wrong about this. I'd rather be right than be first.

FIDEL WAS VERY much alive when I interviewed him in July of 1991. The first Ibero-American Summit was being held in Guadalajara, Mexico, and the disorganized organizers put all the attending presidents and leaders in little cabins on the Camino Real hotel grounds, while members of the press were prowling around the facility without any type of control. For a good reporter it was as easy as shooting fish in a barrel.

If you wanted to interview one of the participating politicians, all you had to do was go up to his cabin and knock on the door. Sometimes, they even answered.

I had just finished interviewing Argentine president Carlos Menem, and I went straight to Fidel. I waited a few minutes, as a number of other reporters were doing, until—without any sort of announcement whatsoever—the legendary Cuban leader emerged from his room surrounded by his bodyguards. I counted six, seven, eight of them. He wanted to go and greet Dominican Republic president Joaquín Balaguer, and without any regard for protocol, he just started walking. So I went after him.

I told my cameraman, Ivan Manzano, to keep it rolling. I caught up to Fidel, and as we walked, I asked my first question. I knew I didn't have much time, so I tried to provoke him right from the outset. And the way to do that was to question the system that he had been defending for years and that yet seemed to be falling apart.

"Comandante," I said, "we just spoke with the president of Argentina, and he said that Marxism is nothing more than a museum exhibit . . ." (In July 1991 the Soviet Union was in the throes of its turbulent dissolution.)

Fidel didn't answer right away. He made eye contact, stopped and then walked toward me and put his left arm around me, his hand on my shoulder. He was much taller than me and walked without looking me in the eye. He clearly felt in control. The image of his long, uncut fingernails extending well beyond the tips of his fingers is etched into my memory.

"In my opinion, [Marxism] is too new to be a museum piece, while capitalism is three thousand years old," he replied.

I could barely concentrate on his answer. There was so much going on around me. As soon as I felt his arm on my back, I turned and pulled away from him. He noticed my movement and lowered his arm. Meanwhile, his bodyguards were gathering around me so close that I could touch them.

Fidel's body language made me very uncomfortable. I couldn't conduct an interview with someone who—for whatever reason—wanted to embrace me. If I had let Fidel put his arm around me without any resistance on my part, the Cuban exile community would never have forgiven me. You can't accept anything from a dictator. Not even a hug.

I think, too, that Fidel knew this—he knew that I worked for Univision in Miami—and that's exactly why he tried to put his arm around me. I know it sounds highly unlikely that someone could have so many thoughts in such a short amount of time, but that's how it was. It's not unlike the notion that a dying man sees his life flashing before his eyes. The difference in my case was that letting Castro embrace me would have signified my death as a journalist.

Meanwhile, Fidel was still talking.

"The three-thousand-year-old pieces, those are the ones in the museums," he said.

"But everything indicates that the world is going in another direction, Comandante."

"Nobody knows where the world is heading right now," he replied.

"Of course that's true, Comandante. But after the fall of the Berlin Wall, there have been a number of changes . . ."

"Yes, there have been changes," he said. "Some have been quite extensive. For example, the wall between Mexico and the United States that is preventing the people from crossing."

Obviously, I realized, he didn't want to talk about the fall of the Soviet Union, his historical ally. He was changing the subject to focus his criticisms on his old archenemy, the United States. It was at this moment that he tried to put his arm around my shoulder again. Again I turned away.

"There are many walls in this world," he continued. "And now there is this great concern over massive migratory movements. A hemisphere away, they're building a wall from the Baltic to the Mediterranean."

I tried to put the focus back on Cuba and the failures of the Communist system.

"But we're talking ideologically, Comandante. Many people believe that now is the time for you to order a public plebiscite."

"Plebiscite" seemed to be the key word here. One of his bodyguards put his elbow in my stomach and got between Fidel and me.

"I respect the opinion of those gentlemen," he said, "but they really have no right to demand a referendum in Cuba."

At that moment, one of the bodyguards shoved me aside. I lost my balance, and I fell to the ground. Castro didn't say a thing. He didn't even turn to look back at me. The microphone went flying. But that didn't matter. I already had my interview with Fidel, the first dictator I ever questioned. It lasted only sixty-three seconds; that's all I could get out of him. I knew that Fidel would never agree to a sit-down conversation during that summit. And in fact, he never did.

FOR DECADES, I thought about the strange way my interview with the Cuban dictator ended. Without receiving a single verbal order from Fidel, his bodyguards came after me as soon as they heard the word "plebiscite." In Cuba, at the time, this was akin to calling for a coup, and the heavies quickly and effectively separated me from their commander in chief. It was a flawless little operation on their part. Just a blow to my stomach, and Fidel would not have to deal with any more uncomfortable questions. But how would that same interview be seen from the point of view of Fidel's security team? I would have to wait twenty-four years to find out.

One of the bodyguards protecting Fidel that morning in 1991 at the

Camino Real hotel in Guadalajara was Juán Reinaldo Sánchez. Ever since he was a young boy, he had been chosen to sacrifice himself in the name of the Cuban Revolution, and for seventeen years, from 1977 to 1994, he was ready to give his life for his Comandante.

I interviewed Sánchez in Miami in 2014. "My family was a revolutionary family," he told me. Starting in high school, he was selected to be a part of the Cuban leader's personal escort.

"It was one of the best security teams in the world," he said. At no time, he assured me, was there ever an attempt on Fidel's life. No threat ever "got through our ring" of security.

His loyalty was bulletproof. "I had blind faith in Fidel. For me, Fidel was as big as they came. He was like a god on a pedestal," he explained. "Not only was I willing to give my life to protect Fidel, I wanted to give my life to protect Fidel."

Because of the close access he had to the Cuban leader, Sánchez saw exactly how Fidel was able to grow his own fortune. "He creates a whole series of unregulated companies," he said. For example, the director of Cubanacan—a state-owned tourism company—"handed Fidel one million dollars in profits. In cash. Right in front of me. On two separate occasions."

"Where does Fidel keep this money?" I asked.

"He keeps part of it in Cuba," Sánchez explained, adding that it was tied to the National Bank of Cuba. "It's called the 'Commander-in-Chief Account,' and it doesn't just contain money but cars, trucks, and other goods." In addition to that, Sánchez said, Fidel also had "encrypted accounts outside of Cuba."

What's more, he owned a number of Cuban properties, including Cayo Piedra, his private island. "Fidel discovered it in 1961," Sánchez told me. "There's a guest house with a pool, an aquarium for dolphins, a sea turtle nursery . . . with an exclusive, three-mile-wide no-sail zone just so Fidel can fish in private."

According to what Sánchez told me, part of Fidel's fortune comes from the drug trade. In 1989, thanks to a listening device hidden in Fidel's office by Fidel's own security detail, Sánchez overheard a private conversation between Castro and his interior minister, José Abrantes. "He was talking drugs with Fidel. For me, that moment destroyed everything. I was stunned. The man I had idolized came crumbling down. I started spending more time with my family than I did with Fidel."

Life started to get complicated for Sánchez when his brother left for the United States on a raft and his sister got a visa to go to Venezuela. He requested retirement from Fidel's security detail—he had already reached retirement age—but not only was his request resoundingly rejected, he ended up in prison in 1994. Fidel had lost confidence in his own bodyguard.

Juán Reinaldo Sánchez told me how, after spending two years behind bars, he made no fewer than eleven attempts to flee the island before he was finally able to reach the United States, in 2008. He wrote all about it in his book, *The Double Life of Fidel Castro*, which was published in 2014 in several languages. Why did it take so long for him to tell his story? "In Cuba, I couldn't talk about these things," he told me. "And then it took me a long time to gather all this material that was brought to the United States in so many different ways."

Sánchez, the bodyguard, and I, the journalist, happened to meet during that first Ibero-American Summit in Mexico in 1991. He was protecting Fidel while I was trying to interview him.

He remembered that day when I approached his commander in chief. "If you're getting too close [to Fidel] and the cameras are running, you have to be very careful," he said. "Fidel was very meticulous about how he came across, in public, on camera." Still, the guard's orders were to protect him, with his life, if necessary, and to keep the journalists at bay. "So I had to be a bit tactful about it," he recalled. "That's why they gave you that shove, but they did it in a way that wouldn't be seen."

A few days after the summit, when Fidel was back in Havana, his security team did an evaluation of their performance and analyzed my mini interview. They didn't like the way I had approached Fidel, Sánchez told me. To them, it represented an imminent threat. But when the opportunity came, they did their job. And I did mine.

Sánchez died from pulmonary cancer a few months after our interview, on May 25, 2015.

FIDEL CASTRO: THE LESSONS

After that brief encounter with Fidel, I never saw him again. Time and time again, I requested a formal interview with him anywhere in the world. But I never received a response. The Cuban authorities didn't even deign to say they wouldn't grant the interview. They didn't even acknowledge having received our request. Cuban bureaucracy is expert when it comes to the art of ignoring things.

For personal reasons, Cuba has always been one of my journalistic obsessions. My two children, Paola and Nicolás, were born in Miami. There is Cuban blood running through their veins, and they have inevitably inherited the family outrage over the Castro dictatorship that is passed down from generation to generation. It's easier to understand what freedom truly is when you grow up in a household where dinner conversations often include very personal accounts of an oppressive and brutal Cuba.

Since I would never have another chance to interview Fidel, I thought about visiting Cuba. But the challenges facing me were much the same. It was impossible for me to obtain a media visa. I often referred to Castro as a "dictator" on *Noticiero Univisión* newscasts, which were broadcast throughout the United States and in thirteen Latin American countries. Other journalists refused to use that term. They argued that qualifying him as a "dictator" meant taking sides and losing objectivity when it came to our news coverage. Still, I always believed that Fidel fit the definition of a dictator—he imposed his will with force, he governed without open, multiple-party elections, he repressed those who opposed him, and he eliminated freedom of the press—and I had to call him what I saw him to be.

The Cuban government had us flagged as Univision journalists—to them, we represented part of the counterrevolutionary movement—and our punishment was, simply, having our access denied. Period. Until Pope John Paul II came into the picture.

For some bizarre reason, the gatekeepers of the revolution believed that the pope's 1998 visit to Cuba would put a damper on our critical attitude toward the island, and—surprisingly enough—we were offered a visa to cover the event. Castro's regime believed that Karol Józef Wojtyła's visit—far from being a threat to the system—would actually legitimize it. They wanted people there to witness the event. Well, what they got was about three thousand journalists.

I spent twelve days in Cuba. I visited Havana, Santa Clara, Camagüey, and Santiago. From the moment we first set foot on the island, I knew we were being watched. My crew and I rented a small car so we could get from place to place. When I went to pick it up, they said to me, "Señor Ramos, here is your car." I was standing in front of a Mercedes-Benz, complete with a chauffeur and two small antennas. I insisted on taking the car we had specifically reserved for ourselves, but it was all to no avail. In the end, I had no choice but to go with a car in which our conversations would surely be overheard.

Whenever we mentioned Fidel, the driver put his finger to his lips. Clearly, someone was eavesdropping. For his part, the driver wisely declined to refer to him by name throughout the entire trip. When he wanted to refer to him, he simply used his fingers to form a triangle underneath his chin, representing the dictator's famous beard.

Of course, I covered the pope's visit to Cuba for what it was: a religious figure passing through an iron-fisted dictatorship. Whatever hopes for change there might have been were instantly crushed. Any protest or sign of dissent during one of the pope's masses was swiftly eliminated by the "*segurosos*," or members of the state-run security force dressed in civilian clothes.

I interviewed half a dozen political dissenters and independent journalists. All of their stories were basically the same: arrests, threats, loss of employment, beatings, torture, incarceration, surprise visits in the middle of the night, warnings to family members . . . and all for simply asking for what amount to basic rights in any other country, like multiparty elections, a free press, the freedom to assemble, and freedom of expression. How could that not be reported?

Across the island the walls of buildings were plastered with official state slogans:

"To Be Efficient Is to Be Victorious"

"Socialism or Death"

"Cuba: The Land of Health"

"We Don't Want Owners Here"

"Revolution in Every Neighborhood"

"Be Like Ché: Pioneers for Communism"

"We Believe in Socialism"

"We Need to Build a Party of Steel"

"We Believe in Fidel"

"Ready to Win"

"Socialism Is the Science of Example"

"Here You Have Freedom, Not Ownership"

"You Have Absolutely Nothing to Fear from Imperialist Men"

"For Life, Not the Blockade"

I reported what I saw, but also what the Cuban government did not want us to see. And of course, they didn't appreciate my work. They were monitoring everything we were reporting and a senior government official, upset by my pieces on dissidents and independent journalists, came to see me at the Habana Libre hotel. In no uncertain terms, he reminded me that we could have problems obtaining media visas to enter Cuba in the future. His warning was clear and direct: if you continue to talk about those who oppose the system, you won't be welcome back.

He then assured me that, in Cuba, political dissidents make up "0.02 per cent of the population," and therefore it wasn't worth the attention of any media outlet. I don't know where he got that statistic, and I continued to do my job and cover Cuba the way I would cover any other dictatorship.

A few days later, I received my second visit at the hotel. This time it was the deputy minister of foreign affairs. "You will not be returning to Cuba," he informed me. He said that my coverage of dissidents had nothing to do with the pope's visit. I debated that point. All voices deserve to be heard, I said. But it was all for naught. Apparently the decision had already been made.

Dictatorships have long memories and old resentments. On several different occasions, I applied for a visa to return to Cuba—in places as diverse as Mexico City; Lima Peru; and Washington, D.C.—but the answer was the same as when I had asked for an interview with Fidel. Nothing. "We can't seem to find your visa application here," was one response I got when I checked on the progress of one request.

The lesson is that dictatorships do not change nor do dictators give up their power voluntarily. This is what we've learned in the more than half a century since the Cuban Revolution. Dictators have to be overthrown, or we have to wait for them to die. But nothing could be sadder for a people than to watch their dictator die in power instead of in a prison cell.

FIVE

The Power of "No": Lessons from Cuban Dissidents

The most important thing is that change is happening from the inside out: Cubans are fed up. —YOANI SÁNCHEZ

Cuba is still in the seventeenth century.

—GUILLERMO FARIÑAS

Life and death are a part of our existence. We live and die in the hands of God. And I will return to Cuba to live or die in the hands of God. —OSWALDO PAYÁ

My husband has worked all these years for people to be able to demand their rights through referendums.

—OFELIA ACEVEDO DE PAYÁ

F IDEL CASTRO NO longer fits into the category of a rebel. There's no denying the footprints he has left across the history of Cuba and Latin America, and his influence is still felt today in several countries. Certainly, he was an important rebel leader when he rose up against the dictatorship of Fulgencio Batista in 1959. But not long after that, the rebellion turned into one of the most repressive dictatorships in our hemisphere.

Rebels can often become dictators. Today, we can unequivocally state that the blogger Yoani Sánchez, the dissident Guillermo Fariñas, and the ideas left behind by the disappeared oppositionist Oswaldo Payá are much more rebellious than the contributions made by brothers Fidel and Raúl Castro.

YOANI SÁNCHEZ AND
THE ISLAND OF THE ISOLATED

Yoani Sánchez knows her weakest point.

The threats aimed by the Castro brothers' dictatorship at the Cuban journalist and blogger were direct. She told me that during an interview in Miami in April 2013: "I've been arrested, I've been beaten, and that didn't hurt me so much. But the last time I was arrested, a state police officer said to me, 'Does your son ride a bike? He should be careful.' And that hit me deeply."

Yoani knew her greatest vulnerability was her son, Teo. He had just turned eighteen, which is the age when you begin your compulsory military service. "Yes, that's my weak point," she acknowledged. She knew there could be serious repercussions for what she was saying. But still she kept on talking. Why? "Of course I'm afraid of reprisals," she said, "but what else can I do? Shut up? They're not going to forgive me. I think the best way to protect myself is to keep talking."

Despite these targeted threats, Yoani went back to Cuba after visiting a dozen countries in eighty days. Go into exile? "That's out of the question," she said. Cuba was her life.

This tireless tour was taken on by someone who had never traveled outside the island and who at the first opportunity she was afforded wanted to take in the entire world. After years of being denied an exit permit, Yoani was finally able to leave Cuba. Whereas she had once been a persecuted political figure inside her own island nation, outside of Cuba she suddenly became—much to Havana's dismay—something of an international celebrity. And I happened to witness it.

When she visited Miami, Cuban American actor and Hollywood star Andy García wanted to meet her. "She is a very brave woman," he told me. He went to see her before a speech she was giving in Miami. They went out to eat together, but their roles were reversed: Yoani was the star. Andy, with great simplicity and openness, just listened.

That's what happens with Yoani. You can't stop listening to her. She tells you what Cuba is like today, not how it's been portrayed from the outside. Wherever she speaks, no matter what country it is, the auditoriums are packed. Hundreds of thousands of people follow her on Twitter (@YoaniSanchez), and the Cuban dictatorship has been stripped and exposed by her courage, her strength, and her demand for transparency.

"Cuba is the island of the isolated," she told me during a rare break. "To me, from afar, Cuba just seems so absurd. I live in a medieval village because there is no freedom, because the government itself acts as a feudal lord. It's sad, and from the outside looking in, you feel it even more.

"Every day there is a growing consensus that we live in a dictatorship," she said. I asked her if she could say that Cuba is a dictatorship without getting into trouble. "I say the first syllable, and I'm already in trouble," she replied. "But I'm a person who wakes up every day and says, 'Today I will behave as a free citizen.' I assume the risks."

Yoani describes herself as nothing more than a "chronicler of reality." But she's so much more than that. She's become the symbol for change in Cuba. Others have tried and failed. Many have tried and died. Nevertheless, Yoani continues with unerring logic, chipping away at a dictatorship that still lacks multiparty elections, that imposes fierce limitations on freedom of expression, that imprisons and assassinates dissidents, and that is heading in the opposite direction from most other countries in the world. Democracy and openness are still the exception in Cuba despite the establishment of diplomatic relations with the United States.

Yoani is constantly defining herself. "My hair is free, and so am I," she said, touching the long black hair that reaches down to her waist. And then she let something slip that seems unthinkable for someone who hasn't stopped talking since she left Cuba: "I'm a very shy person."

She insisted that her mission was to explain Cuba to those who have never been there. And just a short while later, she took us on a brief tour of daily life in Havana: "I'm hyperactive. As soon as I get up, I'm doing things. I'm very much involved in my family life."

Harassment is part of everyday life for Yoani. Her iPhone, given to her by her sister in the United States, is regularly tapped, and she has been detained on several occasions. She is used to hearing pro-Castro sympathizers publicly accuse her of being a CIA agent. It has happened so often that her response to such nonsense is simply to smile: "That's what you call killing the messenger. Don't correct what she's saying: just prove her wrong ethically and morally. No, I don't work for the CIA. I could never work for a foreign agency. I haven't even joined a political party."

Like most Cubans, Yoani makes a living "solving" things. "I'm a typist and I fix computers. And I work as a journalist in many forms of media outside of my country." Her first trip abroad was financed by a number of NGOs and her sister.

I asked her if she believed that change will come to Cuba. "Yes, and I am hopeful," she said. "The most important thing is that change is happening from the inside out: Cubans are fed up." I also asked her whether she thought the Castro regime could endure without Fidel and his brother, Raúl. "The charisma of these leaders is non-transferable," she replied. "In Cuba, the presidency was inherited by blood [from Fidel to Raúl]. . . . It's sad that a nation needs to put its hopes in the death of someone so that the nation may live, but that's where we find ourselves."

Yoani likes to quote Gandhi: "First they ignore you, then they laugh at you, then they fight you, then you win." When I interviewed her, Yoani was living in this third phase. She took on the threats to her life and the lives of her family members as part of her profession as a journalist. But she also knows that she has become the greatest hope for freedom and democratic change in Cuba.

Will she be able to change Cuba?

"Not by myself alone," she said. "But we are many."

GUILLERMO FARIÑAS: DYING FOR CUBA

Guillermo Fariñas believes that if he dies in an act of protest, Cuba could cease to be a dictatorship. Or at least start moving in that direction. It takes an incredible amount of faith to think that one person can end the half-century regime of the Castro brothers in Cuba.

For thirty years, since 1983 when he visited Moscow, Fariñas had been unable to leave Cuba. But in July 2013 he was able to do so because of a new law that made him eligible for a travel visa. "What shocked me the most was the technological gap," he told me during an interview in Miami. "Cuba is still in the seventeenth century."

The blogger Yoani Sánchez felt the same way when she returned to Cuba after her eighty-day whirlwind international tour. Being on the island, she tweeted, is like being in "a time machine to the past."

This journey into the past is both a literal and a political one. "Horse-drawn carts in the interior [of the country] and all the buildings destroyed," is how Fariñas described the current state of Cuba to me. That is the result of more than fifty years of a repressive, ironclad dictatorship.

In the twenty-first century, after so many other nations have managed to overthrow authoritarian regimes, why is such a brutal and repressive dictatorship able to hold on to power in Cuba? According to Fariñas, there are three reasons: "A lack of unity within the opposition, the stubbornness of leaders, and the indifference, even complicity, of many world governments."

Fariñas is very troublesome for the regime in Havana because he knows about the monster from within. He's like a bogeyman to the Castros. He was a member of the Young Communist League, he trained as a military officer in the former Soviet Union, and he even fought—and was wounded—during Cuba's intervention in Angola's civil war that began in 1975. He remained a trusted supporter of Fidel Castro's government until 1989, when he broke ties with the government to protest the execution of General Arnaldo Ochoa, who had been accused by the regime of conspiring to traffic drugs to the United States and was sentenced to death by firing squad.

Afterward, Fariñas worked as a psychologist at a hospital in Havana. In 1995, he accused the hospital's director of corruption and reported her to the police, but in a Kafkaesque turn of events, the police arrested Fariñas and kept him in jail for twenty months. It was his first arrest, and many more followed. Altogether, Fariñas has spent more than a decade behind bars.

Fariñas is best known for his hunger strikes: twenty-three of them by my count. And it shows. When I spoke with him, his health was "quite deteriorated," according to his own diagnosis. In 2010, while fasting to protest the death of Orlando Zapata—a political dissident who died in prison after refusing to eat for more than eighty days—Fariñas suffered a thrombosis on the left side of his neck. He lost all the hair on his head . . . even his eyebrows. When I met him he opened his eyes like an astonished child. He seemed quite tall, a full head taller than me, and although he said he'd gained some weight, his brown skin was still stretched tightly across the bones in his chest. His shirt seemed a size or two too large, and his sockless feet slipped easily in and out of his sandals.

"All my hunger strikes are to the end," he told me. And his body confirms this. He moved very little, as if conserving energy. "With me, there is no middle ground. I go on a hunger strike when the government commits an inhuman act. That's when I take these self-destructive measures, which put the government up against a wall."

Fariñas—who is currently a spokesman for the Patriotic Union of Cuba, a political opposition group that says it has some six thousand members on the island—never even considered staying in Miami. "I respect my brothers who are here," he said, referring to Miami, and without the slightest bit of resentment. "But in this historical moment, a group of brothers and sisters must be fighting in Cuba."

He once wrote, "Now is the time that the world realizes that this government is a cruel one, and that there are moments in history where countries need to have martyrs." And Fariñas—who won the Andrei Sakharov Prize, which is awarded annually to human rights advocates—is willing to be one of those martyrs. "If necessary, I will," he said to me.

Fariñas believes that a "commotion" needs to be created on an international level if the Castro government is going to crack. "There was a time when the world was not listening," he reflected. "Now it is. But there has to be a commotion."

I asked him if such a thing could be achieved by another hunger strike. "I believe that if the Cuban regime were to let a Sakharov laureate die, that would harm the government," he said, "and it would have to make concessions."

Suddenly, as if a cold wind had just swept over me, I realized that I was sitting in front of a man who has made the decision to die for democracy in Cuba. I think this may be the last time we see Fariñas. I never cease to be amazed by men and women who are willing to die in defense of their ideas. There aren't many of them, and they have a unique look in their eyes, unlike that of any other mortal. It's as if they can see right into your soul.

He knows that criticizing the Cuban regime while abroad could have terrible consequences for both him and his daughters, Haisa and Diosángeles. But he refuses to remain silent. "They could kill us at any moment," he told me, without raising his voice or showing any emotion, as if he had repeated that phrase a million times.

But Fariñas does not want his life—and his death—to have been in vain. As the interview came to an end, I told Fariñas that I found his willingness to die for his country to be astonishing. "That is your opinion," he told me, respectfully. "But we consider nothing extraordinary about defending your motherland."

THE DEATH OF OSWALDO PAYÁ

According to official reports, Oswaldo Payá died in a mysterious car accident in Cuba on July 22, 2012. The Cuban government said that the driver of the vehicle, Ángel Carromero, a member of Spain's People's Party, was at fault for the accident and therefore accused him of involuntary manslaughter. Carromero signed a document confirming that version of events. But once he was released from prison and allowed to return to Spain, Carromero reported that he was pressured by the Cuban authorities to sign the document, and alleged that they, in fact, were the ones who killed Payá.

Oswaldo Payá always knew they wanted him dead. When I spoke with him in Miami in 2003, I asked him the obvious question: Do you fear for your life in Cuba? "Look, I fear for my life because I could get shot, I could get struck by lightning," he said. "It could come from anywhere, like one of those security cars that follow me around when I'm riding my bike down the street. Life and death are a part of our existence. We live and die in the hands of God. And I will return to Cuba to live or die in the hands of God."

Payá believed that Cuba could be changed from within. He was one of the founding members of the Christian Liberation Movement, whose aim was to promote human rights and democracy in Cuba. As early as 1992, he campaigned for a seat in the National Assembly of People's Power, Cuba's unicameral legislative parliament, but he was unsuccessful because he did not run as a member of the Communist Party. But he didn't give up.

In 1998 he founded the Varela Project with the simple idea of holding a national referendum. Referencing the existing constitution, Payá realized that Cuban law provides for a referendum if more than 10,000 signatures have been obtained. I spoke with him shortly before he was to present his proposal for change to the National Assembly . . . with some 25,000 signatures in hand.

"The Varela Project is a petition for a referendum," he enthusiastically explained to me. "It calls for all Cuban people to be consulted on changes to Cuban law, so that they can exercise their freedoms of expression and association, so that they can free peaceful political prisoners—and all imprisoned dissidents are peaceful—so that Cubans can have the opportunity to have their own businesses, form unions, contract openly, freely elect their representatives, and hold open elections."

Payá wanted to transform the dictatorship using the dictatorship's own laws. And they wouldn't let him. In 2004, the National Assembly denied his request for a referendum.

Payá was not looking to assassinate Fidel Castro. "Well, it may be a form of regime change, but it's no way to go about liberating Cuba," he said. Nor did he want to overthrow him: "You're using the term 'overthrow' in terms of a coup. I'm talking about liberation, and the way to do that is through a peaceful, popular, civic movement," he explained.

He was not afraid of the Cuban dictatorship—"Yes, yes, of course it's a dictatorship"—nor was he afraid of openly seeking change. "I'm fighting to bring an end to this dictatorship, and for us to have freedom," he said, almost in conclusion.

"You know, you're no pushover," he said, laughing as the interview came to an end.

"Neither are you," I replied, joining in the laughter.

That was the last time I ever saw Oswaldo Payá.

OFELIA ACEVEDO DE PAYÁ: IT WAS NOT AN ACCIDENT

Ofelia Acevedo remembers seeing that interview on television. And she told me so. When we met in 2013, images of her late husband were on every monitor there in the Miami studio. It wasn't an easy place for her to be.

She and her daughter, Rosa María, had moved to the United States just a few months before to escape the harassment they were suffering in Cuba. She had never accepted the official government explanation for the death of Oswaldo Payá.

"I'm absolutely convinced that there was no accident," she said. "That's a total lie."

"They sent someone to kill him?" I asked.

"Absolutely. They sent someone to kill Oswaldo Payá."

"Who did it?"

"State police had been making death threats against Oswaldo for years. They had repeatedly loosened the lug nuts on the wheels of our car. We saw them on a number of occasions."

"Do you think that Raúl Castro and Fidel Castro are behind the assassination of [your husband]?"

"Look, Cuba is a totalitarian regime where the government—the halls of power—makes decisions each and every minute about the lives of its citizens. Nobody in Cuba would dare to do that; they wouldn't dare do such a thing unless they had support from the highest levels of the Cuban government."

After her husband's funeral, state police cars began following her elder son. And they did it in such an obvious way that there could be little doubt that the intent was harassment. This heightened surveillance of her family also had repercussions. A university reneged on a job offer it had extended to her daughter, Rosa María. And it was all because, from the outset, the Payá family never accepted the official explanation of Oswaldo's death. That's why they wanted out of Cuba. And, in that at least, they succeeded.

In 2013, Ofelia decided to leave Cuba with her family and move to Miami. "I was afraid that something would happen to my children," she confessed. "There could have been another accident, they could put something in a backpack, they could put you in jail for any sort of offense. It's very easy to do that in Cuba."

There are certain people who have lived such an intense life that they remain present long after their death. This is the case with Oswaldo Payá. He wasn't there, and yet all the talk revolved around him and his ideas.

At one point, I asked Ofelia why dictatorships have fallen in countries like Chile and the former Soviet Union but not in Cuba. What surprised me about her answer was that she spoke about Oswaldo as if he were still alive. "My husband has worked all these years for people to be able to demand their rights through referendums," she said.

"Do you realize you're speaking about Oswaldo in the present tense?" I asked.

"Yes. I know. It's Oswaldo's legacy. His legacy is present," she replied with a smile. We both fell silent. Oswaldo's many faces were watching over us through the television monitors.

* * *

ÁNGEL CARROMERO WANTED to speak. He had a lot to say, but had kept it bottled up. He'd spent several months in a Cuban prison charged with the death of Oswaldo Payá until negotiations with the Spanish government allowed him to return to Spain in December 2013. But he wasn't entirely free. He had to complete his sentence for involuntary manslaughter under the supervision of the Spanish government. When I spoke with him in Miami in 2014—to mark the publication of his book *Death Under Suspicion*—he was still wearing an electronic monitoring bracelet around his ankle.

On July 22, 2012, Carromero and Payá—along with the Cuban dissident Harold Cepero and the Swedish politician and chairman of the Young Christian Democrats Aron Modig—left Havana on a drive to Santiago de Cuba. Carromero was driving, Aron was in the front seat, and Payá and Cepero were in the back. The government was watching them. A tweet by a member of the regime spread across social networks: "Oswaldo is leaving right now for Varadero. He's going on vacation." No, he wasn't heading for the beach, but he was leaving the capital city in a car.

Suddenly they were struck from behind by another vehicle. Carromero described to me what happened next: "I lost control of the car and we skidded off the road. The next thing I know, they're pulling me out of the car and taking me to the hospital. Then they brought the others—they brought Aron, Harold, and Oswaldo—but they said they were dead. [They had been pulled from the car by] two people who were never identified; they showed up in a van all of a sudden, out of nowhere. It was very suspicious."

What happened to Oswaldo and Harold Cepero? Did they die upon impact? "They said they died in the crash," Carromero said. "That much is a lie. I think they died later, because there really was no accident. They just knocked us off the road. We weren't speeding.

There was no tree like the one the regime says we crashed into. Pictures [show] a tree that's intact. If anyone had hit that tree with any sort of force, the tree would have been damaged."

The official version of the accident, however, was very different. The Cuban government blamed Carromero for losing control of the vehicle, and that's what he appears to be saying in a video. But Carromero assured me that he was forced to give a false report of what actually happened.

"It's very important to clarify this," he said. "After they arrested me, they threw me in prison. I didn't have access to a lawyer; I didn't have access to anyone other than the soldiers who were guarding me. The military forced me to record a video Al Qaeda style. If you watch it, you'll see that my face is bruised, that I can barely speak, that I'm just reading a statement they wanted me to make. In the statement, I say 'transit accident.' No Spaniard would ever say 'transit accident.' We say 'traffic accident.'"

Aron Modig, the Swede who was also involved in the accident, has not spoken publicly about it since leaving Cuba.

According to Carromero, this was not the first time they tried to kill Payá in a car. He told me that two months before his death, Payá and his wife, Ofelia, suffered a similar accident when a car hit their vehicle and knocked it off the road. The perpetrators were never identified, and the military took Payá to the hospital.

Despite his shackles, Carromero shed his fear and used his book to contradict the Cuban dictatorship's official version of the events surrounding Payá's death. But it came at a cost.

"There were all kinds of slurs and threats," he told me as we neared the end of our interview. "As soon as I got back to my country, Spain, I started receiving death threats—over the phone, in the mail, spray-painted on the street—saying that they were going to kill me. It was a real alert when the police told me, 'Be careful wherever you go because there are people who want to do you harm.' But you can't bury the truth, and I have a moral duty to speak up and say what really happened."

That's what life is like when you're fighting a dictatorship.

LESSONS FROM THE CUBAN DISSIDENTS

Yoani Sánchez, Guillermo Fariñas, and Oswaldo Payá always knew that they couldn't overthrow the Cuban dictatorship on their own. Nevertheless, they decided to confront it: through independent media reports (in the case of Yoani), with hunger strikes (in the case of Fariñas), and by demanding a referendum (in the case of Payá).

These three forms of struggle have one thing in common. They're saying no to dictatorships. It is, fundamentally, a powerful moral stance to take: we are not giving in to the killing and the abuse. And it's also an ethical statement: we are on the right side of history, along with others who protect human rights and denounce repression.

"No" is the strongest word in any language, and it's the only one that can cause dictatorships to fold. There is nothing more powerful than saying "no" to a dictator. The cost, of course, can be life itself and that is what happened to Oswaldo Payá. But authoritarian regimes are weakened every time the word "no" is spoken by one of the governed.

No, I do not accept your government.

No, I do not recognize your position.

No, you have no legitimacy.

No, you cannot impose your way of thinking.

No, I will not obey.

No, I will not stop attacking you.

No, I am not going to leave.

No, no, and no.

No.

In her book *A Man*, the Italian journalist Oriana Fallaci wrote that one of the leaders of the resistance to the military dictatorship in Greece (1967–74), Alexandros Panagoulis, took her to the hills of Athens to teach her an important lesson about rebellion. When they reached the top, what she saw was the word "NO" made with stones (*OXI* in Greek).

This was, of course, simply a symbolic gesture, but it was one filled with rage and the desire for change. I have seen that same rage and desire in the ways in which Yoani, Fariñas, and Payá have faced off against the Castro dictatorship. With true heroism—and, in the case of Payá, the sacrifice of his own life—each of them has said, "No." In order to transform a nation (and even a relationship), the first thing you have to do is reject what hurts you.

"No" is the first word you have to say in order to create change, and many times it's the most difficult one to say.

SIX

Hugo Chávez: I Am Not the Devil

I am not a dictator. —HUGO CHÁVEZ

H UGO CHÁVEZ WAS a liar. But at least he was one of those liars who believed his own lies.

The first time I sat down with him, he lied to my face without the slightest hint of shame or discomfort. It was the day before the Venezuelan presidential elections, December 5, 1998. We met in an office in a Caracas skyscraper, and he arrived happily with his two daughters. He introduced them to us and we exchanged smiles.

He was wearing a suit and tie, the sort of outfit that would soon be replaced by a military uniform. Back in those days, Chávez wanted to present himself as a civilian, a democrat, and as a former military officer who would not be taking up arms again.

We started the interview.

Unhurried and amiable, I told Chávez that many people didn't consider him a democrat because of his failed 1992 coup attempt against the legitimately elected president, Carlos Andrés Pérez.

"I am not a dictator," he said.

"Are you willing to hand over power after five years?" I asked.

"Of course I am," he replied. "I've said it before. If, for example, two years from now, I turn out to be a failure—if I commit a crime, a corrupt act, or something else that would justify my removal from power—I would be willing to do so."

That was his first lie. Chávez never relinquished his power, and he ruled as a dictator up until his death on March 5, 2013, having repressed the opposition and personally controlled the army, the National Assembly, the judges, the media, the major state-owned corporations, and even the organization in charge of counting the votes cast during elections. Chávez effectively wrote his own constitution to perpetuate his own position of power. He never intended to hand it over to anyone.

Then came his second lie. Chávez assured me, during that interview in 1998, that he had no intentions of nationalizing any private companies. "No, absolutely not," he said. "We are actually willing to invest even more in the ones we already have, and in the private international capitalists, so that they will come and invest here as well . . . I'm not the devil."

In the first few years of his administration, Chávez nationalized CANTV, the largest telecommunications corporation in the country. Then he took operational control of six foreign companies—British Petroleum, ExxonMobil, ConocoPhillips, Chevron Texaco, Statoil (from Norway), and Total (from France)—who were drilling in the Orinoco Oil Belt. Many more would follow.

And then came the third lie.

"Would you nationalize some forms of media?" I asked. "Some form of private media?"

"No," he said. "Enough with the state-run media. The state already has Channel 8, [the] Venezuelan Television Corporation. I have a wonderful relationship [with] the rest of the stations. We're even interested in expanding them and going into more depth with them."

The sad truth was something else entirely. Chávez refused to renew the broadcast license for Radio Caracas Televisión, which was critical of his authoritarian system and the monopolization of power that was taking place in Venezuela. And he took every opportunity to co-opt or shut down independent media outlets. Globovisión was the biggest example of that.

One day before the elections that would put him in power, Chávez lied to me three separate times. Why did he do such a thing? Without a doubt, it was to appease the voters who were afraid that he would become the very dictator he ended up being.

He lied to gain power.

One thing that always struck me was that, during this very same interview, Chávez said that, yes, "Cuba is a dictatorship." It's difficult to understand, then, why he would take an interest in a dictator like Fidel Castro, and why he would make Cuba his primary ally. I am now convinced that Chávez was never a true democrat. However, that's how he first presented himself to all Venezuelans.

THE BURNING STENCH OF DEATH

In February 2000, Chávez was still pretending to be a democrat. This is what I wrote while on a plane to Venezuela. Getting there wasn't easy. In fact, it almost cost me my life.

In the air between Caracas and La Fría.

"Smoke, smoke!" one of the journalists shouted. "Hey, pilot, there's smoke in the cabin!"

From my seat on this tiny, eight-seat propeller plane, I could see a plume of white smoke—almost like vapor—emerging from the floor in the tail section of the cabin.

"Heeeey, pilot," I said, trying to hide my nervousness. "They're saying there's smoke."

"I heard them," he said tersely. "We're monitoring the instruments."

The first one who noticed the problem was Martín, one of the two cameramen accompanying me on a trip to interview the president of Venezuela, Hugo Chávez. From four seats away, he signaled to me that he could smell something burning.

Angel, our chief camera operator, with whom I've traveled all across Latin America, and our producer, Marisa, both confirmed what I did not want to hear. "It smells like something's burning," Angel said, while Marisa reaffirmed the existence of a sharp smell by scrunching up her nose.

My own sense of smell is quite bad. I've had three operations performed on my nose, and each one took its toll. Now all I can detect are the strongest of odors, but even I was able to tell that something was burning!

The copilot got up from his seat and went to check out the area where the smoke seemed to be coming from. He lifted up the floor mats, found nothing out of the ordinary, and announced, "It's the air-conditioning."

They turned off the heating and cooling system, and immediately it felt much colder there in the cabin. The smell of smoke went away. The plane continued its ascent: sixteen thousand, seventeen thousand, eighteen thousand feet. We had about twenty minutes left in the flight.

Nobody said a word. One of the two women in the group, a public official, pretended to be asleep, as if she were trying to block out the danger.

My insides felt like twisted metal. I couldn't believe that I was on a plane filled with smoke. But there I was. Everything flashed before my eyes: my children, the will I had signed just a couple of days before, my childhood in Mexico, and all the time I wasted on trivial things. What if the plane actually caught fire? The idea of dying in the morning has always bothered me. An entire day wasted! It was only nine a.m.

I was sitting directly behind the pilot and copilot, and although I don't know a thing about aviation, I was obsessively watching their every movement and scanning the unintelligible instrument panel, searching for some little red light that would indicate problems.

Nothing.

I took a deep breath.

The altimeter continued to rise until we reached twenty-four thousand feet. Suddenly, the smoke reappeared, this time with much more intensity. *Oh, shit,* I thought. *Now we're fucked.*

A ray of sunlight came streaming in through a window, and it looked like a little cloud of dust.

"It's just dust," said the public official, awakening from her feigned sleep.

"No, it's not," said one of the others. "I'm a smoker, and I know smoke when I see it."

Without so much as a word, the pilot dropped the plane down to ten thousand feet. Then the copilot—who couldn't have been more than twenty-five years old—checked the instruments and said to us, "I'm going to depressurize the cabin. You're going to feel a pain in your ears, and if you start feeling dizzy or short of breath, let me know and I'll get you an oxygen mask." The air was sucked out of the cabin, and with it the smoke.

"We have a mission," continued the pilot, who was a young officer in the Venezuelan Air Force. "We have to get to La Fría [where President Chávez's tour would begin], so I recommend we continue on at this altitude until we get there."

Marisa and I almost jumped out of our seats. "But how do you know there's not a fire on board?" we asked. "Shouldn't we land and check it out?"

"Because we have a mission," the military pilot insisted. "I gave you my recommendation, and I don't want to have a conversation going on between the passengers and the pilot."

Not even five minutes passed before the smoke came pouring in again. This time nearly the entire cabin was filled with the horrible scorched smell.

Somehow, we were all able to maintain an attitude of relative calmness. But inside, fear was pulling at my guts. I felt my chest and my eyebrows trembling uncontrollably, and my palms were soaking wet. I touched my forehead, and my hand was slick with sweat. My armpits were like two pools of water.

The stench never went away. Some of the passengers started making jokes. "Here comes the Reaper," one said morbidly. We were out of options; we had to make an emergency landing. The pilot forgot about the mission, and, looking somewhat pale himself, he asked the control tower for permission to land at the nearest airport, which happened to be a military base in Barquisimeto. Twelve minutes later, we touched down.

Taxiing down the runway, we realized what had actually happened. "How stupid are we?" we asked ourselves. "We should have told the pilot to turn us around at the first sign of smoke." But, of course, we had failed to accurately assess the danger, and on top of that, we didn't want to risk our chance at interviewing Chávez. "Such idiots," I repeated. I exited the plane and headed toward the hangar, muttering to myself, "I'm never going up in that piece of shit again." Meanwhile, my cameraman Angel kissed the ground like the pope.

After entering the structure, the first thing that I saw was a Catholic priest walking toward us at a leisurely pace. He was dressed in his black cassock and white collar, balding, and with a smile on his face.

Martín and I burst into nervous laughter. "It's like we're in a movie," he said.

Father Angel, as we later learned, visited the military base every Friday morning. I'm not a religious person, but I gladly accepted the little card with the image of the Virgin—the Divine Shepherdess—that he offered me, and I stashed it in my pocket.

Now I know what death smells like. It has a burned stench to it. And I know this because I'm now playing in overtime.

A DAY WITH HUGO CHÁVEZ

City of La Fría, in the state of Táchira.

I know of no other president who does what Hugo Chávez does. Right in front of the terrified eyes of his security detail, the Venezuelan president often breaks protocol and loses himself in a sea of people.

"With Chávez, we have a serious security problem," one of his ministers admitted to me. I was reminded of the case of the former Mexican presidential candidate Luis Donaldo Colosio, who was killed in the midst of a crowd in 1994. All the minister could say was, "What can we do? That's just how Chávez is."

"Chaaavez! Presideeente!" the crowd chants, and he seems to enjoy the spectacle. He asks for and receives requests. He talks and listens to problems: *I lost my home in the floods, I don't have a job, the mayor or town counselor is a thief, my baby is sick.* . . . But, more than anything, the people like to touch him. A lot.

Contrary to most of the Latin American leaders I've met, Chávez does not shun contact with the people. "He likes to be with his court," a journalist with whom I often work said wryly, referring to the Venezuelan people.

They kiss him, they embrace him, they touch his jet-black hair without the slightest hint of resistance on the part of Chávez. For the entire day during which I accompanied him on his tour of La Fría and Guarumito, in February 2000, not once did I ever see the president wipe away the sweat, the grime, the stains—even the lipstick—from his many encounters with the people. Not once.

In a practice that has become more of a ritual, Chávez travels to the interior of the country with several of his ministers and orders them—right there, on the spot—to attend to specific cases where people have asked for help. By now, not even the ministers are surprised. I happened to see several of them, pen and paper in hand, humbly taking note of the problems of people who had never in their lives even seen a minister, let alone spoken with one. These cases, it should be said, are usually resolved, but Venezuela is a nation of 18 million people, and they can't all be given personal access to a minister.

Outside of Venezuela, this style of governing could be described as populist or demagogic. But within these borders, many of the people I met are fascinated.

During one public appearance, Chávez began to read loudly into a microphone from the signs and banners being held up by the audience. In that way, he was able to put students at the Pedro Antonio Ríos Reyna University—who were complaining about not having had a director for months—in touch with the minister of education, and the others who were unemployed and otherwise affected were put to the attention of the special Social Fund.

Children flock to him. "Don't hold that girl like that!" Chávez scolded a man who was bringing his sick daughter up to the presidential stage. "Are you the father? Don't carry her like that!" He immediately called for his minister of health to find out what was wrong with the girl.

Another child, who was missing an eye, made him erupt with more Chavist rhetoric. "Where is the justice in that here we have a child such as this one, who is missing an eye, and for whom I mourn?" he asked, almost in tears. From there, he moved on to one of his favorite topics: how politicians from the country's two major parties have doomed the nation, and that only he, Chávez, could bring it back from the brink.

"Out of every one hundred Venezuelans, eighty are living in poverty," he shouted to a group of supporters who were swarming around the front of the stage. "For forty years, this country was robbed by a band of thieves." Cue the applause. "They stole this country right out from under our very own noses, thanks to cowardice or ignorance." More applause. "Venezuela is like a demolished building, and it is up to us to raise it up again." Much cheering and even louder applause.

Then he shifted to another of his favorite themes: how the Venezuelan oligarchy—both within and outside the country—and the owners of some sources of media are attacking his presidency. "I will not let myself be blackmailed by anyone," Chávez said. "If you listen to the radio and read what's in the papers, you're going to think that this is all a big disaster."

"Nooo!" the crowd shouted in unison.

Chávez has a well-developed talent for the theatrical. He speaks in very simple terms—*"a ver negra, véngase pa'ca."* "Hey, you there in the crowd, come on up here." Like an actor he handles pauses and dramatic scenes perfectly, and he never misses an opportunity to appear in front of the cameras with common folks and low-ranking soldiers.

At the ceremony that was prepared for his arrival at the La Fría airport, Chávez skipped right past the line of high-ranking officers standing at attention and hopped on top of a nearby tank. Much to the surprise of the soldiers, the president started asking them about everything from their families to how their machine guns worked.

Seeing him sitting on that tank, in his olive-green uniform, his black boots, and his red beret, it was impossible not to think that the commander in chief of the Venezuelan military would still be in prison for his failed coup attempt in 1992 if it weren't for the controversial pardon handed down by the president at the time, Rafael Caldera. After that, Chávez did with voters at the polls what he had failed to do with boots on the ground: on December 6, 1998, he won a landslide victory.

Since then, Venezuela has held a number of referendums and written a new constitution, which legally allowed Chávez to remain in power—not for five years, as was the limit in a previous version, but for eventually to stand for election with no term limits at all. And his plan was to take full advantage.

"In ten years," he announced, "you will see the new face of Venezuela. A beautiful face." For him, this "Beautiful Venezuela" project meant a nation without unemployment, with housing, education, and health care for everyone, and with lower rates of crime. But in order to reach that point, he cautioned the people attending the rally, "You have to be revolutionary."

Chávez was constantly mixing his revolutionary rhetoric with biblical passages and references to Christ. In one speech, he compared his job—rebuilding the country—to Christ carrying the cross to Calvary.

Despite his immense popularity in Venezuela, Chávez seemed to be wearing out his welcome just a little bit. In his first year as president, his approval rating dropped from 90 percent to 69.

This was reflected abroad as well. In Miami, for example, where many Venezuelan capitalists had to live since early 1999, you often heard talk about how Chávez was trying to turn Venezuela into another Cuba, and the opinion that the social experiment he began was going to end badly.

A human rights activist in Venezuela agreed. "People voted for Chávez because they were looking for relief from forty years of injustice, corruption, and wealth accumulation," he told me. Now, Chávez was faced with the challenge to transform that hatred and resentment into something that actually worked . . . and to do it soon. Many Venezuelan expats doubted that he could deal with all of that, and their money followed their concerns, by going abroad.

But most Venezuelans were betting that "Chavismo" would eventually take off, because that was their only option.

* * *

IN EARLY 2000, criticisms leveled by the president of the Bolivarian Republic of Venezuela against the media were sounding terribly, terribly bad. There were unmistakable signs of total authoritarian rule.

First the director of *El Mundo*, Teodoro Petkoff, was forced to resign after the government pressured the newspaper's ownership. Other Venezuelan papers—along with private radio and television programs—were under constant scrutiny from Chávez's military advisors.

Then came the new constitution, which put the government in charge of determining what information was considered true and objective. Later there were the furious complaints that Chávez fired at the *Miami Herald* for publishing an article—along with official documentation corroborating the report—showing that the president had not taken necessary safety precautions despite knowing of the imminent danger posed by massive floods in December 1999.

Who would be next? Where was freedom of the press?

OF THE TWENTY-FOUR journalists who accompanied Chávez on Friday, February 18, 2000, eight were Cuban. Obviously, the Venezuelan president's interests in Cuba were such that it would require a number of reporters to cover them all. Eight.

And the journalists, of course, were eager to speak with him, especially since he had stopped giving independent interviews in order to focus on the national stations. In the two weeks leading up to our visit, Chávez had interrupted broadcasts of *telenovelas* (or *culebrones*, as the soap operas are called in Venezuela) no fewer than six times to talk about . . . well, everything.

So, after a grueling, twelve-hour chase involving two separate airplanes and a helicopter, he finally agreed to speak with me for about ten minutes in the town of Guarumito, very close to the Colombian border. This was after having stopped at a dairy plant to pick up some supplies that would later be delivered to flood victims (or "victors," as he referred to them).

It was clear that the weeks and weeks of phone calls and faxes with Chávez's press corps had done us no good, since we had been promised an interview with him on the presidential plane. Instead we were taken to a small border town. Our requests—pleas, really—to speak with him at the Miraflores Palace, his official place of residence in Caracas, were similarly unsuccessful.

"No," one of his spokespeople said. "He is not a president who sits behind a desk. He wants the interview to be conducted among the people." And so it was.

There in Guarumito, surrounded by dozens of "victors," I sat down on a white plastic chair to speak with the Venezuelan president in the middle of a concrete basketball court. The sun was about to set, but even after a full day of speeches, Chávez was eager to keep talking.

Red beret. Green combat fatigues. Black boots. Total concentration.

Chávez had always been a confident person, which I learned from the two previous interviews I conducted with him. But this time I noticed that he seemed impatient and uncomfortable with questions he didn't appreciate. Even so, his desire to maintain total control remained intact. With every question I asked him, his supporters booed me. And they cheered his every response. I'd never done an interview quite like that before.

"Abroad, people are wondering what you're celebrating after your first year [in office]," I said. "They're seeing that the economy decreased by seven percent, that six hundred thousand people are unemployed, that poverty is on the rise, that some of your senior advisors have been accused of corruption, that members of the military have been accused of killing people . . . so what, exactly, are you celebrating?"

"Here in Venezuela, we are celebrating everyone who is here," he began. "The millions of people like him," he said, pointing to a boy.

"Millions like that innocent little girl right there, millions like that woman over there. It's the beginning of a rebirth. We are rising from the grave, and the entire world will have to slowly begin to learn this. That's the challenge. For today's world to understand us. Beyond just what can be said, the truths or half-truths. And I don't care about that anymore. I swear. What does, in fact, matter to me is the reality of my people. I care about their pain and I am moved by the love, the immense sense of love that we feel for all mankind."

On December 15, 1999, Venezuela held a referendum to approve the new constitution. This document, written by Chávez and his followers, would allow the president to remain in power forever.

But like a sign from above in a magical realism novel, that same day saw a series of torrential downpours sweep across the country. The worst flooding Venezuela had experienced in decades followed, and hundreds of people died in the states of Vargas, Miranda, and Falcón.

Far from taking control of the situation, Chávez disappeared from public view during the most crucial moments. Rumors abounded, the most pervasive of which was that in the midst of the storm, Chávez was on the island of Orchila meeting with Fidel Castro. So I asked him: Where were you when your country needed you most? He denied having been with Castro. But he clearly did not appreciate the question, and he began insulting me.

"Well, they're lies. They're lies," he said. "Clearly, you're repeating garbage. You're just here repeating garbage."

"But isn't it true?"

"You're repeating garbage, brother."

"Which is why I want to ask you . . ."

"And I'll respond with my dignity. With the dignity of my people. You're repeating garbage with your own mouth."

"I'm asking you," I replied. "My job is to ask questions."

"It's okay," he said. "It's okay. But you're just picking up people's trash. You're a garbage man, you're hauling manure. Why not bring something else to the table?"

"Well, it's a legitimate question for a journalist to ask, is it not?"

"But, that's how you come across," he argued. "You come here with this trash, brother, and I welcome you as a trash collector. It's not a lack of respect for you, but it's the truth. I have to tell you the truth."

"Which is why I wanted to ask you."

"You're hauling a load of trash. You came all this way—from Miami, right?—hauling this load of trash."

"My question, very simply, is . . ."

"Am I obliged to answer only what you ask?" he interjected.

At this point in the discussion, one of his ministers tapped the president on the back and let him know that the ten minutes allotted for the interview were almost up. "Take it easy," Chávez said. "We're going to talk a little bit longer."

He set the insults aside and quickly changed the topic: "Bring me a coffee, please."

A couple of minutes later, two cups of black coffee arrived. He offered one to me, as a sign of peace, and took the other for himself. He sipped it calmly.

"It's quite good," he said. "Venezuelan coffee is really quite good. Extraordinary."

"How do you take your coffee?"

"Very *guarapo*."

"What does that mean?"

"*Guarapo* means very clear. Almost as much water as coffee. Very smooth. *Guayoyo*, as they say. Well, then, *Viva México*!"

"*Viva Venezuela!*"

Chávez wanted to continue talking. He didn't like losing arguments or leaving anything hanging. We moved on to the topic of Cuba. But even then, in early 2000, he refused to say that his was a socialist revolution.

"In Havana, you said, 'The channel that the people of Venezuela are constructing is the same channel, and it flows towards the same sea, as the one the Cuban people are marching towards.' What were you referring to? The direction you want Venezuela to be headed in?"

"It's the same thing I would say in Mexico City," he replied. "And I have said it. Just as I would if I were in Bogotá or Cúcuta, in Rio or Brasilia, in Buenos Aires or Montevideo or Puerto Príncipe or Santo Domingo."

"But, for example, when you referred to the Cuban leader as 'brother Fidel,' [many Venezuelan expats] felt that you were linking yourself too closely to a dictatorship."

"I'm not worried about what other people are worried about," he replied. "Absolutely not. My concern is my people. . . . If someone wants to see ghosts in the night, he will."

"I was surprised to hear you call [Fidel Castro] 'brother' because back on December 5 [of 1998]—do you remember?—when you and I spoke, I asked you about Cuba and you said to me, yes, 'Cuba is a dictatorship.' And now you're referring to the leader of that dictatorship as a 'brother.' Is there not a contradiction there?"

"Aside from whether you say 'dictatorship' and I say 'yes' or I say 'no'—because you would have to contextualize whatever I said—I'm not one to condemn the Cuban regime or the American regime."

And that's how the interview ended: with the president raising his cup once again—this time for the world to see—with the people applauding, and with the impending evening forcing us back to the helicopter which would take us from Guarumito back to the airport in La Fría.

THE NEW CONSTITUTION had enormous consequences. On July 31, 2000, President Chávez was reelected to another six-year term, easily beating out his former friend Francisco Arias.

A few days later, on Thursday, August 10, Chávez earned the dubious honor of being the first democratically elected leader to visit the dictator Saddam Hussein in Baghdad. "If the United States gets upset, what can I do about that?" he asked rhetorically while in Iraq. Meanwhile, back in Venezuela, the press didn't know whether to highlight the president's independence when it came to foreign policy, or his affinity for meeting with dictators.

47 HOURS WITHOUT HUGO CHÁVEZ

In April 2002 there was an attempted coup against Hugo Chávez. I got on a flight from Miami to Caracas, and this is what I saw . . .

Caracas.

The images were horrible. In a video taken by a Venevisión cameraman, several armed men appeared to open fire on a group of opposition marchers heading down the central avenue of Baral toward the Miraflores Palace. It was chilling to watch at least four men standing on the Llaguno Bridge open fire, reload their weapons, and then open fire again.

The footage itself was not enough to determine exactly who they were shooting at, but the direction in which they were aiming clearly suggested that they were targeting the oncoming marchers.

Chávez ended up banning broadcasts by private television stations, which—before the presidential order was made—had reported extensively on both the march and the victims of the massacre in downtown Caracas. So when the ban did go into effect, it was already too late. Millions of people, both within Venezuela and around the world, had seen the video of these shooters—identified by the local press as members of the pro-Chávez "Bolivarian Circles"—allegedly firing upon the protesters.

The five-thousand-strong march, which was held on Thursday, April 11, 2002, had been organized by the anti-Chavista Workers' Confederation of Venezuela after several employees were dismissed from the Venezuelan state-owned oil and natural gas company PDVSA. Besides demanding the reinstitution of the fired workers, many were also calling for the resignation of President Chávez himself.

Nineteen people died that day, and nearly a hundred were wounded. Among the dead was an eighteen-year-old, Gustavo Tovar. A friend of his family explained to me how the young man was killed.

"They started shooting from who knows where, and he was hit in the head," he said while gently holding on to a photo of Tovar. "Eighteen years old. A boy who was just beginning to live his life."

The next day they arrested a man by the name of Germán Atencio, a former employee of the Ministry of Environment and Natural Resources, who was identified thanks to the video footage as one of the men firing from the Llaguno Bridge. "I know I did wrong and I'm sorry for that," Atencio told reporters shortly after his arrest. "But at no point was I ever shooting at those people."

The day after the shooting, I went up on the Llaguno Bridge myself, and from there I had an uninterrupted view of several blocks of the avenue along which the anti-Chavista protesters were marching toward the Miraflores Palace. The gunmen would have been able to clearly see that thousands of people were heading toward the bridge where they had been stationed. If it were true that these gunmen were not blindly firing into the crowd but instead were firing at other armed men, it would have required exceptional marksmanship to avoid wounding and killing innocent protesters. The video footage shows several gunmen firing wildly in the direction of the crowd without taking any time to aim at any specific target. Furthermore, that same footage shows no evidence of shots being fired back at the pro-Chávez gunmen standing on the bridge.

The events of April 11, 2002, were never fully explained. Chávez's officials maintained that most of the victims were government sympathizers who had gathered near the bridge to stop the opposition march from reaching the Miraflores Palace. They insisted that snipers and members of the Metropolitan Police—allied with Alfredo Peña, mayor of Caracas, and opposed to the Chávez regime—were responsible for starting the shooting. And finally, they estimated that the protesters never came within 380 meters of the bridge, far beyond the range of the Chavista gunmen.

Regardless of what actually happened, the images of those Chavista gunmen firing in the direction of the opposing protesters had enormous political implications. In the power vacuum that arose after the massacre, the version of events that gained the most traction was that the Chávez government had opened fire on the very people who had put him in office. Chávez, his opponents argued, organized the resistance to the march and authorized the use of weapons by the "Bolivarian Circles," or—at the very least—he allowed them to open fire on the protesters with impunity.

To further strengthen the opposition's argument, raids on the homes and offices of the president's supporters, which took place during the two days following the massacre, resulted in seizures of large amounts of arms and ammunition. What was all of this weaponry for?

The legitimacy of the president's power was fading with every passing hour. Yes, it's true, Hugo Chávez had fairly won the most recent election and had received support from a majority of the Venezuelan people to change the constitution and reform the country's institutional principles. But that didn't give him any right to open fire on his own people. And there were videos to prove that he had done so.

From the opposition's point of view, they now had a legal, documented reason with which to justify removing Chávez from power.

Still, though, they needed to find the best way to do it. If he refused to resign, the National Assembly could demand it, and he could even be put on trial for complicity in the murders.

The night of April 11, 2002, was the night Chávez lost control of Venezuela. His authority was being challenged by his opponents, by businessmen, and even by members of his own military. A massacre of civilians was unjustifiable. And all signs were pointing directly at the Miraflores Palace.

That same night, the two primary leaders of workers and businesses—Carlos Ortega of the Workers' Confederation of Venezuela, and Pedro Carmona of the Venezuelan Federation of Chambers of Commerce—got together to talk. An alliance between workers and ownership effectively started a countdown on the presidency of Hugo Chávez. They worked together to find a legal, constitutional way of removing him from power. But in the early hours of April 12, they still hadn't found the means by which to do so. Chávez, they knew full well, would not go willingly.

According to some of the media reports, Carmona left Ortega and other opposition leaders—including members of the Copei People's Party and the Democratic Alliance—and went back to the Four Seasons in Caracas to change. But shortly after, he went to Fort Tiuna to talk with General Efraín Vásquez Velasco. General Vásquez then decided to send a high-ranking military official, General Néstor González, to ask President Chávez for his resignation. The president, as we now know, did not resign, and instead was forced to leave Miraflores Palace under arrest before being transported first to Fort Tiuna and later to the naval base at Turiamo and finally to a military installation on Orchila Island.

This was clearly not a constitutional solution. It was a coup d'état. Period. Carmona, a sixty-one-year-old businessman, along with a group of disgruntled soldiers and rebels, had taken power by force. This was a grave mistake. What had begun as a challenge to Chávez's power after the massacre in downtown Caracas had suddenly turned into a full-blown coup. Chávez, who already had his back up against a wall because of the crimes committed by his supporters, had now become a victim. And a few hours later, that fact would allow him to return to power.

Carmona represented the head of a civilian-military alliance, and his brief tenure as president was a disaster. One of his first acts was to abolish the National Assembly and the Supreme Tribunal of Justice, the highest court in the land. With those actions, Carmona effectively concentrated the three branches of government—executive, legislative, and judicial—which made him a de facto dictator himself. On paper, at least, his alleged power far exceeded that which Chávez had accumulated.

On the night of April 12, I was having dinner with a group of journalist friends at a restaurant in the Altamira neighborhood of Caracas. The mood was, quite frankly, one of celebration. Many Venezuelan opponents of Chávez had gathered, and all of them were thinking that, finally, they had gotten rid of "Fidel's little tyrant buddy." The wine and whiskey were flowing freely amid cheers of "Salud" and "Viva Venezuela."

But the celebration didn't last long.

I had come to Venezuela to report on the fall of Hugo Chávez. I never imagined I would end up covering his return to power.

The prevailing rumor that night in Caracas was that Chávez had resigned and would soon be sent to Cuba. Others, intoxicated by their sudden rise to power, wanted revenge and demanded that Chávez and his collaborators be put behind bars. Throughout the next day, a number of the deposed president's followers were chased down and beaten by opposing mobs.

The problem was that there was a lot of talk about the president's resignation—a version of the facts that suited the opposition, given that they had no legal alternative that could explain the creation of a civilian-military junta—but nobody could produce a document or video footage as evidence that the president had actually resigned. The chief of staff, General Lucas Rincón, had publicly accepted a letter of resignation that Chávez had not, in fact, ever given. That opened the door for Carmona and General Vásquez to abolish Chávez's presidency and create their own transitional government.

But that didn't sound right to Raúl Isaías Baduel, who was in command of the Maracay Air Brigade. "This is a right-wing coup. I'm not involved," General Baduel said to one of his subordinates, according to later reports by the magazine *Cambio*. His position wasn't immediately released by media outlets, many of which were still celebrating the fall of Chávez. But it was, in fact, leaked to other military commanders, who joined the resistance movement started in Maracay by General Baduel. And that's how the counterinsurgency that allowed Chávez to return to power began.

On the morning of Saturday, April 13, many citizens of Caracas were surprised to see storefronts destroyed, people firing shots in the air, and other signs of violence being attributed to Chávez sympathizers who had moved in from the surrounding hills in the night. A mall I visited lay in ruins. The ATM machine at a local bank had been looted. Not a single window remained unshattered; only those businesses protected by metal gates had managed to endure the wrath of the Chavistas. The movement to return Chávez to Miraflores had begun.

The media, which had previously suffered Chávez's repressive whims, refused to report what was happening. They were openly betting against the deposed president, and instead of broadcasting the news, they chose to fill their time slots with movies and entertainment programming. Anyone who was watching private television that day would have concluded—erroneously—that nothing at all was going on in Caracas, and that the president's departure was irreversible. But out in the streets, thousands of Chávez supporters were about to return him to the Miraflores Palace, whether by hook or by crook.

Private television stations could take sides and refuse to broadcast what was going on in the streets of Caracas. But not the international press. CNN en Español, which was providing continuing coverage of the Venezuelan crisis, aired an interview with Chávez's wife, Marisabel, who stated that her husband had never, in fact, resigned. Shortly thereafter, two members of the National Assembly released a document allegedly signed by Chávez that read as follows:

> *Turiamo,*
> *April 13, 2002, at 14:45*

> *To the people of Venezuela*
> *(And whomever it may concern)*

> *I, Hugo Chávez Frías, Venezuelan, President of the*
> *Bolivarian Republic of Venezuela, do declare:*
>   *I have not resigned the legitimate power that the*
> *people gave me.*
>   *Forever!*
> > *Hugo Chávez F.*

The document had apparently been obtained by one of the national guardsmen who were standing watch over Chávez at the Turiamo Naval Base. Any Venezuelans who had access to satellite TV or had otherwise received this information from outside the country now realized that Chávez had never relinquished power, and was defiantly resisting the coup. Carmona and his military coconspirators could no longer prop up their version of events, and their government—literally only hours old—began to crumble.

I spent that afternoon editing my Univision coverage of the night before at the Venevisión offices. On a number of occasions, we had to lock ourselves inside because roving bands of Chavistas would ride up on motorcycles armed with clubs, rocks, and handguns to threaten the station employees. Similar attacks also occurred at Globovisión and Radio Caracas facilities.

Meanwhile, private media outlets insisted on remaining silent. No news, just movies and entertainment. But rumors about the possible return of President Chávez were growing stronger.

Later that night, while I was having dinner at a restaurant in the Caracas Hilton, one of the cooks pulled me aside and asked, "Is it true that Chávez is about to return to Caracas?" He was better informed than I was. "I don't know," I said, "but I'm going to find out." I ordered a plate of pasta, pulled out my phone, and called up some of my contacts.

Something was, indeed, happening. At Fort Tiuna, where a group of Univision reporters had gathered, nobody was allowed in or out. Interim President Carmona was also there to speak with the media. But suddenly he found himself trapped, like all the other civilians. The soldiers who, up to a few hours ago, had controlled the country had lost control of Fort Tiuna. Meanwhile, other military units began joining those who already risen up against the new junta.

After dinner, I called the cook over to me and said, "You were right. It seems that Chávez will be back in power tonight." When the cook returned to the kitchen and told the others what I'd just told him, I could hear joyful chants: "He's coming back, he's coming back!"

When I first sat down to dinner, Chávez was about to be exiled to Cuba, but by the time the dessert course came around, the story had changed and he was on the verge of regaining power.

The lack of hard information was almost overwhelming. Private broadcasts weren't reporting anything, while official state media were only passing along a series of unconfirmed rumors. Carmona and his military leaders were nowhere to be found, and Chávez was still on Orchila Island. Nobody knew whether he was a president or a prisoner.

The violence intensified that same Saturday night. Shots rang out everywhere, and it was dangerous to move about the city. Still, though, we had to get the latest news out, and that meant leaving the hotel. We got a satellite signal with which to transmit, and got ready to broadcast our news live from Caracas. We found a concealed place in the corner of a random house's patio; we didn't want some roving band of Chavistas to see the lights of our cameras and attack us. To them, all reporters and all cameramen were indistinguishable, and all were considered enemies of Chávez.

It was nearly midnight on the night of April 14.

Halfway through the broadcast, one of the producers let me know that he had been in contact via phone with Chávez's defense minister, José Vicente Rangel, and that he was ready to give an interview. It was the perfect opportunity to ask him about the rumors that Chávez was returning to power.

"Very shortly, President Chávez will be leaving the Venezuelan island of Orchila, where he was detained, in a helicopter," Rangel explained to me. "And within the hour, he will be back in Caracas, in the Miraflores Palace, to assume power once again. All the branches of the military—the air force, the marines, the national guard, and the army—are loyal to the President of the Republic. At this time, Vice President Diosdado Cabello is in charge."

The adventure perpetrated by Carmona and his military co-conspirators had collapsed under the weight of its own illegality, and with Chávez still enjoying strong support throughout the military.

"Has the president resigned?" I asked Rangel.

"That is completely false," he responded. "It never happened. That is just one more hoax, one more lie invented by the rebels. President Chávez never resigned."

I told Rangel that many of his opponents blamed the president for ordering the April 11 massacre, and that that would justify removing him from power.

"That is what the leaders said in order to justify the coup," he said. "They wanted to impress the military. Now, the truth regarding that will come out. Most of the deceased—I would say almost ninety percent of them—were supporters of President Chávez. They were police snipers—who have nothing to do with the government—who caused their deaths."

Just minutes after the interview, Chávez reentered Miraflores Palace in front of an excited crowd that had already forced the soldiers protecting Carmona from the property.

Chávez had been out of power for forty-seven hours.

On the night of Monday, April 15, I was able to speak with President Chávez, who was showing clear signs of exhaustion and lack of sleep. I had gotten the cell phone number of Vice President Diosdado Cabello, who—without much hesitation—handed the phone to the president when I called.

"First, I have to tell you that the situation is quickly returning to normal," Chávez told me. "Yesterday, it's true, I was still being detained, being held on the island of Orchila in the Caribbean. But as soon as we returned to the palace, around dawn, the situation began to take on a greater degree of governance. We were working all morning, and the people who had taken to the streets were returning to their homes. I ordered increased police patrols, and in some locations, I ordered military patrols as well."

"Is your life currently in danger?" I asked.

"No, absolutely not," he said. "I'm right here with my wife, my five children, my granddaughters, and I'm working with a number of my ministers, with the vice president. . . . In the afternoon, I went to Maracay to see the commander of the 42nd Paratrooper Brigade, which is the unit that started the popular and military action to restore the law and the constitution, and which reinstituted me as president of the Republic. And that was achieved without firing a single shot. There is no reason to believe that my life is in any danger. These rumors out there about a possible kidnapping are completely false."

"What has happened to Pedro Carmona?" I asked. "Is he under arrest?"

"Yes, Pedro Carmona has been detained . . ."

And with that, the line went dead. We were never able to restore telephone contact, and I was never able to ask him about his responsibility when it came to the April 11 massacre. That was my final interview with Chávez. Despite multiple attempts on my part, he did not want to speak with me again.

HUGO CHÁVEZ: THE LESSONS

After the attempted coup in 2002, Chávez became more radicalized. His flirtations with Castro became a torrid affair. He stopped hiding the fact that his true objective was a socialist revolution, he conducted a purge of the army, and he began to expand his power. That would continue until his death in 2013.

The woman who, perhaps, knew Chávez better than anyone was Marisabel Rodríguez, his second wife. The two had a daughter together, Rosinés.

Immediately following the attempted coup, Marisabel was the first one to come out and say—during an interview with CNN en Español—that Chávez had not resigned from office. This paved the way for him to eventually return to power.

I interviewed her in August 2008, when Chavismo governance had already been reestablished, which was also four years after her divorce from the president. The differences I saw in her were clear.

"Right after the coup [in 2002], we took the opportunity to spend a couple of months together," Marisabel told me. And that was when she realized that Chávez had changed "radically," and now supported a policy based on "retribution and revenge."

"What made him change?" I asked.

"Sometimes, people haven't fully matured by the time they first come to power," she replied. "And in order to sustain that power, they become totalitarian. Some of the people around him filled his head with the idea of perpetuating his power."

And that is how totalitarian Chavismo was born.

During my interview with Chávez in 1998 in which he promised to give up power after his constitutional period, he clearly lied to win the election. That's what dictators do. That's the lesson. When Venezuelans tried to correct their mistake, it was too late. Chávez was already controlling everything.

Hugo Chávez died of cancer, while still in power, on March 5, 2013.

SEVEN

The One Who Loses Is the One Who Tires First: Leopoldo López and Lilian Tintori

If my imprisonment serves to awaken the people, if Venezuela wakes up once and for all . . . then this infamous imprisonment is worth it. —LEOPOLDO LÓPEZ

I married Leopoldo and I also married his commitment to a better Venezuela. I will not stop. I will not stop.
—LILIAN TINTORI

P ERHAPS HE WAS destined for prison. And after that, maybe, the presidency of Venezuela.

When we met in Miami in November 2013, neither Leopoldo López nor I could have imagined that in less than three months he would end up in a Venezuelan prison cell.

He had just arrived from a long tour of his country, and the report was not a good one: Venezuela had become a nation of lines. "Lines at the gas station, lines at the grocery store, lines at the bus stops, lines at the hospital," he began to list. "Four or five hour-long blackouts each and every day. No drinking water. Problems with sewage. We are the least secure country in Latin America . . . an average of sixty murders a day."

But Nicolás Maduro's government was not taking responsibility for the crisis. Instead, it launched a nationwide campaign, complete with posters and televised speeches, accusing the opposition leaders— including Leopoldo, former presidential candidate Henrique Capriles, and assemblywoman María Corina Machado—of being the country's greatest problems.

This is how Leopoldo explained it to me: "Maduro took pictures of each of us and said, and I quote, 'These are the ones responsible if you don't have electricity, if you don't have water, if you don't have enough to eat.' Obviously, the people aren't stupid. The people know it's a campaign move designed to incite hatred. But that's how to reach a certain segment of the population. It's a way—albeit not only irresponsible but also immoral—of handling power."

Leopoldo knew the government was watching him. It wasn't the first time.

LEOPOLDO LÓPEZ WAS mayor of the municipality of Chacao from 2000 to 2008 before announcing his intention to run as a candidate for mayor of Caracas. Polls had him pegged as the favorite.

But President Hugo Chávez did not want an opponent governing the capital city, and so the comptroller general of the republic disqualified him from holding public office for three years because of an alleged conflict of interest (a donation from Petróleos de Venezuela, also known as PDVSA, to his Justice First organization). The disqualification would later be extended until 2014.

The Inter-American Commission on Human Rights took up Leopoldo's case and found in his favor, but the Chávez administration ignored the decision. Leopoldo was clearly positioning himself as a serious threat to the Chávez regime, and they wanted to neutralize him.

After Chávez's death from cancer, presidential elections were held on Sunday, April 14, 2013. The candidate handpicked by Chávez, Nicolás Maduro, obtained 50.61 percent of the vote, according to official figures, beating out his opponent, Henrique Capriles, who had 49.12 percent.

The opposition immediately claimed fraud. And their primary complaint was obvious: the National Electoral Council, which counted the votes, was under the control of the established government.

"Maduro stole the April 14th election," Leopoldo told me in an interview at the end of 2013. "We are convinced that the voters favored unity [the opposition] and stole the election in complicity with the National Electoral Council and the Supreme Tribunal of Justice."

The government, of course, denied any fraud. The opposition had to respond, and they called for a massive march to be held on Wednesday, April 17. The confrontation had been set. Thousands would show up to defend the opposition's vote at a time when it seemed that the Chávez regime might be cracking. The only question was how the army would react to this threat.

According to a number of interviews, there was serious dissent within the opposition. Leopoldo and Assemblywoman María Corina Machado supported the strategy of confrontation, and argued that they had to take to the streets. But, in the end, the decision fell to Capriles, who had been the party's candidate in the election.

Capriles had received reports suggesting the possibility of attacks on demonstrators by both the army and the police that would result in considerable loss of life. The day before the scheduled march, Capriles suspended it.

"I still believe we should have done it," Leopoldo said. "That was my position at the time. Now, I wasn't the candidate. When it comes to the threat of violence during a demonstration in the streets, that burden of that responsibility falls on the Venezuelan state, which has a monopoly on the police force and their weapons."

But the march didn't take place. And with that, the opposition may have lost a historic opportunity to end the authoritarian Chávez regime.

"The opportunity was missed, but it won't be the last one," Leopoldo reflected. Then he tried to put to rest his differences with Capriles. "That doesn't mean that we're not united. We're all united when it comes to change. [But] I do believe that people have to demonstrate in the streets in a nonviolent way."

The primary difference between Capriles and Leopoldo is that the latter was convinced that he had to force the regime to accept change, and the only way to do that was with protests and marches. Capriles's decision not to take to the streets on April 17 had a huge impact on Leopoldo, and it would influence the way he would act going forward.

Meanwhile, President-elect Maduro continued to make mistakes. On one occasion he said that Chávez came to him in the form of a little bird that whistled in order to communicate with him. On another, attempting to quote the Bible in Spanish, he talked about the multiplication of "penises" ("*penes*") instead of "fish," or "*peces*." And the liberties he took with Spanish grammar led to his talking about "*millonas*" instead of "*millones*"—or millions—of women.

The opposition continued to mock Maduro through social networks. They were relentless, especially when he created a Ministry of Supreme Social Happiness. But the fact of the matter was that—despite all his gaffes and a very public fall from a bicycle—Maduro was still in power.

"There are plenty of reasons to mock Maduro," Leopoldo admitted. But this was no laughing matter. "He represents the destruction of our nation, the disaster that we are living today in Venezuela. . . . Happiness by decree? Obviously not."

* * *

MADURO DID NOT fall. But Venezuela went into a tailspin with one of the highest levels of inflation in the world, long waiting lines for basic necessities, and levels of crime approaching those of a war zone. The drop in oil prices and frequent allegations of government corruption created a terrible economic crisis for the country.

"Today, the people governing Venezuela are turning it into a rogue state," Leopoldo said with condemnation. "A state centered around backroom deals, corruption, and even links to drug trafficking." Indeed, what had been one of the most prosperous countries in Latin America for decades was quickly becoming one of the poorest, most dangerous, and most corrupt. (A Gallup poll conducted in March 2014 found that 75 percent of Venezuelans believed that corruption was rampant in the government.)

The opposition did not want a coup. The lesson from the failed attempt in 2002 was well learned. Nothing would be done outside the law. But they were still seeking legal options to force Maduro "to leave." Leopoldo told me of four possible choices: "A reform, a constitutional amendment, [a decree] by the constituent assembly, or Maduro's own resignation."

Clearly, Maduro would neither cooperate nor resign. "In 2016, if you want, you can collect signatures and we can square off in a recall referendum," Maduro said in response to all the challenges coming from his opponents. But the opposition wasn't willing to wait any longer.

In February 2014, antigovernment protests broke out across the nation, but were quickly suppressed by the Venezuelan National Guard and the police. These protests not only were proposing an immediate change of government, but were also a clear rejection of Nicolás Maduro's administration. When the disturbances were quelled, the final toll was forty-three dead (including a number of government officials), more than eight hundred injured, and thousands arrested.

The protests and *güarimbas* (the blockading of streets) gradually began to fade, but the government's intention of putting the organizers behind bars did not. A court in Caracas issued an arrest warrant for Leopoldo on charges of terrorism and murder, among others.

Leopoldo refused to go into hiding or seek asylum outside of the country. Instead, he decided to publicly turn himself in on February 18. He did not trust what he called an "unjust justice system," but his incarceration had a clear political goal: ending the Maduro regime.

"If my imprisonment serves to awaken the people, if Venezuela wakes up once and for all—and if the majority of those of us who want change are able to create it in a peaceful and democratic way—then this infamous imprisonment is worth it," he said in Caracas before turning himself over to members of the National Guard and being whisked off in a military vehicle.

Leopoldo would be held at Ramo Verde military prison.

THE REBEL WIFE

Every morning at five thirty, Lilian Tintori gets up to pray and read the Bible. At the exact same time, her husband, political prisoner Leopoldo López, does the same in Ramo Verde military prison. They made this agreement before his arrest so that every morning, at the same time, Lilian and Leopold can be connected.

I spoke with Lilian in Miami in February 2015, just over a year after the arrest of her husband. Lilian must now speak for Leopoldo because Leopoldo is no longer free to speak for himself.

President Maduro never forgave him for leading the 2014 protests that nearly toppled the regime. The government filed four trumped-up charges against Leopoldo—destruction of property, arson, conspiracy, and public incitement—and shortly after that, Leopoldo surrendered to authorities. His trial was a farce. Several human rights organizations—including Amnesty International and Human Rights Watch—believed his arrest was unjustified, that it was nothing more than a crude attempt to suppress the leader of Maduro's primary opposition.

But Maduro made two mistakes by arresting Leopoldo. First, he created a martyr. Some compared Leopoldo's arrest to that of Nelson Mandela in South Africa. And we all know how that story ended. "Leopoldo is a prisoner of conscience," Lilian said. "Leopoldo was incarcerated for his ideas, for his words, for wanting a better Venezuela. So what do we do? We denounce it. We will never stop denouncing it."

Maduro's second mistake was underestimating Lilian Tintori. He never expected that Leopoldo's wife would be as aggressive as he was. And that was a serious miscalculation.

Lilian has kept Leopoldo's memory, his sacrifice, and his mission alive. She fights every fight there is in Venezuela. She makes an appearance at every international forum there is. Thus, Lilian Tintori, the Rebel Wife, has now become one of the primary threats to the current dictatorship. More people would rather have their picture taken with her than with Maduro.

Lilian's bravery stands in stark contrast to the cowardice of most Latin American presidents, who never dared to criticize the human rights violations taking place in Venezuela. (At the Summit of the Americas, for example, in Panama in April 2015, not one of the thirty-four presidents and prime ministers spoke out against Leopoldo's imprisonment.)

Lilian won't stop talking about Leopoldo. When I interviewed her, she denounced torture in the prison system. "Armed men dressed in black entered and trashed the place," she told me. "They stole his memoirs; everything he had written was taken. That cell inspection took seven hours, then he was thrown into a punishment cell called El Tigrito [the Little Tiger]. . . . One night, at one in the morning, they threw human feces and urine through his window. Then they cut the water and electricity so he couldn't clean himself up. It's absolutely inhumane treatment. It's torture."

I asked her how she saw them getting out of this mess in a legal manner. "If [Maduro] loved Venezuela, if he loved the people, he would resign," she replied. "The system failed. It's an undemocratic system, and it failed."

In the meantime, Leopoldo and his wife continued to make life uncomfortable for Maduro. Before López was imprisoned, Maduro offered him the chance to leave the country. "Please, just leave Venezuela. We have a plane ready," Lilian recalled Maduro saying. "Maduro sent that message directly to our home. We said no."

Maduro is mistaken if he thinks that Lilian is going to give up. "I married Leopoldo," she says, "and I also married his commitment to a better Venezuela. I will not stop. I will not stop."

Lilian Tintori thinks about that every morning at half past five. "Yes, we've had that plan since day one," she said. "If we don't stand up and fight for our country, who will?"

LEOPOLDO LÓPEZ AND LILIAN TINTORI: THE LESSONS

If you can't endure, you can't win. Leopoldo and Lilian knew that even before Leopoldo López was imprisoned for standing up for his beliefs. The two of them could have lived a safe and quiet life in Miami or Madrid. But that's not what they wanted. They wanted to live in Venezuela.

But not in the Venezuela of Nicolás Maduro.

There is no access to Twitter at the Ramo Verde military prison. But even there, within those walls, there are people helping Leopoldo get notes to the outside world. And so, on the first anniversary of the protests and his subsequent imprisonment, Leopoldo sent out the following tweet:

"Today the struggle continues! Venezuelan youth: the one who loses is the one who tires first. I know that you won't, and neither will I. Strength and Faith!!!"

They have chosen the most difficult path. Also the most exhausting. Lilian has taken over Leopoldo's role as the most visible opposition figure. They still share a moment of prayer every morning at the same time and the conviction that Venezuela will be a democratic country one day.

In September 2015 Leopoldo López was sentenced to more than thirteen years in prison for "conspiracy, damaging public property and inciting violence," among other charges. The whole legal proceeding was a charade, dictated by the office of the president, Nicolás Maduro.

Lilian told me in an interview that the day of the sentencing, Leopoldo was moved to a smaller cell and was "psychologically tortured." But just a couple of days later, Lilian was already on the move. She went to Prague, for an international conference on democracy, where she denounced the sentence against her husband as unfair and the process as corrupted.

She is full of hope. "I wake up every day thinking that today is the day Leopoldo will be freed."

EIGHT

Carlos Salinas de Gortari: Mexico's Favorite Villain

Everyone is entitled to their reputation.
—CARLOS SALINAS DE GORTARI

INTERVIEWS WITH THE bad guys are the best. This isn't to say that interviews with good guys are boring, but they rarely end in fights. Talking with bad guys, on the other hand, always gives you the opportunity to speak truth to their power, to expose their lies and abuses, and—most importantly—to leave a historical record.

Bad guys should not be allowed to die without knowing that we all see them for who they are. Better yet, we can pressure them to change the way they operate.

Guatemala in 2015 became a great example of what can be done to corrupt public officials with a mix of public indignation and good investigative work. The president, Otto Pérez Molina, and his vice president, Roxana Baldetti, were forced to resign after being charged with corruption. A United Nations team, embedded in the office of the attorney general, was instrumental in bringing charges to the highest authorities in the country.

From a journalistic perspective, the bad guys are always more challenging than the good ones. The interview is more likely to be antagonistic, and that forces you to prepare more, to study his moves and countermoves, to try to know more about the interviewee than even he himself does. Many a journalist has been destroyed going down this road. If you haven't done your homework, you run the risk of getting run over. But if your questions are well planned out, if you approach the interview as a battle, exploring your interviewee's weak points, if you adopt a concrete strategy, and if you are always on the attack instead of playing defense, you might just reach a draw. Because you also have to remember that bad guys almost never lose. If they're doing an interview with you, they want something and they believe it suits them more than it suits you.

For all of the above reasons, interviewing Carlos Salinas de Gortari is always a journalistic challenge. Gortari was president of Mexico from 1988 to 1994. He is, without a doubt, one of the most intelligent figures in Mexican politics. But he's also one of the least transparent.

The first thing you need to know about Salinas de Gortari is that he speaks only when he wants to. Once, during the self-imposed exile in Ireland that he embarked upon after leaving office, I went to dinner with him in Dublin. I was hoping to persuade him to let me interview him on television. When I got to the restaurant, he was already there, waiting for me at a table at the far end of the main dining room, near the exit. From his seat, he could see everyone entering and exiting the premises, and—if necessary—he could sneak out the back door. After a long and animated conversation off the record, he decided not to do the interview. "Now is not the time," he said to me, smiling. "The mute makes the news when he speaks."

When Salinas de Gortari speaks, it's always news. I've interviewed him four times, and he never hesitated to flash his sharp political fangs. And it didn't always turn out well. He continues to be "the favorite villain" of many Mexicans. He spent all of the years he governed Mexico fighting to restore his name and reputation.

How could someone so intelligent be so hated?

The first time we spoke, it was on the street. I surprised him. He didn't want to talk with me, but he had no choice. He was standing in line, along with his daughter Cecilia, to vote in the July 6, 1988, presidential elections. The whole thing was a charade. Everyone in Mexico knew he was going to be the next president. He had been handpicked. The elections didn't matter; the decision had already been made.

"The president of Mexico chooses his own successor," I said. "So in this case, did Miguel de la Madrid select you? What do you have to say about that?"

"Well, it's a long line here," he replied. "That means a lot of Mexicans are voting to elect their next president."

This exchange lasted exactly thirty-eight seconds. His security team quickly separated us from the Institutional Revolutionary Party (PRI) candidate. Gortari's response to my question was a monumental lie. The Mexican people did not choose their president in 1988. There was major electoral fraud that culminated in the defeat of Cuauhtémoc Cárdenas, an engineer and candidate for the National Democratic Front coalition. Instead, Salinas de Gortari was inducted into office.

He declined to be interviewed for most of his presidency. But finally, on August 29, 1994, when he had just three months left in office, we spoke again. He wanted to announce a new bill that would allow entry to Cuban refugees with relatives in Mexico. I, on the other hand, took the opportunity to ask him about the fraud that took place in 1988, when the computer system "crashed" and went down for six days. When everything came back online, Salinas de Gortari had been declared the winner.

"How did you win one hundred percent of the vote on 1,762 voting machines?" I asked. "Your opponent was never allowed to count half of the 54,000 machines."

"What I think is important to remember," he said, "is that more than three-quarters of the voting machines were covered by more than one party, and that there is documentation to confirm this."

Salinas never publicly acknowledged any fraud in the 1988 elections. But his opponent, Cuauhtémoc Cárdenas, would later declare that "99 percent of us, the Mexican people, are convinced that electoral fraud took place."

But that's not the only fraud in which Salinas de Gortari participated. The day I interviewed him at Los Pinos, the official residence and office of the president of Mexico, his thumb was still stained with ink. The week before, on August 21, 1994, another presidential election had been held, and the black thumb was proof of having voted. His party's candidate, Ernesto Zedillo, had won. But in fact, it was another handmade selection. Another fraud. But Salinas, of course, would never admit it.

"You are not promoting democracy by handpicking your successors," I said, referring first to Luis Donaldo Colosio and then Ernesto Zedillo, both PRI candidates for president. "And I think now is the time to defend yourself."

"Over the past five years, the PRI has introduced new procedures when it comes to selecting candidates," he responded. "In Mexico, what we're experiencing is society's demand that the parties become more modernized. The PRI, of course, and others as well."

"What I'm asking about, more than anything," I stressed, "is the role the president plays in selecting the candidate. In September of 1990, [President] Luis Echeverría said, 'The tradition in Mexico is that the president, in turn, elects his successor.' Has that actually ended in Mexico?"

"I would say that everyone's reflections conform to their own experiences," he said.

"How does it look to you?" I asked.

"In my case, Mr. Luis Donaldo Colosio was the PRI's preferred candidate," he replied. "He had been a senior party official, my presidential campaign manager, a federal deputy, a senator, and party chairman. He also served as Social Development Secretary, handling a lot of governmental social work, and he led major international initiatives, especially regarding the environment. So, again, he was the party's expected, preferred candidate, which is why he was nominated."

No matter how good Colosio's qualifications, his campaign didn't last long. He was nominated as the PRI's candidate in November 1993, and he was killed on March 23, 1994, in a shooting in Tijuana that remains very controversial.

There was still much to ask Salinas about, but he wouldn't allow it. I didn't interview him again until 2000. Several times, I spoke with him on the phone, off the record, and once (as I mentioned) I sat down to speak with him in Dublin. But he always refused to participate in a television interview.

Getting an interview became almost an obsession for me. Gortari had gone off the radar in Mexico, leaving many questions unanswered. But one day, out of the blue, I got a call at my office in Miami. It was Salinas de Gortari. "Now, yes, let's talk," he said. His book, *Mexico: The Policy and the Politics of Modernization*, which he'd written while he was in Ireland, was about to be published, and he was willing to speak with me for an uninterrupted hour without any limitations.

We met at one o'clock on Sunday, October 6, 2002, at the home of his in-laws in the El Pedregal neighborhood of Mexico City. His had been a voluntary exile. No legal charges were ever pressed against him. He hadn't changed much since the last time I'd seen him. He had the same moustache and the same lack of hair on his head. No gray. Dark suit, black shoes, blue shirt, and a green tie. "Irish green?" I asked. "No," he replied. "Mexican." His small, acute, razor-sharp eyes recorded every detail, every movement. Nothing escaped him. *In charge as usual*, I thought to myself.

"Ready?" I asked.

"Ready," he replied. "Which camera is mine?" I pointed to his, and the man who had been silent for years finally began to speak. And the first thing he did was respond to some of his critics.

"What we've had here was a campaign of misinformation deliberately promoted by President Zedillo's government."

"President Zedillo was involved in a campaign to discredit you?"

"What we've had is a concerted action by the Mexican government to convince everyone who suffered the terrible effects of the 1995 economic crisis that the crisis stemmed from mistakes made by my administration."

"What were the causes of the crisis?"

"Look, there was one fundamental factor. It has been documented, and it consists in the fact that between December 19 and December 21, 1994, Dr. Zedillo's administration gave confidential information to a small group of Mexican businessmen, saying that a devaluation [of the peso] could occur."

"And that's why capital began flowing out of Mexico?"

"So much capital flowed out of Mexico that the country's international reserves were drained in a matter of hours."

"Many Mexicans feel as though you've cheated us," I said. "That you lied to us for six years."

"I'm glad you used that word, because yes, basically, many Mexicans believe they've been cheated."

"You can't even walk down the street anymore."

"How could I," he replied, "after Dr. Zedillo has spent the past six years telling people, 'Hey, if you lost your home, it was Mr. Salinas' fault. If you lost your job, it was Mr. Salinas' fault'? And this whole campaign of misinformation was created [by Zedillo] to cover up his own responsibility for creating the crisis."

RAÚL: THE INCONVENIENT BROTHER

"Let's talk about Raúl Salinas de Gortari," I said, changing the subject to one that had perplexed many in Mexico. He was the *hermano incómodo*—the inconvenient brother—of the Mexican president. The president was always thinking about his legacy as a reformer. After all, he negotiated NAFTA, the free trade agreement with the United States and Canada. It is a treaty that to this day has enormous influence on trade relationships in North America. His brother, however, was more concerned with his businesses. The question—the big question—was whether the president was aware of how his brother increased his fortune while he was in power.

"There are many Mexicans who reproach you for not having been aware that your brother was a multimillionaire. The Attorney General's Office said that Raúl owned a hundred and twenty-three properties: thirty-seven overseas and eighty-six in Mexico. How is it possible that you were not aware of this, Mr. Salinas?"

"Some of my brother's behavior was undoubtedly improper—using falsified documents, for example," he said. "And that has caused me great sorrow and I strongly reject it. But at the same time, [Raúl] has stated that his resources have derived from his own private activities."

"But how could you not know that Raúl had ranches, apartments, lands?" I pressed. "That he traveled from country to country, from city to city? It seems unlikely that you wouldn't be aware of this."

"You keep insisting that I should know more about my brother," he said. "Jorge, look, I tried to be a well-informed president. Informed about the key issues facing the country, not about particular family matters. We didn't consider them essential to the task of governing. Now I realize I should have paid more attention."

"Swiss police concluded, after a three-year investigation, that Raúl used his influence to protect drug traffickers, who could have received up to five hundred million dollars in bribes, and that some of this money ended up in your campaign. Did you know this? It's all in a 369-page report from the Swiss police."

"It is what it is," he said. "It's a report based on the testimony of protected witnesses, criminals who only say what they heard. . . . I will not discuss the terms of that accusation."

"He was certainly an uncomfortable brother."

"That nickname was given to him one week before my presidency ended. But let me say one thing very clearly: no decision I ever made— or that one of my primary associates ever made—had anything to do with business funds that Raúl deposited in foreign accounts."

WHO KILLED COLOSIO?

"Daniel Aguilar Treviño, the confessed murderer of José Francisco Ruiz Massieu, said in January of 1999 that the assassinations of Ruiz Massieu and Luis Donaldo Colosio were hatched in Los Pinos," I said. Six months after the assassination of Colosio, the secretary-general of the PRI, José Francisco Ruiz Massieu, was gunned down in Mexico City.

"You want me to comment on a statement made by a confessed murderer whom my government arrested, jailed, put on trial, and, moreover, sentenced for the crime he committed? Jorge, look, the only thing I would say regarding a comment from a completely noncredible person such as this would be to wonder if it's not just one more piece in the litany of fabrications they've made all these years."

"Let me ask you directly," I said. "Did you order the killing of Colosio?"

"Luis Donaldo Colosio was my dear friend," he said. "Luis Donaldo Colosio and I had a fifteen-year relationship during which we developed a deep sense of closeness and political affinity. Those who claim that Donaldo Colosio and I were at odds don't know the intense conversations we had, the straightforward relationship and the common political goals we had throughout those fifteen years."

"But there were tensions," I pressed. "For example, on March 6, 1994, Colosio made a speech in which he distanced himself from you. Ernesto Zedillo, who was his campaign manager at the time, wrote a letter to Colosio in which he talked about the tensions that existed with you. Is this not a line of investigation? In other words, don't reasonable people have a reason to suspect that you had something to do with Colosio's assassination?"

"Look," he said, "if those people knew that—after his family—the person who was most affected by the death of Luis Donaldo Colosio was me, they might have a different perspective. But what have they said? That the March 6 speech represented a rift."

"I have the speech right here," I said. "Colosio said, 'It is time to block the path of influence, corruption, and impunity.' Many people believe that's a direct criticism of you."

"I actually see it as a very strong statement against activities that were being fought out during my administration . . ."

"I want to get back to the question," I said. "You had nothing to do with the assassination of Colosio?"

"I was one of the people who had the most to lose from Colosio's death."

"Following Colosio's assassination, you chose Ernesto Zedillo to replace him [as a candidate for the presidency]. Was that a mistake?"

"I'm convinced that, under the circumstances of handing off Luis Donaldo Colosio's candidacy, all signs pointed to Dr. Zedillo."

"But did Zedillo betray you in the end?" I asked.

"I would say that Dr. Zedillo set aside the platform and the ideas which led him to victory in the 1994 presidential elections," he replied. "That, itself, is a betrayal. These are not personal things. . . ."

FROM PUBLIC SERVANT TO MULTIMILLIONAIRE?

"Mr. Salinas," I asked, "have you always been a public servant?"

"All my life," he said. "Yes."

"How can a public servant become a multimillionaire after spending five years in Europe without a job?"

"First off," he began, "I continued to work even after I fulfilled my responsibilities as president of the republic. You know I was on the board of directors of the Dow Jones company. Plus, while I was fulfilling my responsibilities, I was building my assets."

"But you've always been a public servant," I countered. "Salaries for civil servants are so low, and yet you are a multimillionaire."

"Jorge, let me say one thing," he began. "My life abroad during those years was spent in a rented home, I used public transportation, and I had a quiet life. Yes, I built up my assets throughout my life, and the work that I've continued to develop allowed me to sustain that life when I moved abroad . . ."

"But are you not a multimillionaire?" I cut in.

"What you want, what you want me to say is . . ."

"Whether you have more than a million dollars, or if you have [over] $100 million."

"My assets have allowed me to live my life with my family—abroad, as I said—in a house that I rent, and I use public transportation."

"In June of '97, the PAN faction of the Chamber of Deputies [the lower house of Mexico's bicameral legislature] mentioned the disappearance of $7 billion from privatization and sales to semiofficial state organizations. $7 billion."

"It has been proven that every dollar earned from privatization was used to pay off debt."

"You, during your term, had $854 million in a hidden section of the budget. How was this money spent?" I asked.

"Every government in the world has confidential funds used for tasks responsible to the state. In Mexico, they are established by the Constitution and recognized by Congress."

"But that's a source of abuse," I said. "You could spend $854 million however you pleased."

"I heard you the first time you quoted that figure."

"It's a large sum," I said. "I repeated it, but you spent it."

"Forgive me, but that's state money spent by the state on tasks the state is responsible for. The same thing happens all over the world."

FAITH AND FAMILY

"You were talking about your family," I said. "You have two young children, Ana Emilia and Patricio Jerónimo. Were they both born in Cuba?"

"My daughter Ana Emilia Margarita is Mexican, though she was born in Havana. My son Patricio Jerónimo is Mexican, though he was born in Dublin. And I actually have five children: Ceci, Emiliano, Juan Cristóbal, Ana Emilia Margarita, and Patricio Jerónimo."

"Did Fidel Castro help you stay under the radar in Cuba?"

"I've been there from time to time, yes."

"The fact that Ana Emilia was born in Havana and that you have spent time there yourself . . . has that caused you to lose objectivity?" I asked. "For example, do you consider Fidel Castro to be a dictator?"

"Living in Cuba causes one to lose his objectivity?" he countered.

"In your opinion, is Fidel Castro a dictator?" I pressed. "I want to gauge your objectivity."

"Mexicans, as a principle, do not interfere in the affairs of other nations," he said.

CLEARING HIS NAME

"Will you have to spend the rest of your life trying to regain and clear your name?" I asked.

"Look, I think every human being has a right to defend himself and present himself anywhere," he said. "But the purpose of this book is not to rebuild a reputation. . . ."

"[But you say] that this book will be the sword and the shield for your children. Explain that to me."

"A shield against all the things that have been said during all these years," he replied. "In other words, so that my children can look to the future and not have to be explaining their father. That's the shield. And the sword is so they can bear the family name with dignity and pride."

"Will you be able to shed the nickname of being [Mexico's] 'favorite villain'?"

"Look, nicknames, like any other matters of public opinion, change over time," he said. "In the end, all that matters is the judgment of the people."

CARLOS SALINAS DE GORTARI: THE LESSONS

Salinas is, after all is said and done, a smart guy. He sees and understands. "I know that a lot of people aren't going to believe me," he said, accompanied by his wife, Ana Paula, as we bade farewell once the interview had concluded. "But all I want to do now is create some doubt. That alone is a bit of a win."

Salinas's struggle to regain his reputation did not end there. We spoke again in Washington in 2008. He had just published another book, *The Lost Decade*, which was so enormous that it would be unlikely that many Mexicans would read it in full. Salinas de Gortari wanted to be remembered for negotiating NAFTA—which transformed the business relationship between Mexico and the United States—and the privatization of 350 state companies. But not for the electoral frauds of 1988 and 1994, not for the Zapatista uprising in 1994, not for the economic crisis of 1995, and not for the corruption accusations levied against his brother, Raúl.

"Look, there's no doubt that they brought much pain to my family, my name, my reputation," he said. "But eventually they'll be recanting."

There were still some bills left to pay, however.

"Are you [Mexico's] favorite villain?" I asked.

"Of course, and do you know why? Because they hid their incompetence by blaming others."

"But the implication is that you and your family became rich in doing so."

"But in the end, the facts will demonstrate that many allegations and accusations were false."

"But people want to know how Mr. Salinas lives. Are you indeed a millionaire?"

"I live off the income and the assets that I declare to the comptroller general's office. And, with a little luck, even the sales from my book."

"But you've always held public positions. That's the point," I said. "How can you live like a millionaire?"

"And how can you classify me as such without a shred of evidence?"

"I'm not. I'm simply asking."

"It's not a question. It's more of a statement than a question."

Salinas understood that my own doubts and suspicions were shared by many Mexicans. So I wanted to continue to sow those doubts. His ultimate goal, however, was no longer to protect himself. It was to protect his children.

The book was dedicated to his son Mateo, who had just turned two years old. And what happened next was not by chance. As with everything else, Salinas wanted to have the last word.

"Everyone is entitled to their reputation," he said, looking me straight in the eye. That was the lesson. Regardless of all the power that he had exercised, Salinas de Gortari had lost his reputation. His last name was equated with some of the worst practices in Mexico. "And when there's a debate about [my reputation], everyone has the right to participate in that debate. I am in that debate—in the battleground of ideas—and that is where I intend to stay."

The lesson is that even without power, politicians will try to save their reputations. History is always on their mind. They understand that our lives are limited but that their reputations remain decades after they die.

I was always perplexed by Salinas de Gortari's willingness to talk to me even though he knew that the interview would raise controversial issues. Maybe that's why he accepted. He needed a tough interview to clear his name. And that was ironic because during his presidency he had almost full control of the press.

At the end, he understood history very clearly. He understood the importance of telling his own story and not allowing others to damage his reputation.

Many years after he left the presidency, he was still fighting to clear his name, his reputation, and his legacy. And I think he was absolutely convinced that his narrative would prevail in the end.

NINE

Dilemmas of a Masked Guerrilla: Subcomandante Marcos

Although I will one day die, someone else will pick up the name of Marcos and continue on, continue on with the fight.

—SUBCOMANDANTE MARCOS

The Lacandon Jungle, Chiapas.

ON JANUARY 1, 1994—the same day that the Mexican government wanted to celebrate its momentous entry into the North American Free Trade Agreement—a rebel group of indigenous people led by a masked man known as El Subcomandante Marcos rose up in the southern Mexican state of Chiapas. Nobody thought this group could take power by force, although one of its stated goals was to overthrow President Carlos Salinas de Gortari. But the uprising shook the country, deflected attention from NAFTA, and raised fundamental questions about Mexico's tenuous democratic political system.

For the Zapatistas—as they called themselves in honor of the revolutionary hero and peasant leader Emiliano Zapata—their struggle protested against the idea of modernism, which the government was trying to pitch to the people while more than half of them still lived in poverty, against the imposition of a president elected by electoral fraud, and against a country where the gap between the rich and the poor was widening.

The Mexican army was caught off guard by the revolt, but it was able to regain control of the region within a couple of weeks. What it wasn't successful in doing was killing or capturing many of the rebels, or actually handing the EZLN—the Zapatista Army of National Liberation, to give the formal name—a clear defeat. Calls for negotiations and peace talks arose while the voice and words of Subcomandante Marcos echoed loud and strong, both in Mexico and around the world.

The charismatic Subcomandante Marcos became a high-profile media sensation. At once poetic and insurgent, his communiqués outshone the tepid, inadequate government response. His rebellion was the beginning of the end for the Institutional Revolutionary Party, or PRI, which had been in power continuously since 1929, because the rebellion marked the end of the government's total control over the media, which in turn allowed for the arrival of a true participatory democracy in 2000.

Much to the surprise and confusion of, first, the Salinas de Gortari administration and, later, that of Ernesto Zedillo, Subcomandante Marcos and the Zapatistas established an independent, autonomous territory within the Lacandon Jungle of Chiapas. That territory, though, was completely surrounded by the Mexican army.

The military mounted an offensive in 1995, but neither side emerged victorious. The result was an unwritten agreement limiting the Mexican army's access to the region under EZLN control, and in return, the rebels would limit their authority and activities to a very specific area. Those were the conditions of the cease-fire.

The Zapatistas had no chance of overthrowing the federal government in Mexico City. At least not militarily. But Subcomandante Marcos soon began to win the war in the media. His critiques of the president, coupled with his complaints about the social inequalities hurting the country, resonated deeply with the public and undermined the Salinas administration's already tenuous legitimacy.

Two years after the initial uprising, Subcomandante Marcos remained an enigma. Nobody really knew who he was. He was the most telegenic rebel in Mexican history but very little was known about him. The language he used suggested that he was an educated man with leftist leanings. But everything we thought we knew about him was an assumption. That was part of his mystery.

The military had been unable to stop him, and his communiqués continued to generate headlines. That was when I decided to go into the jungle in search of him.

SUBCOMANDANTE MARCOS ONCE wrote that "patience is a virtue of the warrior." But of necessity that was also a trait shared with journalists who wanted to interview him. After two days of travel, thirty hours of waiting, and countless coded messages, I finally found myself somewhere in the Lacandon jungle with the most visible leader of the Zapatista insurgents. I traveled with a cameraman and a producer. We trusted our contacts, but we were afraid that the army was following us. The rebels were, too. That explained the long wait. Once they realized that no one was following and that we really were reporters, the interview was allowed to proceed.

He was armed with his pipe, maple tobacco, an M16 rifle, a rosy smile encircled by his trademark black ski mask, and a tremendous need to define (and redefine) the dilemmas faced by the Zapatistas and their struggle.

In the days before the interview, in late March 1996, I had been hearing that the insurgent Zapatistas were trying to transform themselves into a political front. But what I learned firsthand was that the group of rebels had a long and winding road ahead of them.

My hour-long talk with Marcos started out with the basics, though it quickly grew more complicated:

"How many people either control or are present here in this territory?" I asked.

"Among the many indigenous communities here in Chiapas, there must be more than a hundred thousand men, women, children, and elders," he replied. "We're talking about several thousand indigenous communities."

"Do you think you're setting the stage for a rebellion to rise up in other parts of the country?"

"Yes, but without any control, without any coordination," he said. "There's a kind of resentment that just erupts and begins to take matters of justice into its own hands. What everyone thinks is justice . . . We started to point to that back in '94. It got more acute after August of '94, with the elections. And then even more so after the crisis in December and January [of 1995], the economic crisis."

"Are you predicting violence in Mexico?"

"Yes," he said. "Disorganized violence. We aren't talking about a planned, premeditated violence like we had with the Zapatista Army of National Liberation, but uncontrolled outbreaks, something closer to turmoil or a riot than a program."

"Turning to the Zapatistas . . . what are you, exactly?"

"Well, look . . . we're not a regular army, not even a guerrilla force. We have land, and we have control."

"Do you still justify violence as a means of achieving your ends?"

"We maintain that the Zapatista movement is a sui generis one in the sense that it is a war to be heard. It is not a war seeking to destroy, to annihilate the enemy and replace him with us."

"Could Marcos ever be president of Mexico?"

"No. God, no. May He spare both Mexico and Marcos from such a problem."

Although he mentioned God several times during our conversation, Marcos wouldn't let himself be labeled. "We can't define our-selves by one religion or another, because then it becomes used as propaganda," he said. But did he believe in a higher power? "We can't say that we do believe in God, but we can't say that we don't, either."

When it came to more earthly matters, Marcos handled them with ease. He spoke at length about how the Zapatistas were using the Internet—which, in 1996, had perhaps 60 million total users, about one percent of the world's population—to spread their criticisms of the current political system into the world. "Twenty-first-century revolu-tions are revolutions of the word," he said, before going on to explain that the same methods of communication used by the powers that be can also be used against them.

It's difficult to understand how a masked, sophisticated urbanite ever became a leader and a symbol of an indigenous rebellion. "When people can't speak, they go and grab a gun," he said by way of ex-planation.

But that did not dispel the apparent differences between Marcos and his followers. His small hands stood out in stark contrast to those of the rural farmers who helped me get to him. Theirs were callused and worn with time, while his were thin, almost white, with trimmed nails showing no traces of dirt. Only the dark circles under his eyes and the gaping hole in his right boot—exposing a bunion—reflected the physical toll that life in the mountainous jungle had taken on him.

Marcos liked to talk about himself in the third person, as if he were somebody else. But despite this grammatical defense, when I tried to delve into more personal matters, I was able to fish out a few short sentences: he owned a Notebook brand laptop, he listened to two shortwave radio stations, he ate once a day, slept little at night, and feared he would be killed. He refused to say whether he had taken another person's life. "One doesn't speak of such things," he said.

Back then, Marcos was reading a detective novel by the Spanish author Manuel Vázquez Montalbán, and he sought inspiration in

Shakespeare's *Macbeth* when it came to writing the history of the Zapatista uprising. After the military offensive of February 1995, and the distinct possibility that the Mexican government was looking to assassinate him, his comrades had persuaded him to write about how his armed rebellion was first conceived.

Of course I asked him about his true identity, and he came back with a formulaic response: "I am not Rafael Guillén," he said. "Rafael Guillén is a lie perpetrated by many." All he admitted was that he hadn't seen his family in fifteen years, and that he had six siblings, not eight, as the government had claimed.

When I showed him the picture of Rafael Guillén that had been widely circulated by the Mexican government, Marcos seemed uncomfortable and was constantly adjusting his mask, as if his nose itched or he had a cold. But it was inevitable that I was going to ask him about his identity.

"Some people, of course, see heroism in that mask," I began. "But you do understand that [others] also see it as an example of opportunism or even cowardice."

"Yes," he replied. "Many people have written me to tell me I'm a coward for not showing my face."

"And don't they have a right to ask about it?"

"Yes, they have a right to demand it. Especially because of the reference: you're not a hero at all, they say, because Mexican heroes always show themselves. They've always had a face."

"Why not just remove the mask?" I asked. "Why not just take it off, right now, right here?"

"Because it has become a symbol," he replied. "It symbolizes the possibility that people who have thus far been nameless, faceless people—common, unimportant people—can take a powerful stance when it comes to facing life and the environment in which they live."

"And how long will you have to wear the mask?"

"When we are finally able to transform into a peaceful and civil political force, both weapons and ski masks will have to disappear," he said. "We are very afraid of becoming the very thing we criticize," he continued, now near the end of the interview. It is that very search for definition in which the Zapatistas find themselves entwined.

Before disappearing once again into the cornfields and coffee plantations that crisscrossed the Lacondon Jungle, Marcos explained the origin of his nom de guerre. "Marcos is the name of a fallen comrade. We always drank to the names of those who have died, not in the sense that they have passed and gone away, but that they continue to fight," he said.

Will there be another Marcos in the future? "Yes," he said. "Although I will one day die, someone else will pick up the name of Marcos and continue on, continue on with the fight."

SUBCOMANDANTE MARCOS: THE LESSONS

The last time I heard about Subcomandante Marcos was from an article in the Spanish newspaper *El País*, back in May 2015. The masked guerrilla had attended a tribute to the philosopher Luis Villoro in the town of Oventic, Chiapas.

The reporter, Pablo de Llano, acknowledged that the EZLN was no longer "the media phenomenon that it was in the late nineties, but it is still present in five areas of Chiapas, with its sense of resistance and political and economic autonomy, plus its paradoxical mix of disciplinary compulsion and sense of humor."

But there was one major change. Subcomandante Marcos was no longer Marcos. Now he was known as Galeano, or Marcos-Galeano, in memory of a Zapatista by the name of José Luis Solis, also known as Galeano, who died in 2014. "He was kidnapped, tortured, and finally finished off," Marcos-Galeano told the Spanish reporter.

Surprisingly, more than two decades after their initial uprising, the

Zapatistas have yet to fade away. They have continued their struggle against capitalism and against the Mexican political system. Also surprising is that several Mexican administrations have tolerated the existence of an insurgent army in their own sovereign territory. Then again, perhaps they tried to do away with it but just weren't able to succeed.

The Zapatistas never became a political party, as they had once seen themselves. And thanks to that separation from the traditional political parties, they are left with a purity and innocence that is rare to see in this day and age. Their independence from everything that's rotten in Mexico has become one of their primary virtues.

The problem for these guerrillas lies in defining their purpose. If they aren't willing to step into the political arena, yet also aren't interested in taking power by force, then what is it that they do want? The debate has been going on for years.

While they seek to define themselves, Subcomandante Marcos has stepped down as the leader of the Zapatistas. He has been replaced by Subcomandante Moisés, the first indigenous leader of the last Latin American guerrilla movement of the twentieth century. But Marcos-Galeano has lost neither his voice nor his image: the mask continues to appear alongside his frequent literary references. He is, without a doubt, one of the most well-read guerrillas in history. A warrior poet.

Guerrillas are, by definition, involved in a marathon operation whose success is measured in years if not decades. And the Zapatistas have been no exception. They have long since ceased to be front-page news, having been replaced by drug traffickers, corrupt officials, and other elements of a country that is not looking down and to the south.

It is evident that they cannot overthrow the government by force, as they tried to do back in 1994. But what's also clear is that they have the intent and the ability to maintain a presence in the political life of the country.

Subcomandante Marcos was right when he said that patience is a virtue of the warrior. The Zapatistas' sense of patience has been as impressive as their strategy for survival: every time an insurgent is killed, another one takes up his name. And so Subcomandante Marcos—now Marcos-Galeano—can live on and continue to fight forever.

At least, that's the plan.

The lesson is that for real rebels who are fighting for their lives, simple survival is success. Marcos could have been killed the first day, the first week, or the first year of the uprising. However, two decades later, Marcos is still alive, still controlling a large area of the Lacandon Jungle, and still having a very active public life.

When I talked to him I expected that one day he would take off his mask and tell us all his secrets. But the mask had become Marcos. The real man one day got lost in the jungle and never came back.

TEN

Enrique Peña Nieto: Saving Mexico?

I have a very clean conscience about all my things being in order, and that they are public. —ENRIQUE PEÑA NIETO

I can tell you that there is no democracy in Mexico.
—ANDRÉS MANUEL LÓPEZ OBRADOR

IT SEEMED LIKE a fairy tale. In February 2014, *Time* magazine put Enrique Peña Nieto, the president of Mexico, on its cover, along with a headline that read, "Saving Mexico." The young president, married to an actress, vaguely reminded many Americans of their dearly departed leader John F. Kennedy.

There had been no bad news in Mexico since Peña Nieto took office in December 2012. How could there be, when he was young, new, and looking to reform what wasn't working? The "Mexican moment" was at hand. Left behind was the image of "rough Mexico" marred by drug violence; it was time to look to the future and to integrate Mexico with the most developed countries on earth.

He had to sell hope, the hope of the nation's green, white, and red flag.

That was the story.

Enrique Peña Nieto wanted to be president. He had been planning it for years; he drew up a strategy, he implemented it, and he managed it. But the costs it would have for Mexico would be enormous.

From 2005 to 2011 he was governor of the state of Mexico, which includes Mexico City and which had one of the highest murder rates of women in the country. In fact, more than nine hundred women had been killed in five years. Peña Nieto had allegedly been part of a highly questionable political alliance with the Atlacomulco Group, a shadowy and influential cabal of leading PRI politicians, a group whose very existence is often denied; and his predecessor, Arturo Montiel, had frequently been accused of corruption, though nothing had ever been legally proven.

Power in Mexico is exerted by groups, not by individuals. When a cadre of politicians rises to power, they protect one another as brothers, and they are all expected to leave power at the same time. To jump from one group to another is considered treason. The Atlacomulco Group was no different. The old generation had its chance and had failed to stay in power. Now, it was their chance for redemption.

Peña Nieto had a very specific formula for governing the state of Mexico—and for electoral success. It consisted of making very concrete promises, and then—much to everyone's surprise—actually fulfilling them. In a country accustomed to politicians who failed to deliver, Peña Nieto represented a different sort of leader.

With the help of a massive advertising campaign—or a campaign of "electoral fraud," according to one of his critics, Andrés Manuel López Obrador of the opposition Party of the Democratic Revolution—Peña Nieto arrived in Los Pinos, the official residence of the president of Mexico. And just as López Obrador had refused to recognize Felipe Calderón as the legitimate president back in 2006, neither did he recognized Peña Nieto when he took office in 2012.

"Free and fair elections were never held," López Obrador told me in an interview after the election. "Peña Nieto and his sponsors bought

President Barack Obama.

President Obama promised to introduce immigration reform in his first year in office.

All photos courtesy of Univision/Fusion

My first interview with a U.S. President: George H. W. Bush.

George W. Bush always tried to speak a few words in Spanish to win the Hispanic vote.

My sixty-three seconds with Fidel Castro, Guadalajara, Mexico, 1991.

Cuban dissident Yoani Sánchez.

Cuban dissident Guillermo Fariñas in Miami, 2013.

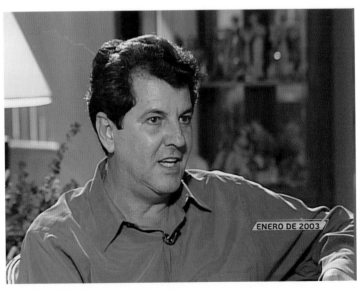

ENERO DE 2003

Oswaldo Payá, who according to government records was killed in an automobile accident in Cuba, in 2012. His wife, on the other hand, does not believe this was the case.

President Hugo Chávez of Venezuela.

President Chávez in his trademark fatigues and red beret: "I'm not the devil."

Interviewing President Chávez surrounded by dozens of his supporters. The crowd jeered at my questions but applauded his responses.

Political prisoner Leopoldo López, imprisoned by the Maduro government in Venezuela.

Lilian Tintori, Leopoldo López's rebel wife, has never stopped defending her husband throughout Venezuela and the world.

President Carlos Salinas de Gortari of Mexico (1988–1994).

"Mexico's favorite villain" defending himself: "Everyone is entitled to their reputation."

With Subcomandante Marcos, somewhere in the Lacandon jungle of Chiapas.

The masked guerrilla, an enigma for more than twenty years: "Why not just remove the mask? Why not just take it off, right now, right here?"

I interviewed Enrique Peña Nieto twice before he became president, but never while in office.

"How much money do you have?"

Alvaro Uribe, President of Colombia, 2002–2010: "I'm a fighter, but I don't sow hate."

The cost of rebellion: FARC kidnap victim Ingrid Betancourt.

Bill Gates, New York City, 2014.

Bill Gates: "The money belongs to society."

Virgin entrepreneur Sir Richard Branson: "Only through exploration of the unknown can we continue to grow and evolve."

Developer Jorge Pérez: "Legacy should never be about money."

The first Latina Supreme Court Justice, Sonia Sotomayor: "I didn't let them discriminate against me."

Dancing "salsa" with Justice Sotomayor after our interview in the Supreme Court.

Spike Lee: "Everybody is an investigative reporter with a phone."

Television pioneer Barbara Walters: "That's my legacy: all these young women in the news."

Interviewing Israeli Prime Minister Benjamin Netanyahu in New York.

During my interview with Palestinian leader Hanan Ashrawi, in the city of Ramallah.

Four DREAMERs:

Cristina Jimenez.

Erika Andiola.

Lorella Praeli.

Gaby Pacheco.

millions of votes. They trafficked in the poverty of the people, which is why we will not recognize him."

The Federal Electoral Tribunal concluded, however, that Mexico had had a "free and verifiable" election, and that López Obrador's allegations of fraud were "unfounded." So I asked him: Whom should I believe?

"I don't lie. I'm very accustomed to telling the truth," López Obrador replied. "I can tell you that there is no democracy in Mexico. I can tell you that both the Tribunal and the Federal Electoral Institute have been taken hostage, and that they answer to organized crime. They're accomplices. They received orders to guarantee electoral fraud." The official count had the Institutional Revolutionary Party candidate beating the Party of the Democratic Revolution candidate by three million votes.

But if López Obrador knew that Peña Nieto had an unfair advantage over other candidates in terms of finances and media exposure months before the 2012 election, then why not withdraw? "Because you always bet on someone beating out the fraud," he replied. "Even when the deck is stacked against you and the dice are loaded, you can still win. We earned sixteen million votes and didn't have to pay out anything in return. You can't withdraw. You have to keep on going."

Any lingering doubts among opponents on the left about the legitimacy of Peña Nieto's election began to fade after he scored a number of notable political agreements—in writing—to reform the oil and telecommunications industries, the educational system, and taxes, among many other changes.

Peña Nieto's communications strategy was very disciplined; he could count on the cooperation of a number of media outlets, which differentiated him from the previous president, Felipe Calderón. He didn't speak publicly about the war on drugs or crime, which is why some of his detractors referred to it as the ostrich strategy. Peña Nieto highlighted only the positives.

Mexico was far more than just drug traffickers, he said. You have to speak well of Mexico, he said. And, for a while, many Mexicans and non-Mexicans believed it . . . until Ayotzinapa. That broke the spell.

On September 26, 2014, a group of forty-three students from the Escuela Normal Rural in Ayotzinapa in the violent state of Guerrero (whose largest city is Acapulco) was detained by municipal police from the nearby city of Iguala. According to the official version of events, the police were apparently following orders from the mayor, José Luis Abarca, who didn't want the students disrupting a public speech his wife was giving.

According to the report released by the federal government, the students were delivered by the police to a group of drug traffickers known as Guerreros Unidos, who suspected that the group had been infiltrated by members of a rival cartel, Los Rojos. This same report states that the students were abducted, killed, and burned at the land-fill in the town of Cocula before their remains were dumped in a river.

This case woke up the nation and demonstrated the inability of the government to handle a crisis of this magnitude. It was eleven days before Peña Nieto spoke publicly about the tragedy, and thirty-three days before he met with the families of the victims. He also refused to speak about it at a press conference or during an interview with an independent journalist.

Marches and demonstrations rocked Peña Nieto's administration. Critics erupted on social networks. Ayotzinapa and the protesters showed Mexico that the central government had quite carefully attempted a cover-up.

Without irrefutable proof, and without ever finding the remains of the forty-three students, Peña Nieto's administration closed the case four months after the crime was committed. The international organization Human Rights Watch sharply criticized the negligence Peña Nieto showed in the Ayotzinapa case and questioned his decision to stop investigating a crime that clearly had not been solved.

Mexico's moment was over. The impunity and corruption of the justice system had been put on full display. But that wasn't all.

A few weeks after the killings in Ayotzinapa, Peña Nieto's administration canceled a multimillion-dollar contract to build a high-speed train from Mexico City to Querétaro, northwest of the capital. The timing raised a few eyebrows. It happened just before Peña Nieto was to travel to China, and it was a Chinese company—along with Mexican partnership—that won the original contract. And the reason for the cancellation would become apparent within a matter of days.

In November 2014, the website aristeguinoticias.com published the results of an investigation into a $7 million home in the exclusive Mexico City neighborhood of Las Lomas that had been bought by the president's wife, Angélica Rivera. It became known as the "Mexican White House." The problem was that the purchase was funded by the Grupo Higa, one of the partners in the construction of the high-speed Mexico City–Querétaro rail, and the recipient of several government contracts that included an aqueduct, a number of roads, and the presidential aircraft hangar.

The conflict of interest was clear. But in a now famous video, the president's wife and the office of the presidency said that nothing illegal had been done as part of this unusual transaction. What Mexican receives funding from a government contractor?

But that wasn't the only conflict. In late 2014, the *Wall Street Journal* reported that one of the president's closest colleagues, Finance Minister Luis Videgaray, had also bought a house through the same company—Grupo Higa—for $532,000 in the town of Malinalco. According to Videgaray, there was no conflict of interest because the purchase had been made in October 2012, just before he became a part of the Peña Nieto administration.

Both purchases were highly suspicious. It was impossible to know if the houses were sold for their fair market value—as the purchasers assured us—or if they had received much more favorable terms in exchange for government contracts, as critics suggested. Grupo Higa had already received multimillion-dollar contracts from the state of Mexico when Peña Nieto was governor of Mexico City. According to both Aristegui Noticias and the *Wall Street Journal*, instead of funding these two houses through a bank, both Angélica Rivera and Luis Videgaray reached a private financial agreement with the construction company and government contractor.

And as if this weren't enough, Peña Nieto had a conflict of interest of his own with a different government contractor. In early 2015, the *Journal* reported that in 2005, while he was governor, Peña Nieto bought a house in Ixtapan de la Sal for $372,000 from the San Roman family, a well-known government contractor in Mexico.

After that sale, the San Román family, received more than $100 million in government contracts between 2005 and 2011. Further, since Peña Nieto became president in 2012, the San Román family business received eleven separate federal contracts totaling approximately $40 million.

Considering all of this, one has to ask: How could a public servant earning a government salary afford to pay cash for a house like this?

Few politicians, regardless of where in the world they live, will openly and honestly answer questions about their personal wealth. During the two interviews I conducted with Peña Nieto before he became president, we talked about money.

The first interview was in March 2009 when he was serving as governor of the state of Mexico.

"How much money do you have?" I asked.

"Well, I don't have an exact figure for how much I have in the bank. But I have declared all my finances and properties."

"Since 1990, your only jobs have been in public office," I said. "If I add up your salaries from 1990 to 2009, won't I come up with what you have in the bank?"

"You will," he replied.

"Nothing more?"

"I'm open to public scrutiny. I am legally subject to public review, and should be."

"Is the sum of your government salaries what you have in the bank?"

"I have a very clean conscience about all my things being in order, and that they are public."

"How much does the governor of the state of Mexico earn?"

"Around 160,000 pesos per month."

"That converts to about 12,000 U.S. dollars."

"More or less. Approximately."

"In other words, you're not a millionaire."

"No, I'm not."

After that interview in 2009, I was left with his statement that, no, he was not a millionaire. But if that were true, then how, in 2005, could he have afforded to pay more than five million pesos in cash for a house in Ixtapan de la Sal, according to his own financial statements? Before buying that home, Peña Nieto had held only two minor positions, as undersecretary of the interior in the state of Mexico from 2000 to 2002, and as a state deputy from 2003 to 2005.

In our second interview, which we conducted in February 2011, we talked about money again.

"How much money do you have?" I asked, repeating my question from our first interview. "It's a very simple question. The public knows that many former Mexican presidents are multimillionaires. But what we don't know is how that happens. If you do become president, how can we be sure that you won't benefit from your position?"

"Jorge, as I said in our previous interview, what I have has been made public. There is even a website where—and I'm not being forced to do this—I basically make my declaration of assets publicly accessible. I clearly indicate all my properties. The ones I had before I became governor. And if I've acquired anything else, it's also indicated there. They're online, and anyone who wants to can see what I have. I think I've been more than clear."

Clearly not. President Peña Nieto's declaration—which is dated January 15, 2013—is available online.* It includes records of four houses, four tracts of land, an apartment, jewelry, watches, and art, but not a single figure regarding how much was paid for these properties. It wasn't until the scandal caused by the purchase of the "Mexican White House" in November 2014 that Peña Nieto made the actual amounts of his financial statements public. That particular declaration lists investment funds totaling more than 12 million pesos, which is equivalent to slightly less than one million dollars.

The Ayotzinapa case, a massacre in the village of Cuadrilla Nueva, Tlatlaya, during a military operation—in which the army executed fifteen of the twenty-two civilians found in a warehouse in June 2014, according to Mexico's own National Human Rights Commission—and accusations of corruption in the buying of properties overwhelmed the administration. It had lost its credibility and moral authority. How could a Mexican president honestly face his people and ask them to fight against corruption when he wasn't willing to do so in his own home?

Mexico has had all sorts of presidents, but never weak ones. Peña Nieto spent his first three years in office trying not to be seen as elusive and impotent. His team was careful not to expose him to unexpected press inquiries. Nothing was left to presidential improvisation.

My two interviews took place before Peña Nieto ascended to the office of the presidency. After that, he didn't want to speak with me.

My questions were simple. How much money do you have? How did your first wife die? But in his answers, Enrique Peña Nieto just gave me the runaround.

* www.presidencia.gob.mx/patrimonio/UGNGFNIK.htm

*　*　*

AT OUR FIRST interview in 2009 it seemed to me that Peña Nieto wasn't prepared. He was accustomed to easy interviews—with preapproved questions and prepackaged answers—and had had virtually no contact with foreign correspondents, even ones who had been born in Mexico.

When I entered his office in the city of Toluca, I noticed two images hanging on the walls: a painting of national hero Benito Juárez, who is known in Mexican history as the first president who was born in Oaxaca and came from the people, not the elites, and a photograph of Angélica Rivera, the actress who would soon become his wife. The subjects of his interest were clear.

There were signs in the bathroom, too. It's a bit of a bad habit, but before an interview, I usually visit the bathroom of the person with whom I'm about to speak. It can give you clues about what you may encounter, because they are usually filled with personal belongings. Here, there were two toothbrushes of differing sizes and colors. Either this bathroom was being used by two people, or it was being used by one person who really enjoyed brushing his teeth.

Another journalist had described Peña Nieto as "young but not new." And that's exactly how he appeared to me. This politician—who was just forty-three—was immaculately dressed in a suit and a very wide tie, and every hair on his head was in place. The "Gel Boy," as many people called him, had a certain elderly air about him, as if he were something of a provincial Ronald Reagan.

The interview went where it had to go. He defended the man who preceded him as governor of the state of Mexico, Arturo Montiel, from the corruption charges that had been levied against him. When it comes to Mexican politics, loyalty is paramount, and Peña Nieto never would have dared to criticize Montiel in public.

Surprisingly enough, he told me that "Mexico is a safe country facing a new criminal phenomenon." Few people would define Mexico as a safe nation. In that year, 2009, more than 16,000 criminal homicides were committed, according to official figures. And Peña Nieto, like any good politician, refused to confirm any intention of running for president.

Toward the end of the interview, more in search of a personal angle than out of any real interest, I asked him about his wife, Mónica Pretelini, who had passed away on January 11, 2007. I wasn't looking to make any waves, and I expected a short, concise answer without much emotion. But his answer—or, rather, his lack of it—left me astonished and put his entire political career at risk.

"It was something . . . inopportune," he said, without finding the right words. "For two years she had a disease resembling. . . . I'm forgetting the name of the, of the . . . the name of the disease."

"Epilepsy?" I offered, trying to help during what was a very awkward moment.

"It wasn't epilepsy, strictly speaking, but something similar," he said, attempting to answer. "Unfortunately, I wasn't with her at the time. She suffered an attack and unfortunately lost her life. When I found her, at that time, in our bedroom, she was already practically dead. The doctor, then, explained all the medical terms that I couldn't put my finger on today, as to what was the cause of death."

This answer was, of course, regrettable at the very least. How could Peña Nieto not know what had caused the death of his wife less than two years before?

The video footage of the Univision interview became the subject of jokes and comments all over the Internet and social networks. Suddenly, the main vulnerability of Peña Nieto's presidential aspirations was centered not on his policies but on his personal life.

So, before officially announcing his candidacy, Peña Nieto decided to grant me a second interview. This time, he and his team were ready.

We met in a luxurious home in the Las Lomas neighborhood of Mexico City, rented by his presidential campaign, in February 2011.

Before the governor arrived for the interview, his aides handed me a letter signed by Dr. Paul Shkurovich, head of the Department of Clinical Neurophysiology at the ABC Medical Center in Mexico City. The "medical report" stated that Mónica Pretelini Peña, forty-four years of age, had suffered a "respiratory arrest" after a "seizure" at two o'clock in the morning of January 11, 2007. The medical report also documented "severe inflammation of the brain tissue," found no trace of drugs or medications, and that—at three in the afternoon of that same day—she was diagnosed as "brain dead."

This had to be the first question of my second interview with Enrique Peña Nieto.

ON THE DEATH OF HIS WIFE

"During our previous interview, back in March 2009, I asked you a question about your wife's death," I began. "And what really surprised me was that you couldn't tell me how she had died."

"It's absurd, Jorge, to think that I didn't know how my wife died. It was a lapse on my part to not be able to say that my wife was suffering from seizures at the time, which resulted in some heart failure, and that that was what led to her death. How could I not have been clear and conscious about this? It was just a slip that certain people took advantage of in order to—I think, even, reprint what you had presented—and to mock me and whatnot, to basically make a caricature out of what was discussed between you and me. Of course I'm fully aware of what happened. It was very painful for our family, my children were still young, and of course we knew what caused the death of my wife."

"Did you have anything to do with [the death of your wife]?"

"No," he said. "When I got home, I found her practically in a state of shock, and not breathing. She was immediately taken to the hospital, where she was revived using all the medical means at their disposal. But, unfortunately, in the end, she was pronounced brain dead from lack of oxygen. That's what happened. And I was deeply hurt by all the offensive insults and accusations that some media sources—irresponsibly, I think—began to make about my wife's death. That she had committed suicide . . ."

"They suspected that you might have even participated."

"That I might have even participated [in her death]. At the time, I asked the attending doctor, who also happened to be her primary doctor—the one who had been treating her for this affliction, this epilepsy—please, I know you're not required to do so, but can you explain the cause of death? And that is also part of the record. I think all these conspiracy theories are starting to fade. [There were] several media sources devoted to slandering my wife's death, to defaming all of this without regard for whom they were hurting. It was very painful. I think it's part of the risk you run when you're stuck in this sort of business."

ON HIS PRIVATE LIFE AND FINANCES

"How deep can we get into your private life?" I asked.

"Look, I have defended the right to privacy and intimacy," he replied. "But I'm also aware that when you're a public figure, your private life ends up becoming public."

"Your wedding [to the actress Angélica Rivera, on November 27, 2010] was very public."

"The fact that I was getting married was very public," he said. "There was no way for me to have done it in a secluded manner. It was public, though I didn't invite the media. Members of the media were there. We chose not to give an exclusive to any particular source. We uploaded a few photos and images of what had been a private event to the Internet. We decided to share them because it had been a remarkably public issue."

"Is it worth it, for example, to talk about the private life of the president of Mexico?" I asked. "You are well aware of the blanket that fell over Congress when it was suggested that former President Calderón had problems with alcohol. Are we crossing the line?"

"I think that, yes, there is a line that separates the public from the private. I think that when someone has a public responsibility, there is a requirement and an obligation to be fully transparent."

"Is it worthwhile asking the president whether he has a drinking problem?"

"I think it's worth asking the president. I think, in order to clear up this issue, it would be worth asking the president about something so controversial. So talked about. In an interview where someone could pose the question [to the president]. Yes."

ON DRUG TRAFFICKING AND VIOLENCE

"Outside of Mexico, when we talk about the country, people think about drug trafficking and violence," I began. "Should we be negotiating with the cartels? Has Felipe Calderón's strategy been wrong?" (Calderón was known for his all-out war on drugs and his frontal attacks against drug traffickers. Tens of thousands died during his presidency due to drug violence.)

"Look, it's unfortunate that the view the world has of Mexico is limited to the subjects of drug trafficking and violence," he said. "I think the government's strategy has been insufficient and inadequate."

"The PRI never negotiates with the cartels?"

"That has been an argument designed to disqualify the PRI. We are now facing a totally different phenomenon. What the PRI experienced when it was in power [from 1929 to 2000] isn't the reality we're living today. It was a different scene, a different reality."

ON PUBLICITY

"One of the main criticisms leveled against you is that your television ads are broadcast nationally," I said. "$100 million has been budgeted [over five years] for advertising."

"I wish it were enough," he replied. "It's still well below what other administrations have allotted. We are the most populated region in the country, with 15 million citizens. I would say that here—both in Mexico City and the state of Mexico—the way to reach the people is by making use of the national media."

"But the accusation is that you're using the state's budget to promote your candidacy for a national office."

"I think that's become a bit of a myth. It's not being used for personal promotion."

"You're the governor of the state of Mexico, but these ads are broadcast nationwide. They're obviously helping to make your image more presidential."

"That's not the case," he simply said.

It's impossible to confirm just how much was spent on advertising during the years leading up to Peña Nieto's 2012 campaign. According to official results, he won the election with 38 percent of the vote.

PEÑA NIETO: THE LESSONS

Enrique Peña Nieto was billed as a new sort of politician. But he never really was. In fact, as the journalist Denise Maerker once said, he's young, but he has old ideas.

There are many things we can learn from Peña Nieto's rise to power. The first is that, yes, you can invent a president. He and his team had a perfectly laid-out path, and he went from being a low-level state bureaucrat to being the president of Mexico. The strategy was one of excessive spending on advertising . . . and of lists.

He made promises, he listed them, and he delivered. The simplicity of this strategy—keep your promises—served him well as governor. In a country where politicians are known not only for failing to follow through on claims they've made, but also for effectively denying them once in power, delivering on your word carries enormous weight.

Second lesson: You can't keep reality behind the curtain forever.

The problem arose when Peña Nieto became president of Mexico. His tactic of ignoring the facts blew up in his face. No matter how hard his team tried, it was impossible to cover up the rampant violence and impunity. The Ayotzinapa tragedy exposed the incompetence of his administration, and the reports of corruption involving the "White House" scandal left it completely vulnerable. How can a president ask his constituents to fight corruption when he's not even willing to lead by example in his own home?

President Peña Nieto requested an investigation into the "Casa Blanca" affair but, instead of allowing for a congressional or independent inquiry, he assigned the task to one of his ministers, Virgilio Andrade. Obviously that was another conflict of interest. Seven months later (in August 2015), as expected, minister Andrade absolved the president and his wife of any wrongdoing. That investigation carried zero credibility and only reconfirmed the suspicions of many Mexicans that corruption in their country starts at the highest levels.

The third lesson is that a lack of leadership is always noticeable. When the Ayotzinapa massacre and the "White House" scandal broke— and drug violence was rising across the country—the president seemed to go into hiding. He gave no nationally televised press conferences, interviews, or speeches to explain his plan going forward. Without direction from the president, the country was left to drift.

And once again, when drug lord Joaquín "El Chapo" Guzmán escaped from the Altiplano maximum-security prison on July 11, 2015, President Peña Nieto didn't know how to react. News of the Sinaloa Cartel leader's escape through a mile-long tunnel came as quite a surprise to Peña Nieto—and his entourage of more than four hundred people—during a trip to Paris. Clearly shocked and paralyzed, he decided to stay in France rather than return home to face the biggest security crisis of his presidency. In other words, the president went missing.

A pattern had been established. Whether it was the death of his wife, the allegations of corruption, or the major crises facing the country, President Enrique Peña Nieto didn't have the answers.

And in the end, all Mexico lost.

When things go badly for the president, they go badly for the entire nation.

Peña Nieto is a weak president. Salinas de Gortari was not. But they both share the traditional vision that one person can rule the country. Mexican presidents tend to think that they are indispensable and all-powerful. That explains the corruption and dishonesty that plagues the office. The big difference is that before the 2000 election, there was no accountability and the media were completely submissive to the office of the president. Not anymore.

Today, the president cannot rule like an Aztec Tlatoani or a Spanish viceroy. He might be able to hold on to power despite accusations of corruption and incompetence. But thanks to social media and a new generation of very brave reporters, he knows that people are aware of his mistakes.

Just as it happened with Salinas de Gortari, Peña Nieto is already fighting for his reputation. Both know that it's an uphill battle.

In Mexico no one is more alone than a former president.

ELEVEN

Alvaro Uribe:
The Irascible Survivor

I'm a fighter, but I don't sow hate. It's like a cow in the swamp: the more it kicks, the more stuck it gets. —ALVARO URIBE

I NEVER GOT ALONG well with Alvaro Uribe. When he was president of Colombia, from 2002 to 2010, he never wanted to answer any of my questions. And when he became the former president, he got angry at my questions. In fact, our first three encounters went so badly that I'm still not sure why I kept requesting interviews, or why he kept accepting them. My questions always seemed to bother Uribe, and I was always frustrated because I couldn't get anything out of him.

Uribe was news. That's why I interviewed him. Even though he always got upset. He needed the international press, of which I was a part, in order to get his message out to the world that Colombia was changing for the better. But there was something else beyond the political and journalistic considerations. To me, Uribe always seemed like someone who believed he had nothing to lose.

After the death of his father in 1983 at the hands of FARC guerrillas, Uribe apparently made a mental promise to himself that he would not rest until he defeated the group to which the murderers belonged. (FARC—the Spanish acronym of the Revolutionary Armed Forces of

Colombia—are leftist rebels who have been active in Colombia since 1964 in a conflict that has taken more than 220,000 lives.) That was the impression I always got from Uribe: he was a man on a mission. And men with this sort of conviction do not bend.

I MET HIM for the first time in New York in the fall of 2007, just after his reelection and just before he was to make a speech before the United Nations. He was half an hour late, but he was doing well. Very well. Smiling. Joking, even. He greeted me enthusiastically. His light blue shirt seemed puffed with energy. It was nine in the morning, and he had already been to two meetings and a breakfast event. And that was after having gone for a run in Central Park for sixty-six minutes. Not a minute more, not a minute less. Sixty-six minutes exactly. And that, it seemed, left him positively euphoric.

I was surprised. In other interviews he had come across as irritable and ill-tempered. But perhaps that was because they always ended with questions about whether he had any ties to paramilitary groups. And I told him that. He took it quite well. "You can't hide it when you're in a good mood," he said, smiling, ready to get down to business.

Uribe had repeatedly told reporters how his father, Alvaro Uribe Sierra, had died on June 14, 1983, while resisting an apparent kidnapping attempt by FARC at his ranch in the state of Antioquia. He was shot in the head and the chest.

According to a report in *El Tiempo*, Colombia's largest-circulation newspaper, one of the guerrilla leaders, Raúl Reyes, said that this was a "false" version of events and that they had had nothing to do with the death of the senior Uribe. But the question remained: How much did the death of his father have to do with President Uribe's belligerent attitude toward FARC?

"My family has suffered, just as fifty percent of Colombian families have suffered," he reflected, lowering his voice. "If I had these reservations, I never could have aspired to become president of the republic. . . . I'm a fighter, but I don't sow hate. It's like a cow in the swamp: the more it kicks, the more stuck it gets."

Before Uribe, many Colombians thought it was impossible to defeat the guerrillas by force. But all that changed when he came to power. His attitude clashed with the prevailing belief. No, they would not clear out one square meter of territory in order to negotiate a hostage exchange with the guerrillas. "That will never happen," he said, even though at the time there had been some 23,000 reported kidnappings in the previous ten years in the country.

But that morning, Uribe had more than kidnappings on his mind. He claimed that paramilitary groups had "totally disappeared" from Colombia. "If they've really disappeared," I replied in disbelief, "that news would be being reported everywhere." He understood my doubts, but still he insisted: "Today there are no paramilitary groups in Colombia attacking the guerrillas."

And then, our roles were reversed. Uribe became the one asking the questions.

"Have you been to Colombia?"

"A long time ago," I replied. "It's been years."

"Go there and then we'll talk," he said. "There are two Colombias: the one that is being painted by the news, and the other one, which is being seen by the visitors. The Colombia of today is a country of joy, a country that has regained her confidence."

Joy and confidence are not the memories I had of Colombia. It had been years since I last visited the country and on my last visit, in fact, I had to flee.

Here's the story: In January 1996, I spoke in prison with Fernando Botero, who had been the chief of staff of then presidential candidate Ernesto Samper. And Botero confirmed to me, on camera, that the campaign had received six million dollars from drug trafficking. "Yes, I knew that large sums of drug money were flowing into this campaign," he said to me. Botero was already serving prison time for that very reason. But he had decided to speak up and confess everything he knew.

That night, I went to the Palacio de Nariño to speak with Samper, who had since then been sworn in as president. He denied everything. "If drug money was coming in [to my campaign], it was all being done behind my back," he said. He also denied allegations of a cover-up, and insisted that Botero was lying to save his own skin.

That ended the interview, but that's also where my problems began. We had been staying at El Nogal, a private club, for security reasons. Two days after the interview, the receptionist answered a phone call with a message for me: "Tell Ramos we will take you down for what you showed on Univision." Two hours later, with police on the scene, another call was made using much the same language.

The threats were direct. It was time to leave Colombia, and that's exactly what we did. Fear doesn't ride a donkey, as they say in Mexico. I went back to Bogotá shortly thereafter to conduct another interview with Samper, but since then I haven't returned. Once, Univision's offices there received funeral flowers with my name on them. The message was clear.

I didn't tell Uribe this, but I'm sure he wouldn't have been surprised.

I always believed—because of the violence, the kidnappings, the poverty, the guerrillas, the paramilitaries, the drug trafficking, and the millions of displaced citizens—that the president of Colombia has the most difficult job in the world. And I said that to Uribe.

"It's not hard work when you do it with love," he said philosophically. And with that, the interview was over.

But over the course of that half hour, the initial energy with which Uribe had come to the interview had waned. He asked one of his assistants what was next on the schedule, said good-bye to a dozen diplomats and other journalists, and headed for a large cushioned couch. He plopped himself down, threw his head back, ran his hands underneath his glasses, and closed his eyes.

Suddenly everyone began speaking in whispers, creating a heavy semi-silence. After several minutes, I got up to leave the room. But as I was walking out the door, I turned to look back: Uribe was still there, motionless, his eyes closed.

WE SPOKE AGAIN in 2009, but with my very first question, I knew I was in trouble. "Do you have anything else you'd like to ask me?" Alvaro Uribe said to me via satellite. Clearly, the Colombian president had no intentions of answering. And he didn't.

I asked him about the accusations levied by Venezuelan president Hugo Chávez that the presence of U.S. troops on Colombian military bases presented a danger to the region and a threat to Venezuela. I wanted to get his reaction, but I couldn't. "No comment," he said. "If you have another topic, Jorge, then by all means [go right ahead]."

Yes, I did have other topics to discuss, and some twenty-odd prepared questions. But it was clear to me that there were several issues that the Colombian president was not about to touch.

Colombia's secret service, the Administrative Department of Security, or DAS, as it's called, had been implicated in an espionage scandal involving the recording of conversations between various government critics and opponents of Uribe. Who gave the order to make those recordings? I asked.

"Do you have another question?" he replied. "This is an honorable government, one that puts all its cards on the table. It is a transparent government. If you have any other questions, I'll be glad [to answer them]."

I did. Former president César Gaviria had said, "Uribe is a dictator who turned the DAS into a criminal machine." But as I expected, Uribe refused to respond. "Do you have another question, dear Jorge?"

Three questions. No responses.

The interview wasn't going anywhere. In fact, we had started at a disadvantage. We had to conduct the conversation via satellite, as the president was in New York and I was in Miami. I prefer to sit down with my guest for an interview in the same room. There is nothing like the personal contact and the chance to read body language. But that's not possible all the time. In this case, I had no choice but to talk to Uribe via satellite.

Things were not going well. We asked him to remove his glasses, because the glare was being reflected into the cameras. That request was kindly accepted. But he looked uncomfortable, anxious, isolated. Several times he raised his hand to his ear, as if he were about to pull out the headset through which he was listening to my questions.

He was upset when I reminded him that the Peruvian writer Mario Vargas Llosa had said that it would be "regrettable" if Uribe were to seek a third term in office, also when I asked whether he felt "indispensable" to Colombia.

No, Uribe didn't want to talk about any of this.

The president didn't know what I was going to be asking. We don't give anyone a list of questions ahead of time. Ever. It's a basic journalistic principle. But clearly Uribe had been hoping for a different sort of interview.

Uribe had changed a lot while in power. He seemed much more impatient than he had during our previous conversation, exactly two years before this interview. He listened less. He didn't want to hear about criticisms of his administration or answer uncomfortable questions. It wasn't the first time I'd seen a president do this. It always happens to leaders who don't know when it's time to step down.

MY THIRD AND final interview with Uribe didn't end any better. He was no longer in office—having been unsuccessful in his efforts to amend the constitution to allow for a third term—but he hadn't stopped talking. On the contrary, on Twitter, in interviews, and in a book—*No Lost Causes*—he challenged incumbent president Juan Manuel Santos and opined on almost everything. He was giving the impression that he hadn't gotten used to being a former president.

Once again we were not in the same room—he was in a studio in Washington while I was in another in Miami. The initial purpose was to discuss the publication of his latest book. But then we started talking about war.

In 2012, a survey found that 77 percent of Colombians were in favor of holding peace talks with FARC. But Uribe was opposed to any such dialogue, and countered with figures of his own. "The same poll says that 80 percent of Colombians don't want there to be any immunity," he replied. "When we came into power [in 2002], the FARC was holding around 30,000 people hostage, and when I left office [in 2010] there were approximately 6,800."

Uribe had made many Colombians believe, for the first time, that the guerrillas could be defeated by force, and it hurt him that his former defense minister and current president Juan Manuel Santos was negotiating with FARC for peace. "I'm very concerned that some of these talks are successful simply because it brings a Castro-Chávez model to Colombia, a model that destroys freedoms and eliminates the possibility of democratic prosperity for the country."

The past was haunting Uribe. I mentioned that about a dozen former officials of his administration—more than in anyone else's presidency—had been brought up on charges. He didn't like the line of questioning, but he responded. "I have put all of my own integrity on the line to defend them," he said defiantly. And then came the attack: "Excuse me, excuse me, excuse me, Jorge. Look, you invited me on to talk about the book, but now I see that all you're interested in is a quick rehashing of allegations."

"I'm basing them on your book," I said.

"No, no, no," he replied. "You're not giving me time, you're not being gallant enough to ask me about each particular case. You're leaving some ideas up in the air, and each of them has its own answer. And they are all honorable answers."

"Lastly, let me ask you about how it feels to be a former president. There are many who say that you were the best president Colombia has ever had, but that you have also been the worst former president because you haven't been able to accept the fact that you're no longer in office."

"What can I tell you, Jorge?" he asked with a smile and a sense of humor.

"I don't know. Whatever you like," I replied, smiling back at him.

"I'm a survivor," he said. "I've survived over a dozen attacks. It's a miracle I'm still alive. Why wouldn't I continue playing a part in the politics of my country, even without any personal ambition? As long as God grants me the energy to do so, of course I have to continue to participate, my dear Jorge."

ALVARO URIBE: THE LESSONS

Colombia's recent history can be divided into two periods: the time before Alvaro Uribe, and the time after him. Uribe effectively reduced the numbers of murders and kidnappings. But even more important than that, he gave the citizens the hope that they could once again live in a safe and secure country.

Before Uribe, there were very few politicians who dared to say that, yes, it was possible to defeat FARC with force. Not only did Uribe say it, he very nearly did it. That's the lesson: Put in practice what you truly believe in. Words are not enough.

The cost of this war strategy, of course, was very high. Administration officials were accused of wiretapping, abusing their authority, and supporting paramilitary groups, among other things. And FARC hasn't disappeared.

Uribe's strategy was always one of war. He was never willing to negotiate peace with his enemies. It must be very difficult to have a discussion with those who murdered your father. But maybe this strategy nudged the guerrillas toward the negotiating table. It's quite possible that the peace talks in Havana, Cuba, between Juan Manuel Santos and FARC never would have come about without the withering attacks conducted under President Uribe.

Colombians deserve peace. Most of them don't know what it's like to live without war. The irony is that—if peace does, in fact, come—one of the people they will have to thank is Uribe, the irascible survivor himself.

Not every president that I have talked to is on a mission. Some see their tenure as an opportunity to change a country; others plan it years in advance and the presidency becomes a part of a natural political process. In the case of Uribe it always felt as if he had no choice but to run, as if there was a moral imperative that forced him to confront the most intractable problems of the country.

Uribe had something in his favor: clarity. You always knew what he wanted, even if his methods were questionable. Also, he was aware of his strengths and was not afraid of using them. He convinced millions of Colombians that peace through force was possible. He just needed more time, and that didn't happen.

What Uribe never understood is that you cannot impose peace. The end of any war is not defined by starting a new one. It's the beginning of peace.

TWELVE

The Cost of Rebellion:
The Case of Ingrid Betancourt

I need some time for me, I need to put down some roots, I need to build a life.　　　　　　　　　　—INGRID BETANCOURT

R EBELLION IS ALWAYS worth it.
　　 It reaffirms the best of you in the face of what you consider the worst of the world.

But rebellion does come at a cost.

And sometimes those costs are incredibly high.

Ingrid Betancourt knows.

She paid in full.

INGRID BETANCOURT TOLD me one day that she was going to become president of Colombia, and that she would personally invite me to the Palacio de Nariño to interview her there. And I believed her. What I never could have imagined, though, was that her life would later become one of the most terrible tragedies in the modern history of Colombia.

Ingrid Betancourt was a rebel. But her rebellion nearly cost Betancourt her life.

I first met her on January 15, 2002, thirty-nine days before she was kidnapped. She was a candidate for the Colombian presidency, but was visiting Miami to promote her book *The Rage in My Heart*.

But the rage she had at the time was directed at another presidential candidate, Alvaro Uribe. "Uribe is a candidate for the paramilitary groups," she told me back then. "I would say that Alvaro Uribe tolerates murders in Colombia as a way of confronting the guerrillas." The irony is that nearly seven years later, it would be Uribe himself who, as president, would negotiate her freedom.

On February 23 of that same year, Betancourt was kidnapped by FARC, while traveling by land from Florencia to San Vicente del Caguán in a demilitarized zone controlled by the rebels. She was taken along with Betancourt's campaign manager, Clara Rojas. Before the kidnapping, the administration of the current president, Andrés Pastrana, had withdrawn her security detail in an apparent attempt to keep her from traveling to the conflict zone, where Pastrana would be holding a press conference of his own.

Those were days of great tension in Colombia. Peace talks between Pastrana and FARC had failed. The government, therefore, was attempting to recover the demilitarized zone that had previously been granted to the guerrillas.

Ingrid the Rebel—the same Ingrid who had bravely denounced acts of corruption since her early days as a senator, who would search for peace with youthful enthusiasm, who would not mince words when attacking unscrupulous politicians, and who was ready to give her life for her country—had been kidnapped.

Her voice had suddenly been silenced.

INGRID BETANCOURT AWOKE in the Colombian jungle just as she always did: before the sun was up. It was July 2, 2008. She switched on the radio, and the first thing she heard was the voice of her mother,

Yolanda, who was traveling to France. Then it was her daughter, Melanie, who was leaving for China. What Ingrid didn't know was that that day would be the last of the 2,330 days she spent as a FARC captive.

From Monday through Friday, at five in the morning, Colombian radio would broadcast messages from relatives of the hostages. The hope was that somewhere, deep in the jungle, they were listening. And Ingrid—who, much to her dismay, was the most famous hostage in the world—heard those messages on the day of her rescue.

"After each message, the moral, emotional, and intellectual wear and tear was devastating," Ingrid's aunt, Nancy Pulecio, who repeatedly spoke to her over the radio, told me in an interview.

She feared that a rescue attempt would end with Ingrid's death. "We were afraid that they would kill her," she said. "It's happened with so many hostage situations: you attempt a rescue, and they end up killing them." But not this time.

"Ingrid is out! Ingrid is out!" That's how Yolanda broke the news to her sister Nancy, who was caught, incredulous, in a bank in Miami.

Along with three Americans, seven Colombian soldiers, and four Colombian police officers, Ingrid was rescued by the army during what was called Operation Jaque in the state of Guaviare. It was an ingenious surprise maneuver in which the guerrillas were tricked into handing over their most valuable hostages safe and sound. The United States did not participate in the rescue. "The operation was one hundred percent made in Colombia," Secretary of Defense Juan Manuel Santos said in a television interview.

"It was a serious moral blow to the FARC," said Clara Rojas, on the phone with me from Bogotá. She had been freed a few months earlier.

At that time, FARC was still holding more than seven hundred people hostage. But the perception that the guerrillas could not be defeated militarily was beginning to wane, and Uribe—who was convinced that his own father had died at the hands of the FARC—acted like someone who had nothing to lose.

The day of her rescue, Ingrid went to bed well past midnight, after a lengthy conference with President Uribe, Secretary Santos, and the eleven other rescued Colombians. A few hours later, at the airport in Bogotá, Ingrid Betancourt was reunited with her twenty-two-year-old daughter, Melanie, and her nineteen-year-old son, Lorenzo. Despite the exhaustion, it was, I suspect, a day on which she would rather not close her eyes, for fear of waking up and believing that the long nightmare was still going on.

I SPOKE WITH Ingrid two weeks after she emerged from hell.

"I'm very tired," she said via satellite from Paris, before starting the interview. And it showed. She looked like she hadn't slept in days. Gone were the joy and enthusiasm we saw shortly after her rescue from the Colombian jungle.

It was ironic, but as I watched her there on the screen, I wondered whether a couple of weeks of freedom—during which time she spoke tirelessly at media and political events, along with an international flight from Colombia to France—had affected her vitality more than the six years and 140 days she had spent as a prisoner of FARC.

The night before, she had fainted after an interview. But she wasn't about to stop. So why do it?

"I think there is a need to keep fighting for those who remain in Colombia," she said, referring to the hundreds of hostages still being held by FARC. "But I do have to admit that this has all been very intense for me. I am very tired. I need some time for me, I need to put down some roots, I need to build a life. . . . These will be my last interviews, because I just need to be with my family and to mentally get myself back together."

I asked her about her hair—a long ponytail that fell most of the length of her back. It was no trivial thing. In fact, it was filled with symbolism. She said that every centimeter of hair was a centimeter of pain.

"It has a symbolic value, because when I was in the jungle I couldn't cut my hair, mainly because we didn't have any scissors," she said, showing her hair to the cameras. "[My hair] is like a biological clock, it's like a mark indicating how much time I spent in another world, a world of suffering. As long as there are still people living that same horror in that same jungle, I have to let it keep a running track of time."

For Ingrid, the jungle represents hell.

The pain is physical.

"It was six years and five months, and every day something hurt, every day I physically felt myself being bitten by bugs. I was itching and scratching, some part of my body was always in pain," she recalled. But beyond the tarantulas, snakes, and scorpions of the jungle, Ingrid's hell also involved her captors: "That horror of horrors, the hostile presence of arbitrariness, of daily cruelty, of the refinement of hell."

Despite this, there were some things that Ingrid wanted to leave in the jungle. When CNN's Larry King asked her if she had been sexually abused by FARC, she preferred not to answer.

"I know that I have to bear witness, that there are things I have to talk about," she said. "All I can say is that I need time, there are still some things I have to let go. . . . One of the things I learned is that I'm a fragile woman. . . . One day I'll have the strength to talk about these things, but right now I don't think I could possibly do it."

When Ingrid traveled to the French capital she traded the dragonflies of the jungle for the lights of Paris, the smell of mud for perfumes and hotels, and a river for a bath for water so hot it burned her skin when she took her first shower after her abduction.

Her presidential ambitions were over.

"For me, after those years in captivity, that's no longer a priority," she told me. "It's not an ambition of mine."

After the twenty-minute interview, Ingrid was clearly exhausted. She would pause to catch her breath and to find the words. But she finished by telling me that she had spent these past few days in Paris with her two children, Melanie and Lorenzo, by her side.

"I didn't sleep much those first few days," she recalled. "So when they would drift off next to me, and I watch them sleep, and when I see in their faces what's left of how they looked as children—they're not children now, of course, they're adults—it is very beautiful."

ABOUT SIX MONTHS after her release, in December 2008, we spoke again, via satellite. She in Paris and me in Miami. She was still not yet accustomed to freedom. It still seemed like a dream.

"Yes, it still surprises me," she said. "Every day surprises me, and I don't think I'm the only one. . . . We're all living with the sense that it's a dream, but it's a beautiful dream, and thank God it's reality."

Then I reminded her of the conversation we had thirty-nine days before she was kidnapped, when she said she would invite me to Nariño, the presidential palace. The 2010 elections were fast approaching. Would she jump into the race?

"No," she said, powerfully and without hesitation. "I've changed a lot, Jorge. I'm not going to run. I love my country very much. But there are things in my country I do not like. I don't like the hatred that I see. I don't like this extreme polarization in which speaking out about something means you're either for or against each other. I would like us to be more open with our opinions, and not trapped in the cages of our extremes."

No, Ingrid Betancourt has learned her lesson. Even for rebels such as she, the risk of being trapped in a cage, yet again, was very high. She would not do it again. Politics, even the presidency, would be just another prison. It was better to be free than powerful.

One imprisonment was enough.

INGRID BETANCOURT: THE LESSONS

I finally got to meet Ingrid Betancourt in person. She had written a book—*Even Silence Has an End*—and in October 2010 she was going to be in Miami to promote it. I was invited to introduce her at an event at Miami Dade College, in the heart of the city, and immediately I accepted.

It was the opportunity I had been waiting for to tell her how many people had fought for her release, how I was struck by a giant poster of her face hanging outside the opera hall in Milan, how I remembered the last conversation we had before her kidnapping.

Her book is filled with honesty and rage. But she told her story as if it were a pending assignment. It was something she had to do. She was "touched," as the Colombians often say. And it was indeed touching to hear Ingrid tell what had happened and to keep alive the memory of those who were still being held by the guerrillas.

When we met, I didn't detect any joy in Ingrid's face. Clearly, she would rather have been somewhere else, with other people. She had lost nearly seven years of her life in the jungle, and she didn't want to waste any more time with strangers.

But there she was, regardless. In front of an audience of hundreds of people who wanted to listen to what she had to say.

Yes, Ingrid was still a rebel. But her rebellion had come at a high price. The lost years, spent without her children, were, after all, unrecoverable.

Beyond whatever hatred she might have harbored for her captors, an attempt at forgiveness and reconciliation was already forming. "No, one can't live with so much venom," Shakira rightly sang while Ingrid was still imprisoned. "Rage weighs more than cement."

Ingrid was being freed, and talking about what had happened helped her in this process.

When I saw her, I went up and gave her a big hug. "What a joy to see you free," I think I said. She thanked me, her eyes wide, brimming with the new wisdom that comes from knowing she is no longer a captive.

But in the embrace, I felt a fragile woman. Perhaps that had always been her secret. Behind the outward image of firmness and strength, there was a woman still being constructed, a woman who had spent all her life learning how to overcome her own fragility.

There are some rebels who are made out of their own sheer will.

THIRTEEN

Daniel Ortega, or the Revolution That Left Everything the Same

If there were something improper, something illegal, then plenty of action would have been taken against me.

—DANIEL ORTEGA

FIRST THEY WERE the Somozas. Now they're the Ortegas.

Daniel Ortega and the Sandinista rebels rose up against the Somoza regime that dominated Nicaragua with three dictators over a forty-year span. The Somoza regime ended in 1979, and that's when Ortega's began.

Daniel Ortega was the de facto leader of the Junta of National Reconstruction, which governed Nicaragua after the fall of the Somoza dynasty. He was president from 1985 to 1990, when the Sandinistas lost the election to Violeta Barrios de Chamorro. Ortega lost the election again in 1996 (to Arnoldo Alemán) and in 2001 (this time to Enrique Bolaños). But he returned to power in 2006 with just 38 percent of the vote. And since then, nobody has been able to knock him off his horse.

In 2009, with absolute control over nearly all the political power in Nicaragua, he managed to amend the constitution to allow for continuous reelections, the first of which took place in 2012. It's impossible to know what his plans are for this power, but either his wife, Rosario

Murillo, or his son Laureano—who is one of the primary proponents of the controversial Interoceanic Grand Canal, the proposed megaproject to build a rival to the Panama Canal across Nicaragua—could replace him should he decide to retire.

Thus, what began as a fight to bring down one nepotistic family—the Somozas—has ended up establishing another, the Ortegas. It's the revolution that left everything the same.

THE ONE EXAMPLE that best reflects the abuse of power in Nicaragua is the house where the Ortega family lives. It's not just any house. And here's why:

The house, and everything in it, was stolen from the Morales Carazo family—"confiscated" according to the government—shortly after the Sandinista triumph back in 1979. That's what I was told by Jaime Morales, one of the primary political figures in the modern history of the country. Morales was vice president of Nicaragua from 2007 to 2012, the former campaign manager for Arnoldo Alemán's presidential bid, and the current deputy to the Central American Parliament.

The house we're talking about is actually more of a fortress, comparable only to the one occupied by the dictator Anastasio Somoza before he was thrown out of the country. The acre of land, on the outskirts of Managua's old center, was acquired between 1967 and 1968 by Morales, who was by then a prominent businessman and collector of some of the most valuable works of art in all of Nicaraguan culture. Morales laid the cornerstone and, over the next few years, he used precious woods to build an impressive hacienda that included six fountains, six bedrooms, two living rooms, an office, and several dining areas. In the end, it covered nearly a quarter of the property. And when it came to the artwork it housed, "the house was practically a museum," according to its first occupant.

The financial group to which Morales belonged supported the Sandinista revolution, and so they never expected that one of their leaders would end up taking possession of their house once Somoza was removed from power. When the Sandinistas took over on July 19, 1979, Morales was in Mexico City. He was one of the leaders of the Nicaraguan Red Cross, and had been sent to Mexico on a mission to collect plasma. Much to his surprise, he learned that—two days after the Sandinista victory—Daniel Ortega and Rosario Murillo had appropriated his home, occupying it immediately.

Morales's wife, Amparo, and their three children were traveling in Miami when all of this took place. Thus, there was nobody to contest the entry of Comandante Ortega. The house was commandeered because it had been "abandoned," according to the Sandinistas' legal justification, and for twelve years, Ortega didn't pay a penny for it, other than the property taxes. Amparo, a Mexican citizen, returned to Managua shortly thereafter to demand that the house be returned to its rightful owner. But it was all to no avail. She argued vehemently with Rosario Murillo, and was threatened. According to Morales, that personal confrontation became "the crux of the problem."

Rosario was not about to let Amparo return home.

Morales estimated that the value of the home, when it was taken, was between $1.5 and $2 million, including the works of art. But Ortega paid a mere $1,500, according to copies of receipts that Morales has received from INDESA, the Nicaraguan Investment and Development Bank.

This one-time-only payment was supposedly made in April 1990, after Ortega's electoral defeat by Violeta Chamorro during the period known as "La Piñata," during which a series of legislative acts allowed estates that had been seized by the Sandinistas to become the private property of certain government officials, including Ortega.

But what does Daniel Ortega himself think of all this?

In late 1996, during an interview in Managua, Comandante Ortega told me that the house had become a "symbol" that he had acquired "through the legal framework," and that thousands of Nicaraguans would feel "helpless" if he were to return the property. But when I asked him how much he actually paid for the property, his answers got all twisted together.

"One of the issues that divides Nicaraguans is La Piñata," I began. "Many people would believe you if you were to return the home."

"Well, then, La Piñata, what did it mean?" he said. "In Nicaragua, La Piñata meant promoting structural changes in ownership. In other words, the democratization of property. Land that was concentrated in the hands of the few was redistributed, which benefited 155,000 rural families. And, really, that undoubtedly upset the sector that saw itself being affected, being expropriated, which is a minority sector of the population. In any case, the fact is that I have a home which I acquired through the legal framework, which, as a Nicaraguan, is simply a right that I have. If there were something improper, something illegal, then plenty of action would have been taken against me."

"They say it's worth two million dollars," I pressed. "How much did you pay for the house?"

"Well, the truth is that it's not worth two million dollars," he countered. "That's an exaggeration."

"How much did it cost? How much is it worth? How is the value calculated?"

"It's not worth all that much. It's a lot less than that."

"A million?"

"No, no, no. Not that much at all."

"I'm not sure. I don't know the house. I'm just not sure how much it's worth."

"Well, it's not worth very much. I can tell you that."

"How much did you pay for it?"

"Well, I paid what it was worth at the time."

"How much was that?"

"Well, the truth is I don't have the exact figure."

"But more or less."

"It wasn't much, then, it wasn't much."

"Thirty thousand dollars? Ten thousand dollars?"

"Yes, it was a small sum because back then everything was undervalued. . . . For me, it would be easy to leave that house. But that would send a bad impression to thousands of Nicaraguans, who would feel helpless if I were to do that."

"Could it be that your house has become a symbol?"

"It is a symbol. Ultimately, I've held on to the house mostly because it's a symbol."

I couldn't get Ortega to give me a clear figure on how much he paid for the house, despite asking him twelve separate times. (I know because I counted.) But based on Morales's version of events, the payment was—I repeat—a mere $1,500, which is about one-tenth of a percent of its true value.

Morales assured me he wasn't interested in revenge. So much so, in fact, that despite their personal differences, he agreed to serve as Ortega's vice president for five years.

Incredible. Only in Nicaragua.

I RETURNED TO Nicaragua in 2006, and Ortega was still living in that same house. And it seemed that Daniel Ortega's main problems were inextricably linked to it.

His stepdaughter, Zoilamérica Narvaez—the biological daughter of Ortega's companion, Rosario Murillo—accused him of frequently raping and sexually abusing her after she turned eleven. And everything allegedly took place under the roof of that disputed residence.

Here is the statement Zoilamérica made to the Spanish paper *El País*: "I was sexually abused by Daniel Ortega Saavedra, starting when I was eleven years old, and these acts continued for nearly twenty years of my life. I remained silent all of this time due to ingrained fears and confusion arising from different forms of aggression that left me extremely vulnerable and dependent on my aggressor."

When I met again with Ortega, I asked him about Zoilamérica. "That chapter has ended," he said. But her testimony was filled with lurid details. "Daniel Ortega raped me in 1982," she stated during public testimony that has appeared on the Internet. "He ejaculated on my body to avoid the risk of pregnancy, and he continued to do so time and time again."

"It's completely false," Ortega told me, his eyes unblinking. "False."

"Is she lying?" I asked.

"She's lying. Of course she is."

Ortega consistently denied these accusations, and in 2007, Zoilamérica dropped the lawsuit she had brought against Ortega and the Nicaraguan state before the Inter-American Commission on Human Rights.

But at the time, in 2006, Ortega was on the campaign trail. It was the fifth time that the Sandinista comandante had sought the presidency, but his rhetoric was the same. He attacked U.S. president George W. Bush—"who committed mass murder in Iraq and beyond"—and defended Fidel Castro by saying, "Fidel, to me, is not a dictator."

He kept no secrets when it came to his friends. "Gaddafi, Chávez, Fidel, Lula [da Silva], and Evo [Morales] are like brothers to me," he said, referring to the leaders of Libya, Venezuela, Cuba, Brazil, and Bolivia. It was the same old Daniel Ortega; he had just changed his tactics in order to return to power. He had lost the presidency in 1990, and his mission was to regain it no matter the cost.

Ortega was frequently seen with Cardinal Miguel Obando y Bravo, the most powerful Catholic priest in Nicaragua, and in September 2005, he decided to marry the poet Rosario Murillo in a Catholic ceremony. "I felt it was a commitment I had made to my mother," he said. "My mother always wanted me to get married. She was very traditional, very Catholic." And so he did.

Before I left, I asked Ortega if he believed he would win the election. "Yes," he confidently replied. "I have faith in the people and faith in God that we will win."

He won. The problem now for Nicaraguans would be how to get him out.

DANIEL ORTEGA'S LESSON

There are revolutions that end up in the same place where they started. And there are revolutions that—once they achieve power—cease to be revolutionary. That is the case with Daniel Ortega.

The Sandinistas started a legitimate uprising against the Somoza dictatorship. The atrocities committed under Somoza's rule are among the worst in the recent history of Central America. And it would be unfair to compare Somoza's repression with the serious and arbitrary excesses of the Sandinistas. But that does not excuse the fact that revolutionaries can fall victim to the same mistakes made by the rulers they replaced: issues of impunity, nepotism, corruption, accumulating power in the office of the presidency, attacking and campaigning against their political opponents, limiting and censoring the freedom of expression, and—above all—the impossibility of democratically removing them from power.

We mustn't exaggerate. The Somozas were brutal and murderous leaders. The Nicaragua of the early twenty-first century isn't what it was during the mid-twentieth century. Ortega's abuses pale in comparison with those of the bloodthirsty Somoza regime. But the sad and serious fact of the matter is that a despot has returned to rule Nicaragua. Was the Sandinista revolution a missed opportunity? To many it seems that way.

The irony lies in the fact that it would take yet another rebellious movement to end the corrupted revolution that brought down the

Somoza regime. Ortega's lesson is that even the most committed revolutionaries—and here we can include Chávez and Fidel as well—succumb to the excesses of dictators once they have concentrated all of a nation's power.

We ask our revolutionaries for democracy and change, and then we ask them to retire. But Daniel Ortega has never been one to say no to power.

I have always been interested in what makes a revolutionary want to live in a wealthy person's home. I don't like to ask personal questions unless they are related to a public matter. But questions about personal homes and wealth are always necessary. A politician's home says more about him than any of his speeches. And then comes the important question of accountability. If a leader ends his presidency with a bigger home than he had when he started, then corruption is a possibility. That's why politicians are always uncomfortable when you ask them about their homes.

I never fully understood the urgency with which Ortega and Rosario Murillo occupied one of the most elegant mansions in Managua just days after the triumph of the Sandinista revolution.

True revolutionaries, I suppose, would reject the luxuries and excesses of the class they just overcame. But instead of doing that, Daniel Ortega imitated his enemies, and did so as soon as he took power. There was no moral justification for taking over a house that did not belong to him. It's as if the revolution changed the rules of the game and made larceny legal.

Ultimately, living in someone else's home comes at a high personal cost: you become someone you're not. I want to believe that Daniel Ortega would have been a different revolutionary figure if he hadn't taken over that house. But that, of course, is something we will never know.

FOURTEEN

Money Isn't Everything: What the Super-rich Can Teach Us: Bill Gates, Richard Branson, and Jorge Pérez

The choices I make are not based on some views of the hereafter. Here on earth there's a lot of lives we can uplift. And my basic view is positive; we are making a lot of progress.

—BILL GATES

This inquisitiveness is a healthy thing, and leads to new innovations. Only through exploration of the unknown can we continue to grow and evolve. —RICHARD BRANSON

I didn't set out to become a billionaire. . . . I started with nothing, or next to nothing. I was an immigrant kid who came to Miami with $2 in my pocket. Today I am a billionaire.

—JORGE PÉREZ

O N MORE THAN one occasion I have pressed a national leader about the size of his personal fortune. Making money is apparently a priority, even for leaders who started out as rebels. The super-rich— and I'm talking about truly wealthy people, those who don't have to work for a living, who generate money in their sleep, who have secured a lavish life for many generations to come—are different. For them, money isn't the most important thing.

There comes a time when they're able to pause for a moment, and all of a sudden, they do an about-face. They decide (through divine inspiration, some would say) that their goal in life is not to make money but to give it away. And at that moment, they become rebels of a different kind.

Something changes in their minds. It's not that they think they were wrong all this time. On the contrary, they understand that they've surpassed all the expectations they and others might have had for their lives. They've secured their places in history, or at least among those who are important to them.

It's a radical change. Instead of living for themselves, they've decided to live for others. This is not to say that they've lived a selfish, egotistical life to this point. No. They earned their money—lots of money—by making things that other people needed: computers, airplanes, buildings. Many have been rebels in the way that they have gone about doing it. Nor does this mean that they're about to stop producing these goods. What's different is that instead of accumulating things, it now becomes time to start giving them away.

It's a complicated process, like trying to pull off all your layers of clothes after a long, frigid walk on a wintry night. But it's not about giving gifts. Nothing could be further from the truth.

One characteristic of the super-rich is that when they donate money, they do so with the same care and discipline with which they earned it. They set a goal, formulate a plan, execute it with precision, and then—only then—release the funds. Sometimes this process unfolds in the blink of an eye, urgently, as if they feel something burning deep inside them. Other times it's more cautious; it has to be pushed ahead slowly, one step at a time.

Either way, in the end, the result is a rewarding one. I've never seen a super-rich person feel sad or unfulfilled after giving away his or her money. It turns out that we were wrong to believe that money was their primary objective.

Money is simply the consequence or by-product of their success. They appreciate it and look after it because they put a lot of work into earning it. It's a symbol of the power they have. But it's liberating—in a rebellious way—for them to give away that which they've spent their entire lives to acquire. It's as close as they can get to being like one of those Indian monks who so impressed me by giving away all their personal belongings except for the bare essentials: their robes, their sandals, and a small bag. That's all.

But let's put things in perspective. When a super-rich person gives away money, he's not taking a vow of poverty like this. He's still incredibly wealthy. He makes sure that he retains enough to live comfortably, luxuriously even, for the rest of his days; he has to leave something for his children and future generations; and he has to ensure that his brand—because ultimately, that's what the super-rich have become, a brand—leaves a footprint on the planet.

When all of this happens, the super-rich person becomes a savior. Literally, even. Whereas he was once accustomed to counting dollars, now he measures his efforts by the number of lives he's saved. And that, no matter how you look at it, leaves him richer than he ever was before. In other words, the super-rich never cease to be exactly that. It is the measure that has changed.

Three members of the super-rich community—Bill Gates, Richard Branson, and Jorge Pérez—in true acts of rebellion, decided to give away a good part of their fortunes. In purely mathematical terms, they might have less money in the bank than they did yesterday, but I have no doubt that they are wealthier and more rebellious than ever.

BILL GATES

Bill. That's it. Nothing else. That's what we call one of the richest men in the world. The simplicity of his name stands in stark contrast to the variety of his interests. He's one of the architects of the revolution that gave us personal computers, which is what made him a billionaire. Yet today he dedicates the majority of his time to dispensing with all the money he accrues

For many, going to Harvard is the goal of a lifetime. Having a child accepted there will make an entire family proud for generations to come. But Harvard wasn't enough for Gates, and he left the university without earning a degree in order to create an operating system for the first microcomputers. And that is when Micro-Soft was born, in 1976. (Shortly thereafter, the hyphen would vanish.)

The first time I met Bill Gates, he seemed shy to me. It was at a meeting with his wife, Melinda Gates, and right from the start, she took control of the conversation. There were clues that Bill Gates felt out of place. His suit, which was of the highest quality, seemed slightly too large for him, half a size, maybe, and it slipped a little to one side. The knot in his tie wasn't quite perfect. He seemed uncomfortable in his own clothes. Yes, that was it. The man wasn't comfortable in his own skin. Or at least not in that particular skin.

Melinda, understanding perfectly her husband's intellectual eccentricities, told us that Bill can get excited when discussing a new, more resistant type of seed for agricultural use, or an innovative drainage system. Clearly, his talent lies in knowing how things work. He's not the one who sells the finished product; he's the one who gets the ball rolling. That's the power of the introvert.

Going back a couple of decades, you'll find that there were two great geniuses of the digital era: Steve Jobs—the creator of Apple— who envisioned a new world of computers, and, eventually, iPhones, iPads and iPods, and Bill Gates, who developed the operating systems that run the vast majority of computers on the planet. Ying and yang. Extrovert and introvert. Both were critically important to the digital revolution.

Gates and Jobs shared the difficult experience that each failed many times and each became his own worst critic. This is how Steve Jobs explained his decision to return to run Apple (to Brent Schlender and Rick Tetzeli for their book, *Becoming Steve Jobs*) a few years after he was forced to leave the company: "If you look at true artists, if they're really good at something, it occurs to them that they can do this for the rest of their lives, and they can be really successful at it to the outside world, but not really successful for themselves. That's the moment that an artist really decides who he or she is. . . . And I finally decided, I don't really care, this is what I want to do. And if I try my best and fail, well, I tried my best."

Gates and Jobs changed our lives. My kids can hardly believe I grew up in a world without cell phones or laptop computers. I still remember a time when we didn't have a phone line installed in our home. The technological leap was due, in part, to the minds of people like Gates.

There comes a moment—at different times for different billionaires—when the thing that consumes their lives doesn't have the same importance that it once did. For Gates, that moment came during 2006. That was when he started dividing his time between Microsoft and the workings of his foundation, which he had set up in 2000. This double life lasted only eight years.

I had the opportunity to interview Gates in January 2014. One month later, he would step down as chairman of Microsoft, remaining simply as an advisor. As improbable as it may seem, the company that had been his obsession for most of his life had drifted into the background. Saving the world was his new passion.

When I interviewed him on a very cold morning in New York

City, he was eager to share two pieces of good news: first, the world is a better place now than it was years ago; and second, no, he wasn't throwing away his money.

I started with the obvious question: How much money does he have? Over seventy billion dollars, he replied matter-of-factly. But then he made a clarification:

"Well, it certainly doesn't matter in terms of personal consumption," he said to me. "But to the degree that my wife and I can assure that the money is spent to help those most in need, to invent new vaccines or new seeds, help with education, then it really does matter. We are very excited about our giving and very committed, to not only put our money, but to put our time into that work."

Bill Gates's plan is to give away nearly all of his money. At the time of this interview, he had donated some $28 billion. But there was still much more to give. Everything, save for a very small part, would go to the Bill and Melinda Gates Foundation.

Then he explained how he and his wife would be generous with their children. He assured me that they had received a great education, but "the money belongs to society."

Pope Francis has said that not to share one's wealth with the poor is to steal from them. That might carry weight with Catholics across the globe, but Bill Gates is agnostic. He has no religious reason to donate his money. And he doesn't necessarily think he'll end up in heaven.

"No. I will be pleasantly surprised if I find myself in heaven," he said. "The choices I make are not based on some views of the hereafter. Here on earth there's a lot of lives we can uplift. And my basic view is positive; we are making a lot of progress."

Gates is an optimist. He doesn't make his judgments based on news headlines about protests and natural disasters. He believes that economic progress is being made in the world's poorer nations, and he predicts that "by 2035, there will be almost no poor countries left in the world."

He is a man of numbers. Decades ago he saw the future and designed computer operating systems that would dominate the global market. That's how he made his money. And although he still serves as a technology advisor to Microsoft, for the last several years he's spent the majority of his time looking for ways to donate his fortune.

His success now isn't counted in dollars, but in lives saved. "The work that we've done has saved more than eight million lives, just from the grants. And that's inventing new vaccines, buying the new vaccines, helping those vaccines get delivered out to very poor children."

About half of the money donated by his foundation goes toward vaccines. Another 20 percent is dedicated to education in the United States. But he has also invested $100,000, for example, in a project designed to make thinner, stronger condoms. This is a way of linking health with women's reproductive rights.

"In general, if women want to have contraception, we think it should be available to them," he told me. "If they want to have a smaller family where they can then have more resources to feed and educate their children, we think that's good for them, we think that's good for the world. We are a big funder of innovation in that area as well."

Despite all of this, some critics suggest that, occasionally, Bill and Melinda Gates are throwing away their money by giving aid to countries that lack democratic systems, where corruption is rampant, and where there's no guarantee of economic stability in the medium-range term. So I told him that some people believe that he's simply a good guy wasting his fortune. He disagreed, of course.

"What I say is that I've come into this with total freedom to give the money anywhere that I want. I'm a big believer in analytics and measurement. I've gone in and looked at these health and agricultural programs and I've decided that this is the best money spent. Even though a very small percentage, maybe two and in some cases as high as five percent, will be corruptly misdirected. . . . You want to pick something that's so impactful—you want to guard that it's not a high percentage—you want it to be so incredibly helpful, like saving children's lives. And we are now saving millions who would have been dying in the past."

For this man who can have it all, is there anything that money can't buy? Apparently there is, when it comes to his children, Jennifer, Rory, and Phoebe.

"You'll always have hope for your children, that they'll find a career that's very satisfying for them, that they'll meet a great spouse. There's no way that you can worry about that. Try and set a good example for them. It's always an element of fate there."

BILL GATES: THE LESSONS

Bill Gates is a very pragmatic man. His rebellion lies in questioning everything and proposing new ways of doing things. I was left with the impression that he is a man who manages his money, not someone who lets his money manage him.

After all, there are far more important things in life than money. But he doesn't just say that. He consistently operates according to that mind-set. He treats his money as if it isn't actually his. In fact, he said exactly that: the money belongs to society.

Bill Gates isn't worried about the things he cannot change. But I was struck by the fact that he ended our conversation by mentioning fate. I never would have expected that from him. Fate, by definition, means putting at least some part of our lives in another set of hands, and that's why I thought it was notable that he would mention it. Someone who has controlled almost every aspect of his own life recognizes that there are a number of areas—especially when it comes to our children—where our own influences are limited.

I was left with a certain sense of peace. If Bill Gates can't control it all, what can the rest of us mere mortals expect of ourselves?

FOR RICHARD BRANSON, THE SKY IS NO LIMIT

Sir Richard Branson is a rebel with a knight's title who wants to go into space. But he doesn't want to do it alone. He wants to take the world's wealthiest adventurers into outer space . . . and bring them safely back to earth. Let's just say his goal is to make what today might seem extraordinary into something normal.

Branson's business is making that dream a reality. He once said, "This inquisitiveness is a healthy thing, and leads to new innovations. Only through exploration of the unknown can we continue to grow and evolve. Going into space is important for the future of transportation, commerce, science, and our imagination—inspiring entrepreneurs, inventors and entire new industries. Just like my generation was inspired by the moon landing, new generations can be inspired by commercial space travel."

The name of his corporation—Virgin Group—derives from his first enterprise, which was selling music. All who were involved, including Branson, considered themselves virgins when it came to business. But in 1972, after selling albums out of their shop on Oxford Street in London, he formed his own recording company, Virgin Records, and in 1984 he took to the skies with the launch of Virgin Atlantic Airways.

But Branson wants to go higher still. In 2004 he founded the world's first outer space tourism company called Virgin Galactic. That should come as no surprise to anyone who has followed the trajectory of his career. He's spent his entire life trying to break records, whether it's crossing the Atlantic Ocean by boat two hours faster than anyone had ever done before, or flying a balloon from Japan to Canada at a speed of 245 miles per hour.

When I spoke with him in early 2014, in addition to taking the first group of tourists into space, he had a new challenge—ending the war on drugs. But, of course, we started off by talking about money. His fortune has been estimated at nearly five billion dollars. And he, much like Gates, was focused on that unique form of rebellion: giving almost all of it away.

"If you're fortunate enough to be successful, with success can come money, and sometimes it becomes too much money for one family to have," he said to me. "I think it's very important you use your money to tackle issues you feel will make a difference in the world. To create organizations to tackle global problems and ultimately, when you do die, to make sure—if you've got money left over—a very good percentage of it goes to good causes. I'm part of Bill Gates' 'Giving Pledge' [described as "a commitment by the world's wealthiest individuals and families to dedicate the majority of their wealth to philanthropy"]. I thought it was admirable he set it up. And I walk in his footsteps and try to see if we can play our part in the world."

Branson has created more than four hundred companies worldwide. Some are more successful than others. Nevertheless, as we talked, he revealed his passion for changing drug policy. And his reason is simple: the war on drugs hasn't worked. He saw the problem from an entrepreneurial point of view: after decades of negative results, it was time to look for a different solution.

"Well, we concentrate on a number of injustices of the world," he explained. "And the war on drugs is one of the biggest injustices in the world. It's been going on for sixty years. As a businessman, if I had a business that had gotten worse and worse. . . . I would have closed it down."

He continued. "It doesn't work and what is happening is millions of people worldwide are suffering as a result. Many of the young people are getting criminalized offenses or being put in prison. Three years ago President Cardoso—who used to be president of Brazil—he set up a global drug commission and he asked if I'd be one of the commissioners. We looked at the war on drugs and asked if there'd be a better way than criminalizing people and putting people in jail."

"Do you think, like President Obama, that marijuana is no more dangerous than alcohol?" I asked him.

"I one hundred percent agree with President Obama. Now, the five percent of people who drink, they can overdo it. The five percent of people who take marijuana, they can overdo it. But for fifty percent of people who smoke cigarettes, they definitely can overdo it and it's very dangerous for them. . . . If I wanted to get a joint, I can walk out on the street and within five minutes I can buy marijuana anywhere. It's much better if it's regulated—check to make sure it's pure and tax it—than to drive people underground and end up having, literally, 1.8 million people in American prisons, a vast majority of them related to drugs—and a lot of them Hispanic or black. The vast majority."

"But by legalizing it, are we exposing our kids—your kids, my kids—to drugs, to marijuana?" I asked.

"Our kids are exposed to marijuana whether we like it or not. The countries that have taken this approach have not seen a rise in the amount of people who smoke it. It's remained almost static. What has happened in those countries is that the money that was going into putting people into prison has gone into health clinics."

"Do you mind if I ask you if you ever smoked marijuana?"

"I've smoked a joint or two in my life. It didn't appeal to me; it makes me feel tired and I've got quite a lot going on in my life. I like to keep a clear mind. I find getting high on fitness is better."

From there, appropriately enough, we moved on to outer space. His Virgin Galactic project—taking tourists into orbit—hasn't quite taken off. He said it would be ready by the summer of 2014, and that "by

September myself and my family will have been into space. I'm ninety percent convinced that will happen."

But it didn't.

After our interview, Sir Richard Branson's ship failed to reach space. In fact, it exploded in midflight. The experimental rocket plane *SpaceShipTwo* broke apart at an altitude of 45,000 feet in November 2014. It suffered serious technical problems upon separating from the mother ship *WhiteKnightTwo*. One of the pilots died in the accident, while the other was able to survive because he was able to deploy his parachute.

If Branson has learned anything in life, it's taking responsibility for everything he does. So he immediately went to the crash site, in California's Mojave Desert, and faced the media just hours after the accident.

"Yesterday we fell short," Branson admitted to reporters. And then, he put the future of his extraterrestrial dream in doubt. "We'll now comprehensively assess the results of the crash and are determined to learn from this and move forward. We are not going to push on blindly."

Richard Branson doesn't do anything blindly. But he has devoted his entire life to putting maximum effort into reaching the things he's imagined. No, for him, the sky isn't the limit. Unlike the vast majority of people, he has learned how to live—happily—without limits.

RICHARD BRANSON: THE LESSONS

Some people have a contagious sense of optimism, and Richard Branson is one of them. It's the only way to explain why some seven hundred people have paid up to $250,000 to be the first space tourists on one of Branson's Virgin Galactic spaceships. For now, they'll have to continue to wait. But the interesting thing is that they believed in

Branson's project from the very beginning, and they paid to become a part of it.

Branson has been sailing against the current his entire life. His rebelliousness has led him to do things differently, whether it's in the music industry or outer space. And his success, I think, lies in the fact that he has avoided becoming his own worst enemy. In other words, he never imposes limits on himself. He imagines things, and then he looks for a way to make them happen.

Money has given him the freedom to dream. But it's his enthusiasm for trying new (and often dangerous) things that has allowed him to take flight.

JORGE PÉREZ CITY

I know Jorge Pérez's closet. Which is why I understand why he decided to create his own museum, the modern, contemporary Pérez Art Museum Miami.

Pérez's house in Miami looks out, of course, over the sea. It sits in an exquisite, exclusive coastal area in South Florida. One night I was lucky enough to be invited there, along with a small group, and immediately I felt the pleasant sensation of having arrived in someone's home. The Pérez house isn't a work of art; it's a place to be lived in, to enjoy, to be with family.

But there ends any sense of normalcy. Pérez is one of the wealthiest businessmen in the United States, and a renowned art collector. Shortly after we arrived at his home, he gave us a quick tour. Works by famous painters were everywhere. Literally.

After strolling through the living room and hallways of the house, we took a peek at his bedroom and closet. In no way was he trying to show off; on the contrary, he was a man who opened his home and his heart to his friends. And there, half hidden among his slacks and shoes, was a work of art valued at several million dollars. I couldn't help but picture Pérez getting out of the shower every morning and trying to decide what shirt to wear, all the while standing right next to that wonder.

The fact is that the walls of the house were covered with art. Painting after painting, jumping from one century to the next, from one continent to another, from Impressionism to simply impressive. Everywhere we looked, there was something that caught our attention. Some of the works were labeled by title and artist, while others were simply there, hanging silently, recognizable only to the experts.

I visited Jorge Pérez's closet several years before he announced the opening of his art museum in an incomparable location just across the bay from Miami Beach. But when I found out about his plans, I can't say I was surprised. When I got home that night, after visiting his home, I thought to myself, *Jorge needs to put all that art into a museum*.

It occurred to me that he could loan his works out to any of the great museums around the world. But that idea just goes to show how little I understood. Why would he give his collection to someone else? No. Instead of donating and loaning out the works of art he's been collecting throughout his life, Pérez went about things the only way he knows now: doing it himself. He had to build his own museum to display the paintings that for years had hung on his walls and sat in his closet. And that's how the Pérez Art Museum Miami came to be.

Jorge Pérez has always thought big. In his book, *Powerhouse Principles*—the foreword to which was written by Donald Trump— you can follow the great arc of his life: "I didn't set out to become a billionaire. I didn't intend to make the top 200 on the Forbes 400 list of richest Americans. But I did . . . I started with nothing. Or next to nothing. I was an immigrant kid who came to Miami with $2 in my pocket. Today, I am a billionaire."

This Argentine-born immigrant was, once upon a time, an economic development director with the City of Miami. So how did a bureaucrat become a billionaire? Investing in real estate and making sure that he always—always—turned a profit. His philosophy has always been crystal clear: a business with no profits is not a good business. In 1979 he created the Related Companies and began building his own urban legend. He lost a sizable part of his fortune in 2008 during the global financial crisis, but what he didn't lose was his keen business acumen. And when the economy—and the Florida real estate market—bounced back, Pérez rose up again like a world-class surfer.

Today, Miami itself is a reflection of his buildings. The skyline before Jorge Pérez was very different from the one that exists now. And in 2014, he described to me how it feels to him to be driving through downtown Miami.

"I love it the most when I'm in the car with my ten-year-old and he says to his friends: 'Daddy, that's yours. Daddy, that's yours.' And you see the great sense of pride in him," he said. "Before, we had a collection of buildings. Now everything is coming together—shopping and offices and culture. We're finally not talking about being a great city, but being a great city."

When someone is rich—as rich as Jorge Pérez—it's hard to imagine them going through hard times. You tend to believe that this is how it's always been. But starting out wasn't easy. The first two buildings he constructed in downtown Miami in the early 1980s had to be financed by a bank in Brooklyn because nobody in Florida was willing to take the risk.

I asked him how many buildings he owned. But that wasn't the right question. Big real estate entrepreneurs don't think in terms of buildings; they think in units. "We built over eighty thousand units," he replied. "Once you sell them, you don't own them anymore, but they're yours. They're always your buildings."

In the wake of the 2008 financial crisis, it was rumored that he had lost a billion dollars. To me, such a thing sounded impossible. But not to him.

"I lost more than a billion dollars."

"How can you lose more than a billion dollars?"

"Because I had a commitment to stay alive, and to have the company remain alive."

"So you went from being a billionaire to being poor?"

"No. First of all, I think with the exile mentality—one always puts money away in one's personal account. I came from Cuban parents. They lost everything, and I think it stays in the back of your mind, them saying: 'This is not going to happen to me again.' And because of that, I pumped a lot of personal money into the company, to rescue the company."

He did. Jorge Pérez recovered. But the money has never been his biggest concern. "I think legacy should never be about money. Legacy should be about what you leave behind and what you do for others, and the buildings that you build and how you contribute."

That's why it was important for the modern art museum he built to carry his name. "Yes. It is important. I know it's probably part ego, but it is important. Just like it was important to the Guggenheims, and it was important to the Whitneys, and it was important to the Smithsons, and it was important to the Tates in London, you know. One wants to be remembered by the good things that one did. . . . And I want to do the things that I want to do, not what is expected of me. So I'm much freer now to actually do what I want to do."

JORGE PÉREZ: THE LESSONS

The super-rich can afford to let their minds wander, to imagine things, and eventually to build them. It would be easy—and also a mistake—to assume that Jorge Pérez spends every waking hour thinking about his business. In fact, it seems as if money has given him the freedom to think about other things.

When I interviewed him in a television studio in Miami, he was worried about the bullying that was reported to be going on in the locker room of the Miami Dolphins, of which he is a shareholder. And he was also concerned about the 2016 presidential campaign. He was a fund-raiser for Hillary Clinton back in 2008, but it wasn't enough.

Money doesn't always guarantee victory. "We raised more money than Obama, and the Republicans raised twice as much as Hillary and Obama," he told me. The lesson was well taken. Money isn't everything.

Ultimately, Jorge Pérez, Richard Branson, and Bill Gates have come to understand something that other members of the super-rich elite never will: it's not about dying rich, but rather about giving (nearly) all of it back while you're still alive, and—above all—having no regrets.

It's just one life, whether you're rich or poor.

FIFTEEN

Don't Let Them Discriminate Against You: Sonia Sotomayor

There are many people who think Latinos don't have the capacity to achieve great things. I didn't let them discriminate against me.   —SONIA SOTOMAYOR

S UPREME COURT JUSTICES don't speak. Rather, they speak publicly only in court, outside of which they generally remain silent. The reason is a simple one: they don't want their personal viewpoints to affect or contaminate the cases they're hearing in the highest court in the land.

But Sonia Sotomayor is no ordinary judge. She speaks fearlessly both inside and outside the courtroom. She refuses to offer opinions that could influence a future case, of course. But even so, she's remarkably candid. Rarely do you hear so much from a justice.

A number of surveys have put her atop the list of most influential Hispanics in the United States. And there's no wondering why.

The best evidence that the American Dream has not been crushed by the economic crisis and discrimination and can still happen is Sonia Sotomayor. Born in the Bronx, New York, in 1954, Sotomayor didn't have much going for her as she faced poverty, illness, and the death of her father from alcoholism when she was only nine. But despite it all, she went on to become the first Latina to sit on the Supreme Court of the United States. President Obama nominated her on May 26, 2009, and she was sworn in on August 8 of the same year. That's making history.

Others facing the same circumstances failed and even died. Her cousin Nelson, for example. But Sonia didn't. I spoke with her in her office in Washington in January 2013, the same month her memoir, *My Beloved World*, was published.

"A lot of people think we can't do it. There are many people who think Latinos don't have the capacity to achieve great things," she told me in Spanish. "I didn't let them discriminate against me."

Growing up, Sotomayor was nicknamed Aji, or chili pepper, on account of her energy and strength of character, traits that would carry into adulthood. But when she was a lawyer, according to her book, a colleague once described her as being a "tough bitch." Why the insult? I asked.

She thought for a moment and gave me her first lesson in being a rebel. "I have a strong character," she replied. "You don't push me around. I won't allow people to think I do not have value. When you value yourself, there are a lot of people who think that's a bad thing if you're a woman, because women aren't supposed to speak up or complain much or demand certain things."

Sonia Sotomayor is the closest thing the Hispanic community has to a true hero. Many young children, whether Latino or not, want to grow up to be like her. But her life wasn't easy, nor was it perfect. She reveals many personal details about herself and her family in her book—both the good and the bad. I asked her why she was so candid. "I don't know any family in this world that is perfect," she replied. "I want people who read this book, in the end, to know the real Sonia . . . someone who has many strengths, but also limitations."

Thinking of her grandmother, Sotomayor said she herself wanted to grow old without going gray. And she changed. From being a very withdrawn person who would almost never go up to someone and give them a kiss on the cheek, she became a much more affectionate woman who welcomes people with open arms.

Sotomayor's childhood wasn't easy. After a fainting spell when she was seven, Sonia was diagnosed with type 1 diabetes, and soon she taught herself to administer her own insulin shots, in case her parents couldn't or weren't around.

"What I understood when I was seven was that my life was going to change and that I was going to lose my independence," she told me. "The fear of dying made me understand that one has to appreciate every moment," she said. "It made me understand that I didn't know how much time I had in this life, and that I wanted to do as much as I could with every day."

Her mother, Celina, would constantly tell her: "You have to get an education. It's the only way to get ahead in the world." She understood it was the only path to success.

That desire to learn and to live life to the fullest led her—even as a child—to devour the *Encyclopaedia Britannica*, and any other book that crossed her path. Her parents spoke Spanish, but from a young age, Sonia learned to master English. That would be the key to her success. Still, though, she fully and openly identified herself as a Latina.

During her Senate confirmation hearings, a problem came up. Certain conservative politicians were critical of her because of something she said during a 2001 lecture at the Berkeley School of Law: "I would hope that a wise Latina woman with the richness of her experiences would more often than not reach a better conclusion than a white male who hasn't lived that life."

The statement suggested to some that her ethnicity could influence her decision-making in court. But she put an end to the matter by saying that regardless of her background and her life experiences a judge has to follow the law. Period. "I think as a United States Supreme Court Justice," she said to me, regarding this controversy. "I'm thinking about our Constitution, our presidents, our system of government."

Still, though, Sotomayor has never had a problem recognizing that being a Latina has left its mark on her.

"Being Latina is a part of every particle of my skin," she said to me. "It is such a part of me, there is no way to separate both. There is no Sonia who is not Latina."

Sotomayor has publicly acknowledged that affirmative action programs "opened the door" for her at Princeton, where she graduated summa cum laude with a degree in history, and also later at Yale Law. "That was a tremendous help," she said. "But what I accomplished, I accomplished myself, and that's the attitude I try to teach. There are many times when doors are opened for us, but the most important thing is what you do when you walk in."

After earning her law degree, Sotomayor—who remembers having been influenced by the television lawyer Perry Mason—was appointed assistant district attorney in New York before entering a prestigious private firm. In 1991, she was nominated to the U.S. District Court for the Southern District of New York. In 1997 she was nominated to the U.S. Court of Appeals, and in May 2009, in an unprecedented move, President Obama selected Sotomayor to be one of the nine Supreme Court justices. It will be the last job she'll ever have.

Sotomayor is a true New Yorker: she's a fan of the Yankees, she doesn't always cross the street at the crosswalk, and when she orders food, she expects it to arrive in fifteen minutes or less, according to the *New York Times*.

And unlike her fellow Supreme Court justices, Sotomayor is willing to talk about her personal life in public. In her book, she writes extensively about her husband, Kevin Noonan, from whom she is now divorced. They met when they were just sixteen, and started dating two years after graduating from law school.

But when they separated, he had some harsh words for her. "I knew you loved me, but I felt you didn't need me," he said.

Was that true? Is that what made her such an independent woman? "I think so," she said. "That's always been my impression. Those words of his helped me understand that there's a difference between being independent and giving others the opportunity to help us. Being needed and being independent aren't mutually exclusive things. We all need a little help now and then. We all need love."

Sotomayor's greatest virtue is what she refers to as her "existential independence." As a child, she learned that she couldn't always depend on others, and that gave her strength. That's how she's always lived.

After the interview, I was left with the impression that nothing and nobody could stop Sonia from the Bronx. The enthusiasm with which she lives her life is truly contagious. Her brother, Juan Sotomayor Jr., was absolutely right when he said, "Sonia lives life to the fullest. If she were to die tomorrow, she'd die happy."

The interview was over, but not the surprises. "You wrote in your book that the best cure for being lovesick was learning to dance," I reminded her. And she learned. My producer put on some music, and without giving it a second thought, Justice Sotomayor said, "Yes, if you get up and dance, I'll get up and dance with you."

So we danced. She was much better than me. For what must be the first time in history, salsa was danced in the sacred halls of the Supreme Court.

SONIA SOTOMAYOR: THE LESSONS

Sonia Sotomayor told me that, as a Latina, she had to demonstrate her value twofold. Many people doubted her because of her ethnicity and gender. But she broke through all the stereotypes on her way to reaching the Supreme Court.

Without a doubt, Sotomayor is a rebel. She learned to live with diabetes from the time she was diagnosed with the disease at the age of seven. With no father and a working mother, she learned to be independent. And she learned the path that leads to the top: studying.

But Sotomayor's most important lesson is this: Don't let people discriminate against you. Never let others define who or what you are. She epitomizes the notion that we must stand up for who we are. Being obedient and following the letter of the law is not necessarily the most direct route to success and power.

Don't let it happen. That's the secret to a worthy and, perhaps, a long life on the Supreme Court.

Now, making sure that nobody discriminates against you could suggest a life of constant vigilance and seriousness. After all, life has never been easy for Latinas in the United States.

But Judge Sotomayor is completely comfortable in her own skin. She can write an argument that could change the way we live in this country but she can also dance. Salsa. Very well.

Life doesn't pass her by. She lives fully. Every moment. That's what you learn when you're struck by a disease early in life: every moment is precious.

Sotomayor broke many stereotypes to become the first Latina Supreme Court justice, and now she is changing the court. I cannot even imagine any other member of the court who would dare to consider dancing in front of a television camera. But for Sotomayor it was not a big deal.

We planned it all along. A few days before our interview, one of my producers, Evelyn Baker, suggested that we ask Judge Sotomayor to dance. It was an awkward request to make, so she thought of something different.

How about if, at the end of the interview, we blast some salsa music and see what happens? It sounded perfect and that's exactly what we did. We brought a very reliable sound system to the United States

Supreme Court and as soon as the interview ended, the sound of Puerto Rico was being heard very loudly in these particular corridors of power.

Actually, it was Justice Sotomayor who said she would dance, but not alone. So we danced, just a few moments, to the Puerto Rican music, as if nothing else in the world mattered.

SIXTEEN

Spike Lee and Doing the Right Thing

I think that it is great for the public that everybody is an investigative reporter with a phone. —SPIKE LEE

THE UNITED STATES isn't just Apple, Google, Hollywood, and Disneyland. It's also Baltimore, Ferguson, Staten Island, and many other towns and cities where police officers—instead of serving and protecting citizens—abuse and murder them.

I was raised in a country where people are often fearful of the police. In Mexico, it's not unusual for members of the police to collaborate with criminal organizations, so, understandably, many people view officers with suspicion and distrust. In the United States, officers face a similar sense of distrust these days, albeit for different reasons.

Police brutality is the problem. And who are the victims? African Americans, Hispanics, immigrants, and other minorities.

There has been a litany of police abuses in recent history. Take one month—February 2015—and three cases involving Mexican immigrants. In Pasco, Washington, three police officers fired seventeen shots at Antonio Zambrano-Montes, 35, who was throwing rocks on a street corner; in Grapevine, Texas, Rubén García Villalpando, 31, was shot by an officer following a car chase when he had his hands on his head; and in Santa Ana, California, Ernesto Javier Canepa Díaz, 27—with four children and two jobs—lost his life at the hands of the police after a traffic stop. All of these victims were unarmed and in no case did any police officers face any charges.

These cases went practically uncovered in the English-language media. But they certainly reflect the tension between the authorities and the Latino community in this country. The Mexican government was so concerned by the three cases that it asked the U.S. Justice Department to investigate. I often hear complaints in Latino communities about how police officers will stop and question an immigrant or a Hispanic resident simply because of his skin color or accent. A simple traffic ticket could mean the loss of a car or deportation. It could even cost a life.

African Americans, however, suffer police abuse in even more disproportionate numbers. There have been several dramatic, high-profile cases—the death of eighteen-year-old Michael Brown in Ferguson, Missouri, in August 2014, at the hands of a white officer, and the mysterious death of twenty-five-year-old Freddie Gray, in April 2015, seven days after he was arrested by police in Baltimore. Gray was unarmed and died from injuries sustained while in police custody.

Baltimore is a racially and economically divided city—the northern neighborhoods are much wealthier and safer than the western ones—and not even the fact that the mayor and police commissioner are black made the city more hospitable to the African American community. An investigation by the *Baltimore Sun* found that since 2011, more than one hundred people won lawsuits filed against the city involving cases of police brutality and civil rights violations. The city, in turn, has had to pay out nearly $12 million in legal expenses and awards for the victims.

It's not easy being black or Hispanic on the streets of Baltimore. Pastor Angel Nuñez, who has spent over two decades helping immigrants in the city, told me in an interview that "many Latinos have been manhandled, winding up in jail; there are many abuses, and almost nothing about them is reported." He's right.

Impunity is a serious problem. Police who kill without justification rarely end up in jail. According to research conducted by the *Washington Post* and Bowling Green State University and published by the *Post* in April 2015, the thousands of fatal police shootings from 2005 have resulted in formal indictments for only fifty-four officers.* And in most of those cases, the officers were declared not guilty or the charges against them were dropped.

The 2008 election of Barack Obama—the first African American president in history—did not signal the arrival of a new, post-racial society. Certainly, advances have been made, but there are still painful open wounds along racial lines and a clear abuse of power in many cases. And for evidence of that, we have to look no further than Eric Garner.

ERIC GARNER RARELY went unnoticed. He stood six foot two, weighed 395 pounds, and had had previous run-ins with the NYPD in Staten Island. He was suspected of illegally selling cigarettes, and his prior issues with the authorities had never been serious. On July 17, 2015, however, that changed.

Garner was questioned by two agents, and a few minutes after the arrival of other officers, they tried to arrest him. One officer, Daniel Pantaleo, approached Garner from behind and put his arm around his neck before both men fell to the ground. Garner can be heard to say, eleven times, "I can't breathe."

We know this because the scene was recorded on a cell phone video by twenty-two-year-old Ramsey Orta, a friend of Garner's.

---

* Kimberly Kindy and Kimbriell Kelly, "Thousands Dead, Few Prosecuted," *Washington Post*, April 11, 2015.

After a lengthy official investigation, on June 14, 2015, the *New York Times* reported the following: "The video images were cited in the final autopsy report as one of the factors that led the city medical examiner to conclude that the chokehold and chest compression by the police caused Mr. Garner's death. Absent the video, many in the Police Department would have gone on believing his death to have been solely caused by his health problems: obesity, asthma and hypertensive cardiovascular disease."

Orta's video is astonishing. In addition to clearly documenting the choke hold, it also shows several NYPD officers taking Garner to the ground before handcuffing him. Garner stops moving. When the paramedics arrive with medical equipment, they take Garner's pulse at his neck, but administer no oxygen. He is placed on a stretcher and loaded into an ambulance when—at 3:44 in the afternoon—the medics report that he is suffering a heart attack en route to the hospital. According to the *New York Times*, at 4:34 that same afternoon, he was pronounced dead at Richmond University Medical Center.

The video also left an impression on the filmmaker Spike Lee. So much so, in fact, that he decided to make a documentary, called *I Can't Breathe*, based on Orta's cell phone video and an extensive interview with him.

Orta: cameraman, reporter, historian, and witness to injustice. In this day and age, anyone can suddenly become a journalist. Not even the best correspondents in the world can get better material if a person using his cell phone is able to record the news as it happens. That's the current reality.

Journalism has changed in two major ways. First, by the way people learn: that is, increasingly through social media on their mobile devices, and not by traditional media. And second, by the way information is collected, both by professional journalists and through videos, blogs, posts, pics, and Internet reports on Facebook, Twitter, Instagram, and other such networks.

Eric Garner's case precisely reflects a time in which new technologies are being used to report cases of abuse. Without the cell phone video, we would not have a record of the event; with it, a brutal case of police violence is met by a new method of live reporting. In the best cases, the combination generates condemnation and leads to justice. But even when the authorities refuse to act, there remains a permanent record of the abuse.

When Spike Lee saw Orta's video, it reminded him of a particular scene in his extraordinary 1989 film, *Do the Right Thing*, in which one of the protagonists, Radio Raheem, dies while hanging from a police officer's choke hold. Twenty-five years later, fiction and reality cross paths again. And no, nothing has changed.

"When I saw Ramsey's footage, it just was very eerie," the filmmaker said to me during an interview in Philadelphia in the fall of 2014. "And I wasn't the only one that said, 'This is like Radio Raheem.' So then I called up my editor, Barry Brown—who's been editing a lot of my films, great editor, he was also the editor on *Do the Right Thing*—and said, 'We got to cut this stuff together.'"

And they did. The documentary shows violent cuts back and forth between the film *Do the Right Thing* and the video of Eric Garner being choked. It's easy to become confused while watching the sequence edited by Lee and Barry Brown: there are moments when you're no longer certain whether the images you're seeing are fictional or a tragic slice of what took place that fateful afternoon in Staten Island.

"What I think that's happened, though, is now with this video camera," Lee said, referring to cell phone cameras. "Before, the only time it was really caught was Rodney King."

In the winter of 1991, King, 25, an African American man, was pulled over in the San Fernando Valley by California Highway Patrol and Los Angeles Police Department officers. After getting out of his truck, King was severely beaten, resulting in multiple skull fractures, a shattered cheekbone, a broken leg, and other injuries. What the officers didn't know was that a neighbor, George Holliday, was awakened by the sirens, took out his newly purchased VHS camera, and filmed everything.

The resulting twelve-minute video became proof of the abuse perpetrated by the LAPD, which the black community had been denouncing for many years. When the four officers involved in the beating were acquitted in April 1992 by a predominantly white jury, violent protests engulfed the city of Los Angeles. After the riots waned, with more than sixty lives lost, the LAPD underwent major changes in the hope of preventing a similar tragedy from happening in the future.

Today, you don't have to go out and use a video camera to denounce injustice. We all carry one in our cell phones. "I think that it is great for the public that everybody is an investigative reporter with a phone," Spike Lee reflected. "People are posting, just like Ramsey, and they're letting the world see what is happening."

When I spoke with Spike Lee in late 2014, massive popular protests were being held in Mexico, Brazil, Venezuela, and Ukraine. They had been organized almost exclusively through cell phones and social networks. The young people who were responsible for them evaded the censoring eyes of their governments by utilizing Facebook and Twitter. "How do you get 250,000 people to show up when it's against the government? It has to be the Internet," Lee affirmed. "It's not going away. In many places—not here in the United States—but they're going to start trying to crack down on these ways of communicating because it's empowering. It's power, it's powerful."

Spike Lee has spent decades raising his voice against racism and discrimination in the United States. His films are a testament to a society that still, even today, refuses to treat everyone equally. And I didn't want the interview to end without asking him about his personal experiences. Are things better now than they were twenty-five years ago? What does Eric Garner's death mean today?

At the time of the interview, Lee's daughter, Satchel, was twenty and his son, Jackson, was seventeen. "What do you tell them about racial problems in the United States?" I asked.

"I don't care who you are, if you're African American in this country, you know what the deal is," he replied.

"What's the deal?" I pressed.

"The deal's that you're black."

"And that means for you . . ."

"Well, it just means that you're black. And the people who get in trouble are the people who forget they're black. You just can't think, 'Well, I'm successful. I've reached another realm and I'm in the so-called . . .' what's the term?"

"Post-racial."

"Yeah, that's bullshit [to think] where because now we have an African American president race no longer matters. And there are times, even today, it's hard for me to catch a cab in New York City."

"For you?"

"Yes."

"So do you feel discriminated constantly?"

"You're made aware of it. I'm not complaining. It's just something that you grow up with."

"You were talking about the possibility of a post-racial society. Now, you're saying it isn't happening?"

"Look, I can't predict the future. But there are a lot of people who believed that when our president put his hand on Abraham Lincoln's Bible and did the oath, that hocus-pocus, abracadabra, poof, we were in a post-racial world."

SPIKE LEE: THE LESSONS

The first lesson we can learn from Spike Lee is that we cannot lie. As a country, we have to face the music. Racism still exists in America, and it is readily apparent in both the death of Eric Garner and the fact that a filmmaker can still find it hard to hail a cab in his hometown of New York City.

No, we don't live in a post-racial society. Once, while talking with President Barack Obama, I mentioned the term "post-racial." With a smile, he told me that I shouldn't expect the election of the first African American president in American history to change everything. And of course he was right.

I am acutely aware of the discrimination that Hispanics and other immigrants like me regularly suffer simply because we speak English with an accent or because our skin tone is darker than that of the majority of the population. In the United States, discrimination does not discriminate. It's something that virtually all minorities have to deal with. That brings us to Spike Lee's second lesson: Speak up.

The fact that discrimination exists does not mean we have to accept it. Spike Lee has already established his place in cinematic history, and he could spend the rest of his days in peace if he wanted to. Instead, he continues to fight.

When he saw the video footage of Eric Garner being strangled, and recalled those eerily similar scenes from his film *Do the Right Thing*, what came to him was a mandate: "We got to cut this stuff together."

And that's where his rebellion lies: in never giving up, in seeing what other people don't see, in making sure others understand what he sees, and in showing things as they really are.

Nothing is more rebellious than telling the truth.

And refusing to accept discrimination and denouncing it in all its forms is also an act of rebellion. When you hear Spike Lee talk, you get the distinct impression that this is a man on a mission. He's not simply floating down the stream of life being carried along with the current. He's living life with a purpose.

I was deeply struck by how someone who has done so much to denounce racism against African Americans in the United States is so often unable to get a taxi in the city he calls home. And that's exactly it: that's "the deal" that Spike Lee first learned as a child, and that he's spent his entire life trying to change.

The lesson is clear:

Speak up, even when you think nobody is listening.

Speak up, in order to be heard.

Speak up, because there's a sense of freedom in listening to your own rebellion.

But above all, speak up.

SEVENTEEN

Do Your Homework—Lessons from Three Great Journalists: Barbara Walters, Oriana Fallaci, and Elena Poniatowska

That's my legacy. All these young women in the news.
—BARBARA WALTERS

REBELLIONS AREN'T IMPROVISED. They're planned, prepared, and executed with great attention to detail. In the case of the world's most famous journalist, Barbara Walters, rebellion is dressed elegantly and illuminated perfectly.

The lights! Yes. The lights Barbara Walters uses during her interviews are marvelous. Her interviewees look ten or twenty years younger than they are, while she looks fresh, energetic, and ageless. And that's important. Nobody ever thinks about how old Barbara Walters actually is. Journalists simply talk about her short, direct, and piercingly clear questions, about how she manages to engage with people who want to speak only about themselves, and about how great she always looks. But never her age. That doesn't matter.

Barbara Walters is a woman in control. She controls how she's viewed. Controls the scene with the lighting. Controls the interview with her questions. Nothing is left to chance.

At the end of her career, all seemed to have made sense, as if logic and gender equality had both managed to prevail. But it wasn't so easy in the beginning.

Barbara Walters is a television pioneer. She broke the machismo mold and never let anyone use her as decoration. She started out writing and investigating on behalf of other reporters before she became known for her own features and interviews. And despite the wall of resistance at the studio where she worked, in 1974, NBC had no choice but to name her cohost of *The Today Show*, which was the most popular morning show of the time. (Although this could have happened only because of the death of anchor Frank McGee.)

Just like that, history was made in the morning. And it wouldn't be long before she did the same thing at night.

In 1976, Barbara changed stations, and was named coanchor of *ABC Evening News*. Once again, she was the first woman to hold such a position. And, in this case as well, she succeeded despite the anger and resentment of a journalist—Harry Reasoner—who didn't want to share the stage on the company's flagship news broadcast.

Walters anchored the news for just two years, but her reputation as a fierce and tenacious interviewer was by then, already well established. In special broadcasts as well as on ABC's *20/20*, she interviewed everyone there was to interview, from artists to politicians: every American president and their wives, Vladimir Putin, Fidel Castro, Margaret Thatcher, the Shah of Iran, Hugo Chávez, Muammar al-Gaddafi, Anwar El Sadat, and Menachem Begin, and hundreds more. Her annual *10 Most Fascinating People* special, which airs before the Oscars, became a broadcasting tradition. The Hollywood stars wouldn't miss it: Katharine Hepburn, Laurence Olivier, George Clooney, Al Pacino, Robert De Niro, Denzel Washington, Clint Eastwood, Dustin Hoffman,

Morgan Freeman, Meryl Streep, Julia Roberts, and Sandra Bullock, and dozens of others.

Walters had an unparalleled talent for gauging the interests of both the people and her audience; she identified the personalities of the day, and—once she had them captivated—she made them cry. Yes, Barbara Walters makes people cry. She's a detective when it comes to our weaknesses and vulnerabilities. In other words, she knows how to find the places where people are broken, and—when she sees an appropriate time during an interview—she asks mercilessly. That requires a lot of courage. I know many journalists who won't dare to ask the hardest of the hard questions during an interview. They hold back, whether out of shame or fear. But that's not the case with Barbara Walters.

The moment when a viewer can't tear his or her eyes from the screen is what executives and producers call a "television moment." Barbara Walters was the master of these. And for that, you need much more than journalism. Finding a person's weaknesses requires a degree in psychology or a special sensitivity when it comes to detecting human frailties, as she did.

Whenever something significant happened in this country, Barbara was ready to talk with the protagonists of history. She became an expert in talking not only about victories, but also about defeats.

Oftentimes, Barbara became the nation's de facto therapist. Politicians and actors, celebrities and musicians went to her to confess their sins, to talk about their addictions, and to explain their behavior. But they also went to her to apologize.

America is a very generous country. People always get a second chance, and sometimes even a third and a fourth. But before you're granted that new opportunity, you have to publicly admit your mistakes and, hopefully, apologize. Barbara was the high priestess who exorcised those demons in exchange for fifteen or twenty minutes of compelling television. Many accepted her terms: their honesty in exchange for our forgiveness. And the results were unsurpassable. If you wanted to speak directly to the American people, you had to sit down face-to-face with Barbara Walters.

Monica Lewinsky knew. After her brief yet turbulent White House affair with President Bill Clinton, she didn't look to give a press conference or write a tell-all column for the *New York Times*. No. The natural, the standard, indeed, the only possibility was to talk with Barbara Walters. And her March 1999 interview on *20/20* was seen by an estimated 74 million people, more than any other interview in the history of American television.

That was always Barbara Walters's secret: making us believe that she was the one and only person who should be doing an important interview at a pivotal time. Certainly, American media have had—and continue to have—many great interviewers. But none of them, even in his or her heyday, could compete with Barbara Walters.

What's interesting is that Barbara Walters never conducted an easy interview, and she certainly never released a list of the questions she was going to ask ahead of time. Her interviewees knew that. An interview with her was an invitation to bare your soul, to make public what was once private, to talk openly about what had for so many years been consciously kept secret.

Watching her interviews was to see an almost magical act of premonition. She knew what people wanted her to ask, as if she had stolen the questions directly out of the collective unconscious. There were so many times when I sat there, watching the television, saying to myself, "That's exactly what I would have asked."

And after the catharsis came the complicity. *Did you see last night's interview with Barbara Walters?* If you hadn't, it was like you had been on a different planet. At a time when social networks did not yet exist, Barbara Walters created global trending topics.

She was a rebel of American television: she defined a style and an era. She broke down gender barriers well before doing so was considered proper, she did the work that had previously been done only by men, and she earned more money than they did. Indeed, success is the best revenge.

There are many things on television I'd rather not watch. But a Barbara Walters interview was never one of them.

TWO OTHER GREAT journalists left their marks on my career: Mexico's Elena Poniatowska and Italy's Oriana Fallaci. Both have shown extraordinary bravery.

I still find it remarkable that a diminutive woman carrying a portable tape recorder could preserve the most important details from the worst massacre in the modern history of Mexico. But on October 2, 1968, Elena Poniatowska did exactly that. And she did it in the face of ironfisted government censorship, and certainly at great risk to her own life.

Her book *Massacre in Mexico* is one of the finest and most painful works in all of journalism. It recalls the night when the Mexican army, under orders from President Gustavo Díaz Ordaz, gunned down dozens if not hundreds of students in the Plaza de las Tres Culturas in Mexico City just ten days before the opening ceremonies of the 1968 Summer Olympics.

"Who ordered this? Who could have ordered such a thing? This is a crime," we read.

Televisions were silent. The mainstream media justified the government's actions and blamed the students for their own deaths. This huge, imposing square was stained red with the blood of the victims, and city workers had the gruesome task of washing it all away the next morning, leaving it as if nothing had ever happened.

But something had. A lot, in fact. That was the night that Mexico changed.

"I heard a sob from time to time from one or another of my men or women comrades, and I remember hearing someone say (or perhaps I only imagined it), 'Don't cry, this is no time to cry, to shed tears: this is the time to engrave what's happening in letters of fire in our very heart of hearts so we'll remember it when the time comes to settle the score with the people responsible for this.'"

In her book, Elena gathers together all the voices of the massacre: those of the fallen students, the mothers and fathers who lost their children, and the members of a government that killed its own young men and women. Most of these testimonies, she reminds us, were collected within two months of the tragedy, while others—those of the students who were imprisoned after the fact—were obtained over the course of the next two years.

Elena knows she was searching in a place where it can be all but impossible to find anything. "Pain," she says, "is an absolutely solitary act. Speaking about it can be almost unbearable, while digging and investigating smacks of insolence." This is true. But sometimes you have to be insolent to get to the truth.

Although most of the book is filled with other people's voices, it does have a particular point of view. The text is not only rife with indignation, it is also critical of the government. The basic principle of journalism holds true: all the data are presented, but there is also a denunciation. When it comes to human rights violations, one cannot remain neutral.

Without even realizing it, Elena has been my teacher. I have interviewed her several times in her lovely home in southern Mexico City. It never ceases to amaze me that beneath her unwavering smile and tremendous kindness lies a warrior who never gives up, who will never let time erase the evidence of one of the worst massacres in Mexico's history.

I own an old copy of her book *La Noche de Tlatelolco* in Spanish. My sister Lourdes sent it to me many years ago, along with a note. I've read the book so many times that the edges of the pages feel polished, and the tips of the cover have been turned skyward. There are pages where I have folded down a corner to remind me of something I liked, something painful, or something that I will never forget. But what impresses me the most is that there are pages that appear almost to be wet, as if someone shed a lot of tears while writing them.

Oriana Fallaci also covered the 1968 massacre. Elena's book contains Oriana's testimony after she was wounded that night: "They shot me, they stole my watch, they left me lying there bleeding on the floor of the Chihuahua building, they refused to allow me to make a phone call to my embassy. . . . I'm going to let the whole world know about what's happening in Mexico, about the kind of democracy that prevails in this country. What savagery! I was lying face down on the ground, and when I went to cover my head with my bag, hoping to protect myself from shrapnel, a police officer pointed the barrel of his gun about an inch from my head and shouted, 'Don't move.' I could see bullets embedded in the floor of the terrace around me. . . . I saw dozens of people being wounded and a lot of blood until I ended up being shot myself, and then I stayed there, lying in a pool of my own blood, for 45 minutes. . . . I was amazed by the stories in the newspapers; they were awful! So afraid to speak out, so little capacity for outrage!"

This capacity for outrage is what made Oriana Fallaci an unparalleled interviewer. She was ferocious. She saw the process as a war which either the interviewer or the interviewee could win. But regardless of the outcome, at the very least, she emerged with a great interview to publish.

Years before Barbara Walters became famous for conducting the best interviews on television, Oriana Fallaci did the same in newspapers and magazines. It was the golden age of print media, when important things were written for the page and not spoken in front of the camera.

In her book *Interview with History* Fallaci faces off—there's really no other phrase for it—with the great leaders of her day, and leaves none of them standing in her wake. I remember the excitement I felt when I first read those interviews. Fallaci was not a simple recorder who accepted everything she was told. No. She questioned, debated, fought, and took chances. She drove her interviews to the breaking point, hovering over the possibility that her subject might just pack up and leave.

"I do not feel myself to be, nor will I ever succeed in feeling like, a cold recorder of what I see and hear," she writes in her preface. "On every professional experience I leave shreds of my heart and soul; and I participate in what I see or hear as though the matter concerned me personally and were one on which I ought to take a stand (in fact I always take one, based on a specific moral choice)."

Having assumed this stance, she launches into twenty-six interviews, including such figures as Henry Kissinger, Golda Meir, Indira Gandhi, Yasser Arafat, and the Shah of Iran, Mohammad Reza Pahlavi.

But without a doubt, the most difficult interview for her must have been the one she conducted with her partner, Alexandros Panagoulis, one of the leaders of the resistance to the military dictatorship in Greece during the early seventies.

In 1973, Panagoulis took Fallaci to a hill in the Peloponnese region to show her three letters etched into the ground among the trees. The letters were OXI, which in Greek means "NO." He tells her how, despite the wind and the rain and the attempts by the generals to have it burned away with lime, the word continued to defiantly reappear.

When I think of Fallaci, I think of the word "NO." There are, of course, all sorts of journalists. There are those who report with skill and attention to detail. There are the shameful ones who sell themselves out by giving away their questions ahead of time and serve simply to parrot the words of the powerful. And then there are journalists like Oriana Fallaci, whose mission was to confront the powerful head-on. These are the most indispensable of all.

Being skeptical of power was part of her nature. "I refuse to accept it," she wrote. "I refuse to dispense with the idea that our very existence depends upon the few, the beautiful dreams or whims of the few, the arbitrary initiatives of the few." Ultimately, Fallaci was a feminist, a woman who understood that all human beings are equal. "I do not understand power, the mechanism by which men or women feel themselves invested or become invested with the right to rule over others and punish them if they do not obey. . . . To the same degree that I do not understand power, I do understand those who oppose power, who criticize power, who contest power, especially those who rebel against power imposed by brutality."

Imagine having to sit down for an interview with a journalist like that! Clearly, leaders who had something to hide—like Kissinger, for example—were debunked and destroyed.

But in addition to the interviews, what I liked about Fallaci—who died in 2006—was what she wrote before each interview. Her descriptions of power are fascinating. And contrary to what was taught in many journalism schools, her writing was full of opinions, judgments, and prejudices. This transparency allowed the reader to know with whom Fallaci was talking. Regrettably, at the end of her life, she took an unfair and unjustified anti-Muslim position.

Fallaci was a strong woman, and she presented herself to the world in that way. Period. So much so that she could be intimidating. I almost met her once. We were both covering the Persian Gulf War, in the aftermath of Iraq's invasion of Kuwait, and we both happened to be in the lobby of a hotel in Dhahran, Saudi Arabia, near the Kuwaiti border. The war was beginning to wane; there were a lot of comings and goings, and she was part of a group of correspondents about to head out for Kuwait.

Fallaci cut an imposing figure. I remember watching her from a balcony, trying to summon up the courage to go up to her and say, "You're the reason I became a journalist." I was quietly going over the lines in my head, but before I could make it down to the ground floor, her group was called away and she disappeared through a door. I never saw her again.

Of course, I was disappointed by my lack of determination. I had just missed out on the opportunity of a lifetime to meet the woman who, more than anyone else, influenced my decision to enter this profession. I knew that Fallaci wouldn't have hesitated. I vowed never to repeat that mistake, and because of her I have never again hesitated when I had an opportunity to approach someone who interested me and ask them what I had to ask.

That's one of Oriana's lessons. My new mantra was this: there are no second chances.

I MET BARBARA Walters a few months before she retired from television in May 2014. Her producers had invited me to be a guest on *The View*—the program she created back in 1997—and I wasn't about to pass up the opportunity to sit at the same table as Barbara, especially since I knew that she would soon be retiring.

The View is a program where anything and everything is up for discussion. As a guest, you know in advance what the topics will be, but still it's impossible to predict where the conversation might go, and you constantly have to be ready to improvise. On the morning of the show, all the cast members had their program notes handy for quick reference. But I was surprised to find that Barbara had her own clearly written note cards containing all of her questions and every comment she might want to make. She wasn't leaving anything to chance.

I had thought that a journalist of Barbara's caliber would no longer need any sort of reference material when she appeared on television. But when I reviewed the program the next day, the results were clear: Barbara's comments were accurate and to the point, and her questions were direct and delivered without hesitation. She had memorized what she wanted to say, and only occasionally—and very naturally—would she glance at her notes. By comparison, the other panelists seemed somewhat amateurish . . . or at least not as well prepared as Barbara. She was clearly the star of the show.

During commercial breaks, Barbara would consult her notes. But I took advantage of a moment when she looked up to tell her that I was curious about the fact that she seemed to always be in control during her interviews. "No," she replied. "That's not the important part. The important thing is to be truly curious about what they're saying. Control isn't what matters." Then she looked down at her notes again and continued studying.

In the days leading up to her retirement, the great interviewer decided to give some interviews of her own, and I was lucky enough to land one of them. Even so, we had to do it on her own terms: in her New York studio, with the lighting and film crews with whom she'd worked for decades.

When I reached the studio, it was as if I were entering the magical world of Barbara Walters, the place of secrets and confessions. The room itself was dark, and in the center sat two chairs with two enormous rectangular Stellar Diva brand lights hanging over each of them. The light was almost touching my head, but it wouldn't be visible on camera. Around us was another battery of lights filling in any potential shadows. It was impossible to look unflattering.

That halo of light in the middle of that dark room is where Barbara sits her interviewees, and—for a few brief minutes—separates them from their daily lives. I remember thinking that it was like a confessional, with Barbara as the priestess. Bathed in that glow, it was all but impossible to see what lay beyond the camera. All that was left to you was introspection. Talking with Barbara in that atmosphere was like stepping away from the rest of the world, and the heat of those lights in the cold room might provoke in the interviewee a maternal desire to huddle together and to trust. Plus, once you enter that bubble, you can't just walk away. The only way out is to talk, and in doing so, to pop the bubble.

And so it was that I interviewed the interviewer.

Barbara was running late. A group of colleagues had thrown her yet another retirement party; she'd lost count of how many there had been. But once she sat down in that chair, I saw in her eyes the look of serenity and security of someone coming home. Barbara seemed to feel more at ease in front of the camera than away from it, even if she wasn't asking the questions this time.

"I'M REALLY HAPPY that I'm the one asking the questions," I began.

"Well, I like it the other way," Walters joked. "I'm so used to asking the questions that it's strange for me when I have to answer them."

"Is it a matter of control or power?" I asked.

"I'm controlling. I'm powerful. I'm greedy. I'm authoritative." She pauses here and grins before continuing. "It's just that I've been asking the questions for so long that it is where I'm most comfortable."

"I read that you don't like giving interviews."

"Well, this is it. I like asking very personal questions; I do not like answering very personal questions."

She was, perhaps, the most famous journalist in the world, and it was strange to hear her say that she was retiring. But you never stop being a journalist. "I'm not going to come back every week and do an interview," she said. "But if the pope said he would do an interview, would I come back? You bet." The same would be true for Queen Elizabeth, and for Monica Lewinsky, if she ever wanted to talk with her again.

"I'm still in touch with Monica," Barbara said. "I like Monica Lewinsky. . . . She is an intelligent woman and a nice woman."

There were what seemed like a thousand anecdotes. She spent ten days with Fidel Castro, but "I don't get too close to anybody," she said. She even once said that she could have been "Mrs. Clint Eastwood," admitting that "I had a crush on Clint Eastwood, and after I did the interview he asked me to have dinner. And I said no, no, no, I have to go back to work."

Barbara opened doors for many women, both inside and outside the United States. "That's my legacy," she mused. "All these young women in the news. There were not that many when I began, there were very few. . . . The fact that I can open some doors—inspire, maybe—that's a wonderful legacy."

From the perspective of her eighty-four years, Barbara could see how difficult it was for women in the media. "I don't think women can have it all," she said. "I don't think men can have it all. . . . It's very hard balancing, these days, your professional and your private life, and more and more women are having to do this."

I wanted to learn more about Barbara's interviewing style. I mentioned that her questions were short and wonderfully clear, like a knife. There was never any doubt about what she was asking. Her mantra: no forbidden questions.

What's her secret? "I do a lot of homework," she said. "I think it's very important. I sometimes know more about the person than they know about themselves." Suddenly I understood: the secret was that there is no secret. Just a lot of work.

I finished the interview with a pair of questions she often poses to her own interviewees:

"What's the biggest misconception about you?" I asked.

"I think the biggest misconception was that I was very serious and very authoritative because that's the kind of interviews that I did."

And how would she like to be remembered?

"As a good journalist, a good mother, a good person."

My time with her was up, and with it the honor of interviewing the

243

Queen of the Interview. It was only noon, and she still had a ton of things to do. Barbara Walters didn't look like she was about to retire.

I managed to get in one more question in the end: What will you do the day after you retire? "Sleep. I'm going to sleep. Probably the next day as well." But still I was left with the impression that whenever Barbara wakes up, she'll still be asking questions. A lot of them.

BARBARA WALTERS: THE LESSONS

When I asked Barbara Walters what her secret was, I don't know why I was expecting some sort of magical, out-of-this-world answer. In fact, it was quite grounded. She does her homework. Period.

Barbara Walters opened doors for many women, she got the interviews everyone wanted to get, and she met the people who were changing the world. How did she manage to do it? She did her job better than anyone else. That's all there is to it.

I noticed it when I was on *The View*, and when I went back and rewatched several of her old interviews. Those cards she held in her hands . . . written on the cards was the evidence of her secret. She had hundreds of potential questions prepared days or weeks in advance, whittled down to a final list of ten or twenty, of which two or three were destined for history.

What distinguishes Barbara from other interviewers are her questions. Some people take so long to ask something that, in the end, nobody knows what they're talking about. It's not like that with Barbara. Her questions are almost painful: she pulls her knife out of its sheath and plunges it into you without any anesthesia. It's a particularly special talent.

Plus, her interviews are about her interviewees, not about her. There are times when, note card in hand, Barbara knows more about a person's past than even the subject himself can remember. And that sort of knowledge takes days of preparation.

Barbara leaves nothing to chance with her preparation. The extensive description of the lighting that she uses during her interviews simply reaffirms the fact that she understands the business as few people do. Intelligence is not enough. When it comes to visual media, it's important that what you see is attractive.

Another important lesson is that Barbara Walters was constantly promoting her interviews and specials. Some of this, I admit, might have seemed a bit exaggerated. But at the end of the interview, she explained it for me. "If nobody sees what you do, it is useless," she said.

America's Queen of the Interview had no choice but to field a few of her own questions. And in her answers, there is a lot of wisdom to be found.

I gave her some words, and asked her to simply react to them. The first of these was "love."

"Love . . . probably the most important thing you can have," she said. "And it's not necessarily romantic love."

"Money" was next.

"It's nice to have, but it isn't everything. You can be very unhappy with money."

Then came "power."

"You have to be very careful how you use it."

And finally "journalism."

"The best career you can have."

EIGHTEEN

Devoting Your Life to a Dream: Benjamin Netanyahu and Hanan Ashrawi

*Today, we, the Jewish people, have the power to defend our-
selves. We will defend ourselves against our enemies on the
battlefield.* —BENJAMIN NETANYAHU

*It takes courage, it takes strength to keep struggling for peace
despite tremendous odds against you.* —HANAN ASHRAWI

THERE IS NO region of the world that is more fascinating—or more controversial—than the one shared by the Israelis and the Palestinians. There, everything is complicated, everything has a history that dates back hundreds or thousands of years, and—on top of that—everything is divided by two diametrically opposing points of view.

The mere fact that Israeli prime minister Benjamin Netanyahu and Palestinian leader Hanan Ashrawi are being discussed in the same chapter will be seen by some as controversial. Why bring these two adversaries together here?

We should listen to two of the most representative voices from the eternal debate surrounding the Middle East. In fact, they have a great deal in common. Netanyahu and Ashrawi share a passion for their respective causes; indeed, they have both dedicated their lives to those causes. They have devoted their lives to a dream. Additionally, it is difficult to find two people with such dramatically different viewpoints who are both absolutely convinced that they are in the right. This, of course, also implies that each believes the other to be irredeemably wrong.

In a way, this is one single interview involving two separate voices. I posed very similar questions to each of them, and it is in their responses that the seemingly insurmountable differences come to light.

I don't think it's an exaggeration to say that Netanyahu and Ashrawi are enemies. But I do think, as many have said before, that if you want peace, you have to negotiate with the enemy. Both are part of a generation of leaders who have failed multiple times over the past few decades to find a solution to the Israeli-Palestinian problem. That generation is still in power, it has yet to yield to a younger element, and—to this point—it has failed to find a formula for peace.

When journalists get involved in this conflict, it's like walking through a minefield. One wrong move, one misinterpreted word, or one misunderstood gesture could spark an international conflict. But we have to try, regardless of the risks.

In fact, my original idea was to bring Netanyahu and Ashrawi together. When that proved to be impossible, I tried to convene their ambassadors or representatives at the United Nations. That idea never got past the first stages of planning. There was always an enormous amount of resistance on both sides. So, in the end, I had no other choice but to talk with each of them separately.

The interesting thing about these two interviews is that—even though I was the one asking the questions—it seemed as if they were sending messages back and forth from one to the other. They had a lot to say.

NETANYAHU: TOUGH TALK WITH A SOFT VOICE

The first thing that struck me about Israeli prime minister Benjamin Netanyahu was the softness of his voice. It was almost inaudible at times. I had to lean in to hear him. But his quiet demeanor stood in stark contrast to his strong words and hard stance on many issues. In fact, during our talk, Netanyahu refused to concede a single point to his critics.

It happened quickly. We spoke in early October 2014 in New York. He had just arrived in town from Washington, where he had been meeting with President Barack Obama.

I had never gone through as many security checkpoints as I did before meeting with the Israeli prime minister. I was screened even before I entered the hotel, and the process was repeated in the lobby, on the elevator, on two separate floors of the hotel, and in the suite where the interview would be taking place. I was asked the same questions time and time again. I had to show my identification and have my name checked and rechecked on several lists. Every move was monitored, and I was never more than a few steps away from a team of bodyguards or a security chief.

Netanyahu arrived in a hurry, though still composed. And he was hot. The sun had yet to set, but the room there at the Palace Hotel, where we would be conducting the interview, was quite cold. When he arrived, though, he asked for the air conditioner to be turned even higher. Then we sat down to begin.

Is it true that he doesn't get along well with President Obama? I asked. "We're like an old couple," he replied. They'd met more than a dozen times, and, as Netanyahu said, "We've had our differences [but] we agree on a lot more things than we disagree on."

Iran was not one of those issues on which Obama and Netanyahu could agree. Israel was concerned that international organizations among six countries and led by the United States would allow Iran some measure of nuclear capability. In July 2015 Netanyahu's fear was realized when the nuclear deal was struck.

"Iran has sworn to destroy Israel and is seeking to develop atomic bombs," he had said seven months previously, "so naturally I as the Prime Minister of Israel am concerned that history is not going to give the Jewish people another chance. This is it. And we're closer, we're smaller, we're more vulnerable. It's not merely enough to deprive them of nuclear weapons; it's important to deprive them of the capacity to make nuclear weapons in a very short time."

Netanyahu had come to New York to defend himself before then going on the offensive. Palestinian president Mahmoud Abbas had, in a speech before the United Nations, accused Israel of "war crimes" and "genocide" after more than 2,200 Palestinians, including civilians and children, were killed in Gaza during fighting between Hamas and Israel.

I asked Netanyahu if he took that as a personal attack. "I take it as absurd," he replied. "Israel was targeted by these Hamas terrorists, firing thousands of rockets into Israeli cities. . . . And not only were they firing rockets on [our] civilians, they were hiding behind their civilians, using children as human shields. Obviously we had to defend ourselves."

I pressed on. "They're accusing you of war crimes," I said.

"The war crimes that were committed were actually committed by Hamas," he countered, placing the blame on the group that controls the Gaza Strip and seeks the destruction of the state of Israel.

Netanyahu had brought a photograph with him to the interview. It showed a hooded man whom he described as a Hamas terrorist about to execute a kneeling Palestinian. "ISIS beheads people," he said, referring to the extremist group that calls itself the Islamic State, which controls much of Iraq and Syria. "And Hamas puts a bullet in the back of their heads. But to the victims and their families, the horror is the same. So they share the methods and the goal. [Hamas and ISIS] agree that there should be an Islamic-rule order. But they disagree on who among them would be the master of that ruled-order."

I told him that I had listened to his speech at the United Nations, and that it seemed devoid of any hope for peace. There wasn't a single word or even a sign that he would be willing to open new negotiations with the Palestinians. "On the contrary," he replied, "I think we should have two nation-states: one for the Jewish people, one for the Palestinian people . . . [But] we have to have not only mutual recognition but security arrangements that prevent a repetition of Hamas or ISIS takeover of the areas we vacate in the West Bank."

Netanyahu paused to reflect for a moment before looking me squarely in the eye and saying in no uncertain terms, "You say, do we want peace? Let me tell you. I've been to wars. I myself was wounded in a battle against terrorist raids, rescuing civilians from a hijacked plane. I nearly drowned in the [Suez] canal during the firefight with Egypt. There is no one who wants peace more than Israel. We know the horrors of war. We know the pain of losing loved ones. I lost a brother. There is no one who wants peace more. A real peace, a peace that will endure."

Netanyahu, who was sixty-four at the time of this interview, was full of anecdotes. His father—a historian who specialized in medieval Spain—suggested he read *Don Quixote* in the original Spanish. But he never learned Spanish. He hadn't learned to use social networks either, and every Friday evening, in observance of Shabbat, he forbids his family members from having cell phones at the dinner table.

I had time for one more question. Yom Kippur, the most holy day of the year for Jews, the day on which they atone for their sins, was approaching. What wrongs had Netanyahu committed that were in need of forgiveness? I asked.

"I need many Yom Kippurs for that," said the tough-talking man with the gentle voice, smiling ever so slightly.

ASHRAWI: PEACE IS NO SURRENDER

Hanan Ashrawi does not know what it is like to live in peace. She has spent her entire life fighting for the right to have a country.

She was born in 1946 in Nablus in the British Mandate for Palestine, now part of the West Bank. One year later, the UN General Assembly passed a resolution to divide the territory known as Palestine into two states, one Arab and one Israeli. But the 1948 war that began one day after the creation of the state of Israel forced her family to settle in Ramallah, which at the time was part of the Jordanian-annexed West Bank.

Geography is destiny. But in Ashrawi's case, her destiny—her mission in life—had been to change the geography of the place where she happened to have been born and raised. She has been a historian, a university professor, an activist, a legislator, and a spokesperson for a movement that, decades later, still has yet to achieve its goal: the creation of an independent Palestinian state.

In order to interview her, in February 2015 I had to travel to Ramallah, where the Palestinian National Authority operates. And like everything else in this part of the world, it wasn't easy. The Israeli driver who accompanied me in Jerusalem could not enter Ramallah, so we hired a Palestinian to cross the Israeli border with us into the West Bank.

Her office is on one of the upper floors of the Palestine Liberation Organization building, where she is a member of the PLO's executive committee. Security there was minimal; there was just one person in the lobby. We signed in and got in the elevator without any security escort.

While the crew members were setting up their lights and cameras in her spacious office, Ashrawi was sitting at her desk, working quite calmly, as if accustomed to being surrounded by noise, interruptions, and problems.

It was the first time I had ever seen her in person, though for years I had gotten to know her presence through the wonderful debate programs put together by the journalist Ted Koppel for ABC's *Nightline*.

Ashrawi was already made up and ready to go when I arrived. She welcomed me warmly and helped me to pronounce the soft "h" sound in her first name—"I teach languages," she said—and she asked the cameraman what kind of a shot he would be using. She didn't want a very tight close-up. "That's too invasive," she said. The cameraman opened the shot up to show a view from the waist up, and with that, we began.

I told her that I had been following her career since 1991, when she represented a Palestinian delegation attending a peace conference in Madrid. I asked her why it has been so hard to achieve peace with the Israelis.

"Very simply," she began, "because, number one, this is not a situation of a border dispute between two equals. This is a situation of occupier and occupied, a military occupation that enjoys total blind support from the U.S., from the strongest country in the world. . . . And on the other hand, you have the Palestinians under occupation with no rights whatsoever. People get killed every day. Palestinians are killed by Israelis daily without any kind of accountability: Israel destroys our homes, Israel steals the land, Israel builds apartheid walls. Israel builds more settlements. Israel annexes Jerusalem. . . . The asymmetry of power is [such] that we are the only people on earth who [have] to ask the permission of our occupier to be free."

"Does that mean the two-state solution is unreachable?" I asked.

"The two-state solution is being destroyed deliberately by Israeli policies," she replied. "Unless there is immediate, rapid, decisive intervention based on international law and the imperatives of justice, the two states will be gone, yes."

"Then, what would be the solution?" I asked. "Would it be one state—Israel—with a large Palestinian and Arab population in Gaza and the West Bank? Is that the future?"

"If Israel persists in attempting to superimpose greater Israel on historical Palestine, then there would be two results," she began. "One, the Palestinians will ask for historical Palestine; not the two-state solution where we gave away 78 percent of historical Palestine and we're asking to build our state on 22 percent of historical Palestine . . . [And, two,] if they continue with this dangerous and irresponsible policy, they would destroy the two-state solution and have a de facto one-state solution, which is a very painful situation: Palestinians will remain in a state of captivity, enslavement by Israel, with no rights, no freedoms, nothing."

"As I told you, I spoke with Prime Minister Netanyahu. He told me that he's willing to accept a Palestinian state. But first, he says, Hamas has to recognize Israel's right to exist. Is that ever going to happen? He's equating Hamas with ISIS."

"This is ridiculous," she said. "Hamas is our political opposition, but that has nothing to do with ISIS."

"[Netanyahu] says that ISIS beheads people and Hamas puts a bullet in the back of their heads," I continued. "That's what he told me."

"Look, this is ridiculous," she repeated, clearly exasperated. "The bullets that we have seen have been Israeli military bullets. And just finding a scapegoat and putting all the faults on Hamas does not exonerate Israel from its full responsibility in its military occupation. No. Hamas is one constituent of a large, political, pluralistic reality in Palestine. . . . Do you want to go to every Palestinian individual and every Palestinian movement and party and say: Okay, all of you have to repeat the same thing? No, we are not a nation of sheep."

"You're a Christian working with Palestinians and with Jewish people," I said, changing the subject. "Is everything here based on religion?"

"Not at all," she replied. "To us, the fact that we are Christians is a sign of authenticity. . . . We are the representatives of the oldest

Christian tradition in the world. This is where Jesus was born. This is where he lived. . . . Unfortunately religion is being abused. [But] I do not think that this is a religious conflict at all."

"Can you describe for me how it is to be a Palestinian woman living in the West Bank?" I asked.

"Look, being a Palestinian woman living anywhere is very difficult."

"Why?"

"Because you're already framed with preconceptions and you are born with a historical burden, you know. We are trying constantly to work against these stereotypes and misconceptions."

"Which are?"

"Oh, about the Palestinians being violent or terrorists, you know. . . . I don't want to be on the defensive to prove my humanity."

"To finish, I get the sense that you're not hopeful at all about the possibility of peace. I wonder if your children, Amal and Zeina, will ever live in peace."

"Look, when we started the peace process in 1991 my daughter said, 'I'm lending my mother to the peace process so she can come home and spend more time with us and we can have a peaceful future.'"

"It's been twenty-five years."

"It's been twenty-five years. We've lost more lives, more land. My daughters are now mothers themselves. And they've lost their IDs. And they cannot come home and live with me."

"You cannot see them regularly?"

"Only if they come with a visa, because Israel took away their Jerusalem IDs. So I cannot have my children or my grandchildren live with me. They cannot even inherit our family land, our family home. . . . And I can trace my ancestry here for centuries. So my daughters have to come on a visa as visitors while anybody else who happens to be Jewish can come and have instant citizenship."

"Will they see peace one day?"

"I hope so. The thing is we cannot give up. We will not capitulate. . . . Peace is not capitulation. It takes courage, it takes strength to keep struggling for peace despite tremendous odds against you."

"You haven't given up on peace?"

"I still hope that we can make peace. But it has to be a just peace, a human peace, a moral peace, a legal peace."

BENJAMIN NETANYAHU AND HANAN ASHRAWI: THE LESSONS

It's hard to think of two people more unlike than Hanan Ashrawi and Benjamin Netanyahu. Geographically, they live just a few miles away from each other. But their worldviews are separated by centuries of differences and conflicts.

The admirable thing is that both of them have dedicated their lives to a cause much greater than themselves. Both have suffered huge personal losses, and both have certainly sacrificed their family welfare to pursue their political struggles.

Ashrawi and Netanyahu have devoted their lives to dreams. They are, at first glance, two different, incompatible dreams. But ultimately Ashrawi and Netanyahu want the same thing: a safe, independent, sovereign nation to call their home. The problem arises when one dream takes precedence over the other.

Reporting on the Middle East has always fascinated me. It's a part of the world where you always feel that you're covering something important, something of consequence, something with life-or-death implications. The intensity of the political rhetoric is striking, the history carries extra weight, and the conflicting realities are a constant slap in the face. I returned from my trip to Israel and the West Bank with the feeling that I had left a powder keg, a conflict with no possible solution.

Perhaps it's a generational issue. Maybe the current Israeli and Palestinian leaders are too mired in the past to imagine a future without conflict. The weight of politics threatens to drown everything else. But it doesn't always have to be that way.

Before I left, I made a couple of trips that left me with a sense of hope. In both Ramallah and Tel Aviv, I visited technology centers where young people gather to design apps and programs for cell phones and computers. Dozens of students and entrepreneurs were spending their lives exploring new ideas. Their work was completely depoliticized. Yes, it was dependent on electricity, a good phone network, and high-speed Internet access, but no politics were required. In that particular sense, they were quite different from their leaders.

One of them said something that really stuck with me. "Conflict is a waste of time." He explained that the resources devoted to fighting between Israelis and Palestinians could be put to better, more productive use in industries that have nothing to do with the war.

Yes, war is indeed a waste of time. But when you're involved in one, it's all but impossible to see anything else. Netanyahu and Ashrawi know this. War is a black hole that sucks away everything. Even dreams.

NINETEEN

Know That You Will Win:
Desmond Tutu

One very important [lesson] is to know that you will win.
Injustice can't continue forever.   —DESMOND TUTU

I FIRST VISITED SOUTH Africa in January 1996, nearly two years after Nelson Mandela took over the office of the presidency. Yet even then, it was still incredible to think that a prisoner who had spent twenty-seven years behind bars for opposing the white minority government was now the face of the nation.

Black South Africans were still exploring—with a mixed sense of caution and astonishment—the spaces left by the barriers that were falling, one by one, in their country. No, racism and discrimination hadn't suddenly ended with Mandela's election. But the system of apartheid was being dismantled piece by piece.

One of the first things I did upon arriving in Johannesburg was to find someone who could take me to Soweto—which is short for the South Western Townships—to see the house where Nelson Mandela had lived. It wasn't hard. Outside my hotel, Al Mambuto offered to do it for the equivalent of $23.

Just a few years earlier, he could have ended up in jail or worse for traveling along the road connecting Johannesburg to Soweto without a special permit. The first twenty minutes of the ride were spectacular.

"That's the first black movie theater," Al told me. "And there's the first supermarket for people of color, the first hospital, the first nursing home . . ." Everything in Soweto seemed to be taking place for the first time.

My tour was a history lesson. Here were the homes of Nelson Mandela and Archbishop Desmond Tutu. Vilakazi Street in the Orlando West area is the only street in the world that two Nobel Peace Prize laureates have called home. And nearby stands the Hector Pieterson Memorial, commemorating the child who was killed by South African police during the 1976 Soweto uprising.

And in all the time I spent in Soweto, I didn't see a single white person.

I was equally surprised one night when I went to the Victoria and Alfred Waterfront shopping center, and saw almost no black people at all. Apartheid was no longer the official policy of the South African government, but the shadow it cast was patently evident.

I did my homework before traveling to South Africa. Whites (people of Dutch and British origin) make up only 12 percent of the population, yet they earn 58 percent of the nation's income. In stark contrast to that, people of African descent account for 77 percent of the population, yet they receive only 29 percent of the revenues. This disparity didn't change in one fell swoop with the election of the country's first black president.

But differences were beginning to crop up in unexpected places. A number of black families were starting to move into the Hillsboro suburb, which—before Mandela's election—was a whites-only area. And Mandela's house had been turned into a museum. It was two dollars to enter, and for eight, you could take a bit of soil from the garden.

* * *

FOURTEEN YEARS AFTER my first visit, I would be returning to South Africa to cover the World Cup in 2010. Beforehand, I was fortunate enough to meet with Archbishop Desmond Tutu in Miami.

Tutu had been Bishop of Lesotho and Johannesburg and Archbishop of Cape Town, but he was retired when I met with him. Along with Mandela, he had been one of the strongest and bravest voices speaking out against apartheid. He had favored the boycott against his own country when former U.S. president Ronald Reagan proposed his policy of "constructive engagement" with the racist South African government. Justifying his decision, Tutu said that now, at least they would be suffering with a purpose.

"If you are neutral in situations of injustice," Tutu once said, "you have chosen the side of the oppressor. If an elephant has its foot on the tail of a mouse and you say that you are neutral, the mouse will not appreciate your neutrality."

Tutu received the Nobel Peace Prize in 1984 for his fierce struggle against the institutional racism that was pervading his country. Nelson Mandela, understanding his bravery, described Tutu as "Sometimes strident, often tender, never afraid and seldom without humor."

And there it is: the humor. The first thing I noticed about Desmond Tutu was that he was always laughing. It was something I didn't expect from a man who had seen so much suffering.

I spoke with him a few weeks before the start of the World Cup. Mexico and the host nation, South Africa, would be meeting in the tournament's opening match, so of course I would be asking for his thoughts on the game. But I wanted to start out with a different sort of question.

What can Latino immigrants struggling against discrimination in the United States learn from the fight for human rights that took place in South Africa?

"One very important [lesson] is to know that you will win," he said, teaching me my first lesson. "Injustice can't continue forever. And when people are unjust and treat others unjustly, they suffer as well. They discover later that it is much, much better if we accept one another as members of one family."

That faith in justice and the antiapartheid campaigners' ability to win the fight against apartheid eventually brought about the end of the dominant white minority and allowed the transformation of South Africa into a pluralistic nation with eleven official languages. "It's saying 'Let's celebrate our diversity,'" Tutu said. "I mean, we've said that we are a rainbow nation."

Yes, the apartheid system in South Africa is now ended, and equality and civil rights for all are enshrined in the country's constitution, but signs of rejection of and discrimination against black people were still very much present.

Changing that takes time, he said. That's when he taught me my second lesson. "You remember how Martin Luther King said you can't legislate for people to love one another but, he said, it is important that you can legislate to say, 'Don't lynch me.' You hope that people are going to begin to understand that it is better to live in harmony rather than as enemies."

Tutu liked to talk about something he called "ubuntu." What was that, exactly? "Ubuntu is the essence of being human. It says: 'I am a person because you are a person.'" Mandela was the political leader who first implemented the concept of ubuntu by proposing the reconciliation of all ethnic groups in the country.

I asked Tutu what other leaders should learn from Nelson Mandela. "It's a gift that God gives you to be a leader," he said, beginning his third lesson. "And the great gift is to remember that you are a leader for the sake of the led. You are not a leader for self-recognition. It's not that you can enrich yourself. You're there for the sake of the ones that say, 'You are our leader.'"

At this point, our time together was nearing an end, and Tutu had made me feel so comfortable and at ease, without any of the stress that generally comes when you interview someone as wise and influential as him. So I dared to risk asking him the toughest question of all: Who would win the opening match of the World Cup, Mexico or South Africa?

"You know I'm from Mexico," I started to say, but Archbishop Tutu interrupted me almost immediately.

"Tough luck," he said, with a laugh that echoed throughout the room.

Our conversation had come to an end. I shook his hand. He held my hand between both of his, fixed his frank, direct gaze on me, and said, "May God bless you." And he kept on laughing.

Mexico and South Africa tied, by the way, with one goal apiece.

DESMOND TUTU: THE LESSONS

Bishop Tutu's first lesson was the most essential one: You must always maintain faith in your cause. Tutu is convinced that injustice is only a temporary thing. This belief that justice can be achieved enabled Nelson Mandela not only to survive twenty-seven years of imprisonment, but also to eventually become the president of South Africa. This principle can be applied as much to dictators and oppressive regimes as it can to the situation facing immigrants in the United States and Europe.

The second lesson is that we must be practical in our pursuit of justice. As Martin Luther King said, you can't require people to love one another. It is, however, not only possible but also desirable and necessary to enact laws that prevent lynching and violence. Tutu assured me that—sooner or later—people will choose to live in harmony rather than in a constant state of conflict.

The third and final lesson is that leaders should never seek positions of power in order to achieve their own personal goals. Instead, they should be looking to improve the lives of others. That was the life led by Nelson Mandela, and by Desmond Tutu as well.

On a personal level, it was encouraging to learn that a man who had seen so much violence and negation in his life could nevertheless maintain his optimism, his hope, and his sense of humor. Yes, one day, I will learn to laugh like Desmond Tutu.

TWENTY

America's DREAMers:
The First Step Is Losing Your Fear

The first step is always letting go of your fear.
—ERIKA ANDIOLA

It was the first time we did something like that. But we weren't going to be afraid anymore.   —GABY PACHECO

Ever since I was a child, my dad talked to me about mental toughness. You have to be consistent, and you have to keep moving forward.   —LORELLA PRAELI

When I first started out, we were a group of five. I never thought we'd grow to number in the thousands.
—CRISTINA JIMÉNEZ

DREAMERS ARE MY heroes. Or, should I say, my heroines. The majority of the leaders in this movement of undocumented students here in the United States are women. Young, brave, fearless women.

Well, it's not that they're fearless. What they've done is learn to overcome their fear.

The ones who took the biggest risks were the ones who had the most to lose—their families, their education, their friends, even their country—and they stood up to fight for themselves and others like them. It wasn't easy. But so far, they're winning.

Nothing in this country is more difficult than being an undocumented immigrant. You have barely any rights. You live in the shadows, persecuted, under the constant threat of being arrested, deported, and separated from your family. Many politicians refer to you as a "criminal" simply for having entered the country illegally, and if you're killed by the police, almost nothing ever happens. Nothing.

Since President Ronald Reagan granted amnesty to more than three million undocumented immigrants back in 1986, not a single new law has been passed to legitimize the eleven million who currently live here in the United States. The immigration system is broken. States are making decisions that belong at the federal government level, and meanwhile, discrimination and abuse are inflicted upon the immigrant community. We need new laws to deal with our immigrants.

Despite talks about an immigration agreement between Mexico and the United States that were taking place around the turn of the century, the September 11 terrorist attacks derailed everything.

The anti-immigrant climate that spread across the nation after 9/11 was reflected in a series of punitive laws targeting foreigners, which were enacted in several states. In practice, these laws meant that many immigrants could not get driver's licenses, that the police could act as de jure immigration agents, and that college students could not continue their studies.

Frustrations ran high. Imagine a young person who was illegally brought to the United States when he or she was just a baby, who speaks more English than Spanish, who feels more American than any other nationality, and who—all of a sudden—is told that he or she can't attend college because the necessary documents are not in order. For the first time in their young lives, these people realize that they are very much at risk of being deported to a country they've never known.

This is the predicament faced by the DREAMers.

And it's a huge problem. We're talking about more than four million young people under the age of thirty who are in the country as undocumented immigrants, according to a Pew Research Center study.

It is possible to blame undocumented adults for voluntarily coming to the United States without a permit or a visa to do so, but not the children they brought with them. They were too young to know what was happening. It's obviously not their fault that they're here.

For decades—since the time of labor leaders like Cesar Chávez and Dolores Huerta—it was the responsibility of the adult members of the Latino community to fight for their youth. Then, as the number of Hispanic members of Congress began to grow, politicians took up positions of leadership. But now as never before, we are seeing young Latinos breaking with established leaders, questioning their strategies, and launching their own fights with their own means and methods.

It was a true changing of the guard. The traditional politicians were out, and the DREAMers were in.

DREAMers are rebels. They're not waiting to grow up before they begin their fight. They're not listening to their elders. They're not heeding the calls for patience and resignation. And they're questioning everything that Latino leaders have done before. Why? For the simple reason that those leaders and their tactics have produced no real results—none—when it comes to legalizing them and their parents.

Something new has to be done.

When Gaby Pacheco, Carlos Roa, Juan Rodríguez, and Felipe Matos decided to walk from Miami to Washington to denounce the situation faced by undocumented immigrants, many believed they were making a big mistake. Three of them had been brought here by their parents at a very young age, and therefore were running the risk of being deported.

"It was the first time we did something like that," Gaby said to me. "But we weren't going to be afraid anymore."

They left on January 1, 2010, from the so-called Freedom Tower in downtown Miami and prepared themselves for the worst. "We readied ourselves for three things: being arrested, being deported, and even being assaulted. We studied the civil rights movement and the marches led by Cesar Chávez. The important thing was to react without violence," Gaby told me.

Much to my surprise, and to that of many others, immigration authorities allowed the group to reach Washington on the first of May. They weren't able to meet with President Obama, as they had intended, but they were able to draw national attention to a problem that was affecting millions of students just like them. Tens of thousands of people began following them on social networks.

María Gabriela Pacheco was born in Guayaquil, Ecuador, and when she was eight years old, her parents illegally brought her to the United States. "When I was little, I looked a lot like my dad. I had very indigenous features; I was the tough little *chola* girl," she recalled.

But she also remembered a phrase—"girl from Guayaquil, a warrior made from wood with Quechua blood in her veins"—that her father used to recite to her, and that proved to be very important to her during that 1,500-mile march to Washington. "To me, it meant that I could do whatever I wanted to do," she told me, "and that I came from a long line of fighters."

She needed that warrior's spirit in 2001, when she spoke publicly for the first time about her immigration status. By 2005, she had become a student leader and had begun defending other immigrants like herself.

Gaby doesn't know exactly who reported her to Immigration and Customs Enforcement (ICE), but in 2006, eleven agents conducted a raid on her home in Miami, arresting her parents and her two sisters. She was also home at the time, but managed to avoid being detained.

This is going to continue, she thought. *Next time, they could deport us all.* Gaby had two options: go into hiding or fight back. Being a rebel, she chose to stand and fight.

As political director for the national youth group United We Dream, she pursued the objective of getting Congress to pass the DREAM Act, which would legalize millions of young, undocumented students like herself. They managed to get the act brought up for a vote in the Senate in December of 2010, but it fell five votes short of passing.

Gaby was angry and frustrated. And she let Senate Majority Leader Harry Reid, a Democrat, know. "What you did isn't enough," Gaby told him when she met with him. "President Obama can stop deportations and create a deferred action [DACA, or Deferred Action for Childhood Arrivals] program for us."

And then, looking directly at Reid, she said, "We're going to hold you accountable." Gaby remembers that Reid then stepped aside and left. "I stood up to him," she told me. It was quite an exceptional moment: the Senate majority leader was being challenged and questioned by an undocumented immigrant student barely a third his age.

How did she do it? "I've never understood why I am the way that I am, but it gives me an adrenaline rush," Gaby said. Today, she's the program director of TheDream.US program. "When I see people in positions of power as equals, I lose my fear and speak to them as fellow human beings."

BY THE END of 2010, legislative means had failed. The Senate, even with a majority of Democrats, didn't have the votes needed to pass the DREAM Act, while in the House, dominated by the Republicans, it wasn't even brought up for debate. The GOP was intent on blocking any effort to legalize the status of undocumented immigrants, regardless of their age. There had to be another way.

Obama. The new strategy was to pressure the president to sidestep

Congress, halt deportations, and issue work permits to millions of undocumented immigrants. But there was a serious obstacle in the way: President Obama himself.

In interviews and speeches, Obama said that he lacked the constitutional authority to stop deportations of any particular group, and that he had to follow the law. But the DREAMers—supported by a number of Hispanic attorneys and organizations—were convinced that the president, who is a graduate of Harvard Law School, was mistaken.

Lorella Praeli is one of the immigrants who forced Obama to change his mind. Lorella came to the United States in 1999 from Peru. She was just ten years old at the time, and she was brought here in search of medical treatments that would enable her to walk better. When she was two years old, a car pushed her up against a wall, which resulted in her right leg being amputated.

Her parents were hoping that here, in the United States, they would have the opportunity to consult with new doctors and also they hoped that their daughter wouldn't be defined by her accident. They were right.

"When I was down," Lorella told me, "my dad wouldn't lift me back up. He wouldn't let anyone lift me back up." He wanted to teach her to be able to stand up on her own. But the lesson went well beyond the physical therapy sessions. "Ever since I was a child, my dad talked to me about mental toughness," she recalled. "You have to be consistent, and you have to keep moving forward."

That's exactly what Lorella and a delegation from United We Dream did when they met in 2012 with two of President Obama's top advisors on immigration issues, Valerie Jarrett and Cecilia Muñoz. The meeting, strangely enough, was held in a Washington, D.C., church, owing to the fact that undocumented immigrants were not, at the time, allowed to enter the White House.

Jarrett and Muñoz were very clear. White House lawyers had told them that the president had no legal authority to suspend deportations in favor of DACA to undocumented students. But Lorella argued that they were mistaken. "It's a political decision," she said, before offering a warning: "We're going to make sure the Latino community knows the truth."

What happened next was unprecedented. Rather than arguing endlessly, the DREAMers managed to get their attorneys to talk with those from the White House. After this meeting, it became clear that—despite his initial negative reaction—Obama could, in fact, do something for them.

On June 15, 2012, in a White House Rose Garden ceremony, President Obama announced the implementation of new actions designed, as he said in his own words, "to mend our nation's immigration policy, to make it more fair, more efficient, and more just—specifically for certain young people sometimes called DREAMers." As we have seen, President Obama had his own reasons for taking this action, but the results were what mattered to the DREAMers. According to the Pew Research Center, this meant that 1.7 million young, undocumented students like Lorella Praeli would be getting the security they needed.

Her mental toughness had produced results.

THE DREAMERS HAD achieved a very important goal. But they wanted more. Much more. They could legally work, and in most states, they could obtain driver's licenses. They weren't going to be deported. But their parents were still in constant danger of being removed from the country.

After handing DACA to the DREAMers, the White House focused on building immigration reform in the halls of Congress. It would be an uphill battle. The Senate appeared to have the necessary support, including the votes of a handful of Republicans. But opposition in the House was tremendous.

That was the challenge for Cristina Jiménez, managing director of United We Dream, the first and largest immigrant youth–led organization in the country. But first, the deportations had to stop. Barack Obama was deporting nearly 400,000 undocumented immigrants per year, more than any other president in history. His intention was to demonstrate that, yes, he was enforcing immigration laws, and therefore he could pressure Republicans to agree to reform.

But the short-term outcomes were destroying thousands of lives. And Cristina's family could be next.

Cristina came to the United States from Ecuador just after her thirteenth birthday. "I grew up as an undocumented immigrant in New York, wanting to go to college," she told me. "I remember being fourteen and going with my dad to the car wash where he worked. I had to be an interpreter between him and his boss so that they could pay him. Those experiences had a big impact on me."

Cristina's father had been a trade unionist in Quito, and she hoped to become a lawyer. But despite her good grades, a guidance counselor at her high school gave her some of the worst news of her life. "You can't go to college," she told her.

It was a tough punch to take. "I'd always heard that this was the land of opportunity," she recalled. This rejection "wasn't what I'd heard about this country. All of a sudden, I find myself faced with this contradiction, and now the doors are being slammed shut in my face."

But Cristina didn't just sit back and do nothing. At eighteen, she began organizing protests along with other students in New York. "When I first started out, we were a group of five. I never thought we'd grow to number in the thousands, and achieve results like DACA."

In 2013, a change in policy finally allowed undocumented students to enter the White House. And Cristina was in one of the first groups to do so.

The president needed the support of the DREAMers to pressure the Republicans on immigration reform. The DREAMers said yes.

But Cristina wanted the president to go one step further. "We need you to do something to stop deportations," she told him. "They're going to continue being a key issue for us. The pain they cause is felt every day." If there wasn't going to be any real immigration reform, Cristina wanted the president to use an executive action and put a halt to deportations, including that of her own father.

The president was listening. The following year—on November 20, 2014—Obama announced an executive order to stop deportation proceedings for an estimated 4.4 million undocumented immigrants.

Cristina didn't study law. But she did end up in political science. She never accepted the "no" answer when it came to attending college. And along the way, she changed many people's lives. "We've changed a lot of people. Young people and families. People who didn't feel respected and who didn't dare to speak up for themselves," she told me. "We've been able to change the mind-set that we're isolated and powerless."

DREAMERS ARE NOT members of Congress or diplomats. They're not interested in being politically correct. What they're interested in is getting results. If they don't like someone, they'll say so to his or her face. If they have a message, they'll deliver it in person. And if they're afraid, they certainly don't show it.

DREAMers started doing things that nobody else dared to do. They didn't just march and protest—as farmworkers' organizations have been doing for decades—they adapted their strategies to include twenty-first-century technology.

They quickly realized they didn't need television and traditional means of communication to get their message out. Social networks enabled their videos and protests to go viral and reach millions. But then they decided to do something even more radical.

They drew up lists of people they wanted to call out for not supporting comprehensive immigration reform, they sought them out, and—when their targets least expected it—they hit them with tough questions. And of course, everything was recorded in a cell phone video, and would quickly be making its way across the Internet.

They staged sit-ins in the offices of a number of congressmen and senators, and they wouldn't leave until they were heard. House Majority Leader John Boehner was confronted by a young undocumented immigrant while he ate breakfast in a Washington diner. And one of the harshest critics of undocumented immigrants, Congressman Steve King, was accosted by Erika Andiola, codirector of the DREAM Action Coalition in Arizona.

Erika arrived in Mesa, Arizona, when she was eleven years old, along with her mother and two brothers. Her two older brothers came here before them. They are all from Durango, Mexico, where their mother was the victim of domestic violence, according to what Erika told me. "She's a very brave woman," she said. "She left my dad and took it upon herself to come here with her five children. It was an act of valor."

For Erika, her mother was the example to follow. "I attribute a lot about the way that I am, and the way that I act to her," she told me. "She always questioned things and looked into things." That was her first lesson in thinking like a rebel.

"The first step is always letting go of your fear," she said. "Accepting that we're here, in this country, is nothing to be ashamed of."

But she didn't just lose her fear. "I was pretty angry," she said, remembering the time in 2014 when she confronted Representative Steve King, who opposed President Obama's DACA program. "I know you want to get rid of DACA, so I want to give you the opportunity," she told him. "If you really want to get rid of it, just rip mine." And she handed King her identification card. The congressman dared not tear it up, and instead he simply congratulated her on speaking English so well. "I like to confront them with this moral dilemma and make them say things to me that they wouldn't say in public," Erika said.

That's the DREAMers' strategy. Up front and in your face. I'm certain that Representative King, Speaker Boehner, and many others won't soon forget their encounters with these students.

Life has gotten somewhat better for Erika. Her DACA status protects her from being deported for the time being. Still, though, she still can't get a driver's license. She wanted to go to law school and be a normal young woman. But she can't. She has to keep fighting.

"I was proud to be able to empower other guys," she reflected, "and to teach them to lose their fears."

DREAMERS: THE LESSONS

DREAMers, like all undocumented immigrants in the United States, have become experts in the art of survival. There are moments in life where the single most important thing is not to die. In the case of the undocumented, their top priority is to avoid being deported. Plain and simple. There is the hope that, sooner or later, the United States will do what it has done throughout history and protect them. Meanwhile, they have to survive.

Sometimes this means remaining silent. Sometimes it means going into hiding. In many cases, it means putting their dreams on hold. This is the reality for eleven million people here in the United States.

But the DREAMers have gone from playing defense to playing offense. Their parents may be underground, but they are not. Their elders may be living in the shadows, but they seek out the media's attention. Their leaders call for prudence and negotiation; they demand respect and concrete solutions. Those who came before them were willing to wait, but the DREAMers want it now. The adults asked them to follow the rules, but they simply rejected the old rules and imposed their own. Hispanic congressmen suggested that they work through the legislative process in order to achieve comprehensive immigration reform, but the DREAMers knew that road would lead to nowhere, and instead they asked the president for protection.

One of the hardest things for any undocumented immigrant to do is to publicly proclaim that you are here illegally. It goes against everything you've ever learned since childhood. But the DREAMers have gained strength from this public declaration. They've decided they won't stay hidden any longer, the way their parents and their elders did. They're not ashamed of their illegal status.

That's why, for them, the first step is shedding their fears. The first step for any true rebel is recognizing that you're a rebel and knowing why you're fighting.

The DREAMers have taught us real heroism in the twenty-first century. We have a lot to learn from them. Their rebel spirit is based on authenticity. Their parents chose not to be visible to protect the family. But those tactics didn't work. Now, the DREAMers are choosing the opposite—to be in our faces. Hiding is no longer an option.

You cannot fight if you hide. So the first thing they did as rebels was to accept publicly who they were. And they survived. Then they rejected all kinds of derogatory terms and discriminatory attitudes. And at that point they defined their own name: dreamers. They controlled the language and therefore they controlled their own story and their own destiny.

Finally, they lost their fear. That was when they started winning.

TWENTY-ONE

Final Lessons: What I Learned from Thirty Years of Interviews

WHAT DO ALL the men and women who appear in this book have in common? They rebelled against something: a country, a president, a system, a tradition, a myth, an injustice, or even just a stupid idea. Or they forcefully exerted their power in a way that—for better or for worse—left a mark upon history.

These are some of the phrases that remained with me long after the interviews were over:

"The first step is always letting go of your fear. Accepting that we're here, in this country, is nothing to be ashamed of."

—ERIKA ANDIOLA, codirector of the DREAM Action Coalition in Arizona, on the attitude that many DREAMers share

---

"Girl from Guayaquil, a warrior made from wood with Quechua blood in her veins. . . . To me, it meant that I could do whatever I wanted to do, and that I came from a long line of fighters."

—Gaby Pacheco, DREAMer and program director of
TheDream.US, remembering a phrase that her father used to
recite to her and that proved to be very important to her
during her 1,500-mile march from Miami to Washington

------

*"When I was down, my dad wouldn't lift me back up. He wouldn't
let anyone lift me back up. . . . Ever since I was a child, my dad
talked to me about mental toughness. . . . You have to be consistent,
and you have to keep moving forward."*

—Lorella Praeli, a DREAMer who lost a leg in a car accident
when she was very young, on her father teaching her to stand
up for herself

------

*"We've changed a lot of people. Young people and families. People
who didn't feel respected and who didn't dare to speak up for themselves. We've been able to change the mind-set that we're isolated
and powerless."*

—Cristina Jiménez, managing director of United We Dream,
who wasn't able to attend law school, ended up with a career
in political science, and changed the lives of many other
DREAMers like her along the way

------

*"A lot of people think we can't do it. There are many people who
think Latinos don't have the capacity to achieve great things. I didn't
let them discriminate against me . . . I have a strong character. You
don't push me around. I won't allow people to think I do not have
value. When you value yourself, there are a lot of people who think
that's a bad thing if you're a woman, because women aren't supposed to speak up or complain much or demand certain things."*

—Sonia Sotomayor, United States Supreme Court justice

———————

"I don't care who you are, if you're African American in this country, you know what the deal is," he replied.

"What's the deal?" I pressed.

"The deal's that you're black."

"And that means for you . . ."

"Well, it just means that you're black. And the people who get in trouble are the people who forget they're black. You just can't think, 'Well, I'm successful. I've reached another realm and I'm in the so-called. . . .' What's the term?"

"Post-racial."

"Yeah, that's bullshit [to think] that because now we have an African American president race no longer matters. And there are times, even today, it's hard for me to catch a cab in New York City."

"For you?"

"Yes."

"So do you feel discriminated constantly?"

"You're made aware of it. I'm not complaining. It's just something that you grow up with."

"You were talking about the possibility of a post-racial society. Now, you're saying it isn't happening?"

"Look, I can't predict the future. But there are a lot of people who believed that when our president put his hand on Abraham Lincoln's Bible and did the oath, that hocus-pocus, abracadabra, poof, we were in a post-racial world."

—SPIKE LEE, filmmaker

———————

"I do a lot of homework. I think it's very important. I sometimes know more about the person than they know about themselves."

—BARBARA WALTERS, journalist, talking about her "secret" to conducting interviews

---

"I'm a person who wakes up every day and says, 'Today I will be-have as a free citizen.' I assume the risks."

. . . Will she be able to change Cuba?

"Not by myself alone," she said. "But we are many."

—YOANI SÁNCHEZ, journalist, blogger, Cuban dissident

"All my hunger strikes are to the end. . . . With me, there is no middle ground. I go on a hunger strike when the government commits an inhuman act. That's when I take these self-destructive measures, which put the government up against a wall."

—GUILLERMO FARIÑAS, Cuban dissident

"I fear for my life because I could get shot, I could get struck by lightning. It could come from anywhere, like one of those security cars that follow me around when I'm riding my bike down the street. Life and death are a part of our existence. We live and die in the hands of God. And I will return to Cuba to live or die in the hands of God."

—OSWALDO PAYÁ, Cuban dissident who died in 2012 in a mysterious "accident," according to the Cuban government

---

"I'm absolutely convinced that there was no accident," she said. "That's a total lie."

"They sent someone to kill him?" I asked.

"Absolutely. They sent someone to kill Oswaldo Payá."

"Who did it?"

"State police had been making death threats against Oswaldo for years. They had repeatedly loosened the lug nuts on the wheels of our car. We saw them on a number of occasions."

"Do you think that Raúl Castro and Fidel Castro are behind the assassination of [your husband]?"

"Look, Cuba is a totalitarian regime where the government—the halls of power—makes decisions each and every minute about the lives of its citizens. Nobody in Cuba would dare to do that; they wouldn't dare do such a thing unless they had support from the highest levels of the Cuban government."

—OFELIA ACEVEDO DE PAYÁ, the wife of
    Oswaldo Payá

"Today, the people governing Venezuela are turning it into a rogue state. A state centered around backroom deals, corruption, and even links to drug trafficking."

—LEOPOLDO LÓPEZ, leader of the opposition in Venezuela who
    has been imprisoned since February 18, 2014

"Leopoldo is a prisoner of conscience. Leopoldo was incarcerated for his ideas, for his words, for wanting a better Venezuela. So what do we do? We denounce it. We will never stop denouncing it."

—LILIAN TINTORI, leader of the opposition in Venezuela, and
    wife of Leopoldo López

"I'm a survivor. I've survived over a dozen attacks. It's a miracle I'm still alive. Why wouldn't I continue playing a part in the politics of my country, even without any personal ambition? As long as God grants me the energy to do so, of course I have to continue to participate."

—ALVARO URIBE, former president of Colombia

"It was six years and five months, and every day something hurt, every day I physically felt myself being bitten by bugs. I was itching and scratching, some part of my body was always in pain. . . . That horror of horrors, the hostile presence of arbitrariness, of daily cruelty, of the refinement of hell. . . . Yes, it still surprises me. Every day surprises me, and I don't think I'm the only one. . . . We're all living with the sense that it's a dream, but it's a beautiful dream, and thank God it's reality."

—INGRID BETANCOURT, Colombian writer and political leader who was kidnapped by FARC guerrillas

---

"Well, it certainly doesn't matter in terms of personal consumption. . . . But to the degree that my wife and I can assure that the money is spent to help those most in need, to invent new vaccines or new seeds, help with education, then it really does matter. We are very excited about our giving and very committed, to not only put our money, but to put our time into that work."

—BILL GATES, founder of Microsoft, on his personal fortune

"If you're fortunate enough to be successful, with success can come money, and sometimes it becomes too much money for one family to have. I think it's very important you use your money to tackle issues you feel will make a difference in the world."

—RICHARD BRANSON, founder of Virgin Group

"I love it the most when I'm in the car with my ten-year-old and he says to his friends: 'Daddy, that's yours. Daddy, that's yours.' And you see the great sense of pride in him. Before, we had a col-

lection of buildings. Now everything is coming together—shopping and offices and culture. We're finally not talking about being a great city, but being a great city."

—JORGE PÉREZ, real estate entrepreneur and founder of the Related Companies

---

"I cannot guarantee that it's going to be done in the first 100 days. But what I can guarantee is that we will have, in the first year, an immigration bill that I strongly support, and that I am promoting, and that I want to move forward as quickly as possible."

—PRESIDENTIAL CANDIDATE BARACK OBAMA, on May 28, 2008, at a school in Denver, Colorado

---

"Why not sit down with Saddam Hussein and negotiate a solution to this crisis?"

"You might make that case. But you have to see all the people that have tried it. What he wants to do is to present this as Iraq against the United States. It is not. It's Iraq against the world."

—PRESIDENT GEORGE H. W. BUSH, on November 20, 1990

"In my opinion, [Marxism] is too new to be a museum piece, while capitalism is three thousand years old."

—CUBAN DICTATOR FIDEL CASTRO, in 1991

I have my father's eyes but my mother's mouth."

—PRESIDENT GEORGE W. BUSH

———

"I am not a dictator," he said.

"Are you willing to hand over power after five years?" I asked.

"Of course I am," he replied. "I've said it before. If, for example, two years from now, I turn out to be a failure—if I commit a crime, a corrupt act, or something else that would justify my removal from power—I would be willing to do so."

—Venezuelan president Hugo Chávez, one day before his election in December 1998. He would remain in power until his death in March 2013.

———

"Why not just remove the mask?" I asked. "Why not just take it off, right now, right here?"

"Because it has become a symbol," he replied. "It symbolizes the possibility that people who have thus far been nameless, faceless people—common, unimportant people—can take a powerful stance when it comes to facing life and the environment in which they live."

"And how long will you have to wear the mask?"

"When we are finally able to transform into a peaceful and civil political force, both weapons and ski masks will have to disappear."

—Subcomandante Marcos, Zapatista leader in Chiapas, Mexico

———

"How much money do you have?" I asked.

"Well, I don't have an exact figure for how much I have in the bank. But I have declared all my finances and properties."

"Since 1990, your only jobs have been in public office," I said. "If I add up your salaries from 1990 to 2009, won't I come up with what you have in the bank?"

"You will," he replied. . . .

"In other words, you're not a millionaire."

"No, I'm not."

—Mexican president Enrique Peña Nieto, in 2009

―――――

"Are you [Mexico's] favorite villain?" I asked.

"Of course, and do you know why? Because they hid their incompetence by blaming others."

"But the implication is that you and your family became rich in doing so."

"But in the end, the facts will demonstrate that many allegations and accusations were false."

"But people want to know how Mr. Salinas lives. Are you indeed a millionaire?"

"I live off the income and the assets that I declare to the comptroller general's office. And, with a little luck, even the sales from my book."

"But you've always held public positions. That's the point," I said. "How can you live like a millionaire?"

"And how can you classify me as such without a shred of evidence?"

"I'm not. I'm simply asking."

"It's not a question. It's more of a statement than a question. . . . Everyone is entitled to their reputation, and when there's a debate about [my reputation], everyone has the right to participate in that debate. I am in that debate—in the battleground of ideas—and that is where I intend to stay."

—Former Mexican president Carlos Salinas de Gortari

―――――

"How much did you pay for the house?"

"Well, the truth is that it's not worth two million dollars," he countered. "That's an exaggeration."

"How much did it cost? How much is it worth? How is the value calculated?"

"It's not worth all that much. It's a lot less than that."

"A million?"

"No, no, no. Not that much at all."

"I'm not sure. I don't know the house. I'm just not sure how much it's worth."

"Well, it's not worth very much. I can tell you that."

"How much did you pay for it?"

"Well, I paid what it was worth at the time."

"How much was that?"

"Well, the truth is I don't have the exact figure."

"But more or less."

"It wasn't much, then, it wasn't much."

"Thirty thousand dollars? Ten thousand dollars?"

"Yes, it was a small sum because back then everything was undervalued. . . . For me, it would be easy to leave that house. But that would send a bad impression to thousands of Nicaraguans, who would feel helpless if I were to do that."

"Could it be that your house has become a symbol?"

"It is a symbol. Ultimately, I've held on to the house mostly because it's a symbol."

—NICARAGUAN PRESIDENT DANIEL ORTEGA, talking about the house in which he lives and which he confiscated from Jaime Morales in 1979

"You say, do we want peace? Let me tell you. I've been to wars. I myself was wounded in a battle against terrorist raids, rescuing civilians from a hijacked plane. I nearly drowned in the [Suez]

canal during the firefight with Egypt. There is no one who wants peace more than Israel. We know the horrors of war. We know the pain of losing loved ones. I lost a brother. There is no one who wants peace more. A real peace, a peace that will endure."

—Israeli prime minister Benjamin Netanyahu

"Look, when we started the peace process in 1991 my daughter said, 'I'm lending my mother to the peace process so she can come home and spend more time with us and we can have a peaceful future.'"

"It's been twenty-five years."

"It's been twenty-five years. We've lost more lives, more land. My daughters are now mothers themselves. And they've lost their IDs. And they cannot come home and live with me."

"You cannot see them regularly?"

"Only if they come with a visa, because Israel took away their Jerusalem IDs. So I cannot have my children or my grandchildren live with me. They cannot even inherit our family land, our family home. . . . And I can trace my ancestry here for centuries. So my daughters have to come on a visa as visitors while anybody else who happens to be Jewish can come and have instant citizenship."

"Will they see peace one day?"

"I hope so. The thing is, we cannot give up. We will not capitulate . . . Peace is not capitulation. It takes courage, it takes strength to keep struggling for peace despite tremendous odds against you."

—Palestinian leader Hanan Ashrawi

"One very important [lesson] is to know that you will win. Injustice can't continue forever. And when people are unjust and treat others

unjustly they suffer as well. They discover later that it is much, much better if we accept one another as members of one family."

—ARCHBISHOP DESMOND TUTU, winner of
    the Nobel Peace Prize

Videos of the interviews that appear in this book are available at www.jorgeramos.com.

Author's Speech to the Committee to Protect Journalists New York, November 24, 2014

I love being a journalist. It is the only profession in the world in which your job description is to be rebellious and irreverent. In other words, journalism keeps you forever young. As Colombian writer Gabriel García Márquez used to say, this is the best profession in the world. But we can, and we should, use journalism as a weapon for a higher purpose: justice.

The best of journalism happens when we take a stand: when we question those who are in power, when we confront the politicians who abuse their authority, when we denounce an injustice. The best of journalism happens when we side with the victims, with the most vulnerable, with those who have no rights. The best of journalism happens when we, purposely, stop pretending that we are neutral and recognize that we have a moral obligation to tell truth to power.

I believe in the basics of journalism. I have nothing against objectivity. Our profession is based on finding the facts, on reporting exactly what happened, on being obsessed with details. We should not get it wrong. If five people died, we have to say five, not six or seven. We should get the name right, the quote right, the numbers right. Our credibility depends on this.

I have nothing against being balanced. Every story has at least two points of view and we have to report both. This has to be like a reflex. If a Republican says something, I bet you a Democrat has a response, and vice versa. If a president proposes a new law, the opposition should also have a say. This has to be second nature.

But to get all the facts and to present both points of view doesn't mean that we got the story right.

When we deal with the powerful, we have to take a stand. Yes, we have to take an ethical decision and side with those who have no power. If we have to decide between being a friend or an enemy of the president, of the governor, of the dictator, it should be an easy choice: I'm a reporter and I don't want to be your friend.

When I'm doing an interview with someone important, I always assume two things: First, that if I don't ask the tough questions, nobody else will. That's my job. And second, that most probably I will never talk to that person again. Some of the worst interviews that I've seen happen when the reporter refuses to ask difficult questions just to maintain access to his sources. That's self-censorship.

Yes, I'm arguing here for "point of view journalism." It means being transparent, it means recognizing to our audience, to our readers, that we have opinions and a code of ethics. We don't live in a vacuum. All the time, we are taking moral choices right before the interview, right before the investigation or the coverage. It is perfectly okay not to be neutral and to openly take a stand.

We have many great examples of courageous journalists who decided to take a stand:

- Edward R. Murrow confronted biased Senator Joe McCarthy.
- Walter Cronkite openly criticized the Vietnam War.

- The *Washington Post* reporters got rid of a corrupt president, President Nixon.
- Christiane Amanpour denounced President Clinton's flip-flop policies and held him accountable for what happened in Bosnia.
- And Anderson Cooper showed the incompetence of the Bush administration after Hurricane Katrina.

If they did it, I can do it. Therefore, I think I can call Fidel Castro a dictator (even though I can't get a visa to go to Cuba). We were right to report early this year that the Venezuelan government was behind the killings of dozens of students. Obviously President Maduro hasn't given us an interview.

And we are right to report now that there is a huge conflict of interest in Mexico because a government contractor is financing the seven-million-dollar home of the president's wife. That's not saving Mexico. That's corruption.

Can you imagine what would happen here if a government contractor would secretly finance the private home of Michelle Obama? Well, that is happening in Mexico and, believe it or not, there is not even an independent investigation on this matter. Because of the so-called "White House" in Mexico and the disappearance of forty-three students, thousands of Mexicans want President Peña Nieto to resign. We have to report that. No, Peña Nieto doesn't want to talk to me either.

Now let me tell you what it means for me to be a journalist and to be an immigrant. This defines me. I came to the United States after they tried to censor me in Mexico. So this country gave me the opportunities that my country of origin couldn't give me. And, of course, when it comes to immigration, I take a stand.

As an immigrant myself, many times I speak up for other immigrants who don't have a voice. That's why I told President Obama that he didn't keep his promise on immigration and that's why I told Speaker John Boehner, to his face, that he blocked immigration reform in the House. I think I was just doing my job. As a journalist, part of my job is to make visible the millions of immigrants who are invisible to the rest of America.

I don't believe in being partisan. But I believe in taking a stand. As Nobel Prize winner Elie Wiesel once said: "We must take sides. Neutrality helps the oppressor, never the victim." In front of genocide, dictators and politicians abusing their power, we can't be neutral

The worst in our profession is when we stay silent. Sadly, we stayed silent before the war in Iraq, and thousands of American soldiers and tens of thousands of Iraqi civilians died unnecessarily. We have to learn from that. Silence is the worst sin in journalism. But the best journalism becomes a way of doing justice and speaking truth to power.

That's why tonight I want to dedicate this award to all the journalists who have been recently killed in Syria and in Mexico. You were our eyes. Now you are part of our soul.

ACKNOWLEDGMENTS

This book is for so many people, especially those who agreed to speak with me. In every interview—as in both war and love—you need at least two. I'm grateful to all the respondents who agreed to sit down with me for these encounters, all of which originally appeared on television.

After the interviews, some may have regretted having accepted in the first place. But they still have my thanks for their time, for their vision of the world, and for their answers, even if we weren't always in agreement. I learned a lot from all of you during my first three decades in television. You represent one of the many reasons why I chose this profession. I wanted to be able to talk with the people who were changing the world, and many of you are right here, in these pages.

This book is dedicated to my mother, María de Lourdes Avalos Blanco. And I'm using her full name here because ever since she was young, she fought so hard to get ahead and be unlike anyone else. She lost her own mother when she was just fifteen years old, and had me just ten years after that. She was the first rebel I ever knew, both at home and in school.

I'll give you an example of one of her rebellious acts: when she was young, she wasn't allowed to go to school—back then, girls like her were preparing for marriage—so when I went to college, she decided to enroll as well. I often ran into her in the hallways at the Universidad Iberoamericana in Mexico City. That's my mom for you. Today, at eighty-something years old, she's still teaching me the art of living.

Thank you, Chiqui, for the time I stole from you. (If you think it's hard to juggle multiple jobs, two families, and a home, just imagine the stress that's added when you spend several months writing a book, pushing the boundaries of almost all the compromises we make in order to have a well-working relationship.) Thank you for the space you gave me to write, and I apologize for my absences, especially the mental ones. I love you. You were the first person to read this book— we're still accomplices—and your advice and comments are all here.

Nicolás and Paola, I hope that at this stage of life you understand that almost everything I do is for the two of you. I write in order for you to learn more about me and the wonderful profession of journalism. This book contains a number of lessons in rebellion that I've learned from you. You two are my favorite rebels. When I see you rebelling at home, imposing your decisions and your personalities, I know deep down that that's the way things have to be. You're doing what I did at your age, and your rebellion is a necessary part of a happy and intense life. I do believe in this sort of karma. I love you both so much.

To say that this book was made possible by Univision is no exaggeration. Practically every interview that is included here first appeared on television, and without the permission and support of Univision, this book would have remained on the air instead of on the page. Univision has been my home away from home; I've spent more time with the network than I did living in my parents' house in Mexico.

Thank you, Isaac Lee, Daniel Coronell, and Randy Falco for unconditionally supporting my work as a journalist at Univision and Fusion. You have given me absolute—absolute—freedom of expression in my daily work. And there's nothing better than working alongside fellow journalists who understand the moral dilemmas we often face.

Isaac is an extraordinary boss who almost always says yes. Thus, the responsibility falls on one person. Isaac simultaneously protects you while pushing you to new limits. Thank you, Isaac, always.

Thanks to Patsy Loris, Gabriela Tristán, Sabrina Zambrano, and the extraordinary team that puts together the weekly show *Al Punto*. That's my starting point. Many of the interviews in this book were conceived, researched, produced, and edited first for *Al Punto*.

I owe so much gratitude to Dax Tejera and the whole team that put together the *America* program on Fusion. Even though you're all much younger than me, you have been my teachers and forced me to reinvent myself on English-language television. Thanks, *Americans*.

Rene Alegria, my friend, my colleague, and my agent . . . you have been invaluable, as always, both in publishing this book and in the complex decision-making process that occurs before the first word is written and the final period placed. All my appreciation and respect for you, Rene.

Ezra Fitz is my voice in English. He has translated most of my books. If you're reading this in English, it's because Ezra took care of translating and interpreting each and every one of the words I wrote in Spanish. Even though I've lived in the United States for more than thirty years, I still prefer to write in Spanish. It's clearer for me, and the words flow more quickly from my heart. The hard work comes later, when Ezra has to put down on paper—or on the computer— what I really wanted to say in a different language. Ezra is my other self. My admiration for you, Ezra.

Miriam Aris is the one who—with a smile on her face—coordinates my life, from the news and videos to the scheduling and the interviews. She always makes sure I don't lose my head, that I don't show up at the airport on the wrong day, and that I don't get the guest's name wrong on the show. Thank you for your efficiency and your infinite patience.

Karim Fuentes is my Web genius. He handles the www.jorgeramos

.com site, but he mainly handles the technology of the future. The interviews contained in this book are available online thanks to him, and you can learn more about this cyber-wizard at K4rim.com.

Each of the interviews here was coordinated by an army of producers, camera operators, and assistants. Television is one of the most unfair industries in the world because only a few people are given credit for the work of so many. In order for me to sit down and talk with a president or world leader, dozens of people have to do an incredibly difficult job. There's a different crew for every interview, and they know who they are.

I said this in one of the chapters, but it bears repeating: the DREAMers are my heroes. Despite having all the odds stacked against them, they rebel against the circumstances of their youth and stand up to the leaders who refuse to allow them to fully integrate into the United States of America. They have shown us the best example of nonviolent rebellion. Thank you for the example you've set.

Thanks so much to Ray Garcia from Celebra who fought so hard to publish this book. I really appreciate your enormous effort and solidarity. Ian Jackman was my talented and incredibly efficient editor. I owe him the final structure and the flow of the book. Both saw what I didn't see.

Finally, on a more personal note, this is the first book that I ever wrote without my cat Lola. She had been at my feet, by my side, or in front of me since 1998, when I wrote my first book. We did that eleven times together. I figure she would have been about twenty years old—there's no way to know her actual birthday—and she passed away slowly, sadly, gently.

Yet somehow, she was here, curled up in a corner next to a window, warm in the sun. But now I've finished this book and it's time to let her go.

Photo by Aníbel Mestre

Jorge Ramos is an Emmy Award–winning journalist, syndicated columnist, and the author of ten books. Hailed by *Time* magazine as one of "the 25 most influential Hispanics in the United States," Ramos has been the anchorman for *Noticiero Univision* since 1986. He also hosts the weekly show *Real America with Jorge Ramos* and the Sunday morning public affairs show *Al Punto* on Fusion. In 2017, he was awarded the Walter Cronkite Award in the US and the Gabriel García Márquez Prize in Colombia for his excellence in journalism.

Ready to find
your next great read?

Let us help.

Visit prh.com/nextread

Penguin
Random
House